Contents

	Acknowledgements	vi
1	Problems and context	1
2	Shimla: city of migrants	12
3	How the study was conducted	32
4	Urban households	40
5	Housework and housewifery	63
6	Household management: material resources	85
7	Women, education, and the household	103
8	Women and paid work	119
9	Networks, cooperation, and social life: sources of information	152
10	Networks, cooperation, and social life: patterns of sociability	170
11	Conclusion	187
	References	199
	Name index	204
	Subject index	206

Acknowledgements

The research upon which this book is based was funded by a grant from the Social and Economic Research Council. I acknowledge their support with gratitude. I would also like to thank those at Keele University who were involved in the administration of this grant, especially Doreen Clowes and Graham Bytheway.

Om Prakasha Sharma and Balvinder Gill worked with me as research assistants in Shimla. Their hard work and good team spirit was a great help to me and I hope that they enjoyed our time in Shimla as much as I did. Credit is also given to Om Prakasha Sharma for the photographs in the text.

Fieldwork in Shimla was indeed a happy experience, and while writing this book I have often thought of our many friends there. Without their help and encouragement it would have been difficult to complete the research in the limited time at my disposal. Special thanks are due to Mrs Sujaya Alok (IAS), Mr S. K. Alok (IAS), Mrs Bhavani Negi, Mr P. S. Negi (IAS), Mr B. R. Jamwal (HAS), and to Mr and Mrs V. Kahol for their practical assistance of many kinds. Many thanks also to Mrs K. Shirali of Himachal University and Mrs V. Srivastava of St Bede's College for their constant intellectual encouragement. Mrs Shipstone of the Shimla YWCA and members of the Shimla All India Women's Conference also provided me with much help and enthusiastic support. Many other individuals took an interest in my research and facilitated it in various ways; I remember their help with gratitude.

Finally, let me thank Joy Kendrick and Caroline Baggaley for typing interview transcripts and the manuscript of this book.

Ursula Sharma
University of Keele, 1985

WOMEN'S WORK, CLASS, and the URBAN HOUSEHOLD

A study of Shimla, North India

Ursula Sharma

Tavistock Publications

LONDON and NEW YORK

To Radha,
a Pahari woman

First published in 1986 by
Tavistock Publications Ltd
11 New Fetter Lane, London EC4P 4EE

Published in the USA by
Tavistock Publications
in association with Methuen, Inc.
29 West 35th Street, New York NY 10001

Printed in Great Britain at
the University Press, Cambridge

British Library Cataloguing in Publication Data
Sharma, Ursula
    Women's work, class, and the urban
    household.
    1. Women – India – Social conditions
    I. Title
    305.4'2'0954   HQ1742

    ISBN 0-422-79320-5
    ISBN 0-422-79330-2 Pbk

Library of Congress Cataloging in Publication Data
Sharma, Ursula, 1941–
    Women's work, class, and the urban household.

    (Social science paperbacks; 332)
    Bibliography: p.
    Includes index.
    1. Housewives – India – Simla – Social conditions.
2. Home economics – India – Simla – Social aspects.
3. Wages – Housewives.   4. Women – Economic conditions.
I. Title.   II. Series.
HQ759.S4616   1986   305.4'3   86-11296
ISBN 0-422-79320-5
ISBN 0-422-79330-2 (pbk.)

1 Problems and context

In this book I shall explore the nature of women's household work in a modern Indian city, and show how it contributes to the maintenance, and sometimes mobility, of the household.

By 'household work' I do not mean housework alone. Naturally the members of a household cannot easily survive unless their physical needs are met – food must be prepared, the dwelling cleaned and maintained, and children must be cared for. In India, as in the west, most of this work is done by women. But there are many other kinds of work which must be done if the household is to maintain itself and prosper, activities which do not relate so immediately to the physical needs of members. For instance, expenditure must be organized; bills need to be paid, cash banked or withdrawn, credit arranged. Social relationships must be kept going; contact with 'family' friends or common kin must be maintained, presents given on festivals or ritual occasions, invitations extended and hospitality provided. I will not try to specify all these different kinds of household work here since they will be discussed in detail in later chapters. All that I wish to establish at this point is that besides the more obvious case of housework, there are many other kinds of work involved in the servicing of a household and these require study if we are to understand how households persist as groups.

I am not going to argue that these activities are invariably performed by women, but in the community I studied women certainly played the more important role and it seems valid to concentrate on the effects of their input on household viability. Ultimately, I shall contend, this work has consequences outside the household and has implications for the process of class formation.

Before embarking on an account of my research, let me explain what I think can be gained by exploring the connections between women's work, class, and the urban household, and say something about the concepts I shall be using.

The household: a real social group or alliance of individuals?

Feminists can claim some credit for the fact that the household has become a productive focus for research in the social sciences in recent years. It was largely the surge of feminist enquiry into the domestic sphere beginning in the early 1970s which drew attention to many neglected aspects of domestic life: the nature of housework, the power structure of the family, the differential access of women to household resources. Until that time, the study of domestic life had more usually taken family relationships as the starting point for research, not an unreasonable practice since in most societies households are still more often constituted on the basis of kinship links than on any other kind of tie. But focusing on the 'household' rather than the 'family' enabled researchers to apprehend the household group as a *resource system*, a group with its own internal economy yet also linked with the wider economic system.

The household as a concept has the advantage of being down-to-earth, but at the same time it raises problems which cannot easily be dismissed. An obvious difficulty is that of arriving at a definition of the household which will stand up to cross-cultural application (see Netting, Wilk, and Arnould 1984). More important from the point of the view of the problems dealt with in this study is the question of whether the household, however defined, really constitutes any kind of collective entity. Does it have any reality as a social group, as opposed to a group of individuals who happen to share a common hearth, budget, or other resources?

Paradoxically, if it was feminist research which stimulated the study of the household it has also been feminists who have questioned the way in which the household is taken for granted as a group with real joint interests or status. Research on the internal power system of the household shows that women generally do not have access to household resources on the same footing as men (e.g. Whitehead 1981:109). Work on the allocation of money in the household indicates that whatever the details of the budgeting system adopted, there is usually differential access to cash income which reinforces women's dependence on their husbands (Pahl 1983).

Turning to the matter of status, the unity of the household is questioned further. Ann and Robin Oakley criticize official statistics for conflating a wife's social class status with that of her husband. If class position accrues to *individuals* by virtue of their occupation (or lack of one) then there can be no such thing as household status, and consequently no sense in trying to derive such a joint attribute from the status of a male household 'head' (Oakley and Oakley 1979:178).

Feminists have indeed done a good job of deconstructing the household and have discredited what Whitehead calls the 'black box' treatment (Whitehead 1981:89). In feminist discourse the household is no longer an irreducible unit; it has an inner politics of its own which is not divorced from the politics of the society in which it is embedded. So how can such a group claim to have any real collective interests or standing which women promote through their household service work?

It is not only from the feminist point of view that a critique of the view of the household as an irreducible unit can be mounted. There may be differential allocation of household resources according to age as well as gender with young people, and sometimes the very old, having less access to or control over the goods and services which theoretically belong to the household as a group. There may be different degrees of communality at different points of the household cycle; for instance in Britain young people are expected to set up their own households at marriage or earlier, and in preparation for this separation from the 'parent' household they may accumulate funds or goods of their own to which other members of the household do not have free access or overriding claims. Where marriage is a fragile relationship, there is the greater possibility of one or both partners developing resources of their own to which the other partner does not have access and may not even know about. Does the household therefore represent anything more than the coincidence of individual trajectories for a time before they disperse to form other alliances? I think that usually it does, but this is a matter which must be established empirically, not merely assumed.

If we take this deconstruction job seriously, as I am sure we must, how then are we to formulate the relationship between the household and class? Since Bernstein's (1973) work on language, class, and education we are familiar with the idea that part of the business of reproducing class structure begins in the home. Socialization practices of various kinds, even those as subtle and unconscious as language acquisition, shape the initial orientation of the child to school and school-work, and the education system continues with the work of 'placing' the child (Bernstein 1973:44ff.). The family is seen as an institution through which class experience and ideology are channelled, even if few writers have been able to break down the process and demonstrate precisely which activities of men and women in the home ensure that this transmission takes place. If this view is taken, does not the household turn out to be a very real social entity after all?

Certainly no-one has tried to deny the household as a *subjective* reality, that is as a unit with which women actually identify their interests, even when it realizes these interests less effectively than the interests of men and is a major site of their oppression. Indeed it is to the chagrin of many feminists that women continue to see household solidarity as serving them better than generic solidarity with their own sex,[1] although this is not surprising in view of the fact that in many societies there is no satisfactory life for women outside the 'shelter' of a household group. If the household group has this degree of reality for its members, the functions which have been identified by sociologists cannot arise fortuitously by the mere co-residence and shared consumption practices of its members. Perhaps it is time for a reconstruction of the household as a unit of study, this time informed by a feminist scepticism about any supposed symmetry of rewards or indivisibility of interest among its members.

In India, as in many other countries, there are few institutional sources of support outside the household and its immediate circle of kin. There is little public welfare provision in the form of state insurance schemes, pensions, and unemployment benefit, and the free health services provided by the state are severely overburdened. In crises such as sickness, widowhood, or loss of livelihood, individuals (both men and women) have to rely on whatever resources the household can muster internally, or else upon the external sources of aid and information which its members have been able to cultivate and maintain – kin networks for the most part, but also neighbours and other contacts. The household 'works' most effectively as a group where its members have been able to cultivate and make available to each other such social as well as material resources. The maintenance of social resources is, in the long run, almost as important as the maintenance of material resources such as wages, property, housing, tools, and household equipment.

The work through which these social resources are maintained has largely been neglected in studies of the Indian family and household. This may be an effect of the 'invisibility' which seems to cloak so many of the activities of women and delay their recognition by social scientists. Possibly also it has been due to the fact that many of the servicing tasks I have referred to are not explicitly recognized as forms of work by those who perform them and may be difficult to isolate for the purpose of study from the various other activities of women.

Household service work

It was in the course of research on rural households that I became aware of this category of work, and of the fact that in India it is largely performed by married women. In the villages I studied it was they who were primarily responsible for seeing that the household was represented at ritual events held by neighbours or related families, an important task if useful links between households are to be kept alive and in good shape (Sharma 1980a: 150). It was women who took the leading role in maintaining and extending the network of gift exchange relationships in which the household participated, seeing to it that gifts of cloth, sweets, and cash were presented in the correct amount or quality on appropriate ceremonial occasions. The business of arranging marriages among young people was also largely the work of women, for it was they who assembled information about available partners and initiated matches, even if much of the subsequent negotiations were performed by men.

These activities could not be seen as entirely individual initiatives, although they were often described in such terms by the women themselves and they might certainly bring personal satisfaction or allow the application of individual talents and resources. They are really *household* duties, for in the end the household's maintenance, growth, and standing depends on its members attending to these activities. The detriment to the household were they not performed would not be so immediate as that which would follow if, say, the wife failed to cook the food or attend to her children's health and safety, but it would be real enough in the long run, as it would lead to a drying up of the sources of aid and esteem which guarantee the group's vitality, even survival. This element of constraint or necessity would seem to justify the application of the term 'work' to these activities, even if women do not always perceive them as work in the sense that cleaning, cooking, or farm labour are easily perceived as work.

This work is part of the process of reproduction in the sense that modern Marxists have used the term. That is, first, it contributes to the reproduction of the labour force, albeit not in such a direct or concrete manner as the work which is conventionally termed 'housework'. Second, inasmuch as the household unit is important to the way in which relations of production are structured, this work helps to 'reproduce the conditions of existence of the relations of production' (Edholm, Harris, and Young 1977: 106).

I am certainly not the only observer to have noticed the importance of these activities for the household in South Asia, but they have generally been described incidentally in relation to accounts of kinship or religious and ritual institutions, and therefore their significance as a form of household work has not been pursued. Indeed, accounts of women's work in the west suggest that this residue of unclassified household work is not confined to agrarian societies. For example, Jane Marceau (1976) writes of the social capital which French middle-class women bring to their marriages in the form of useful social and professional contacts. This enables them to provide practical support to their husbands' careers, but such contacts have to be serviced through visits, gift exchange, and so forth if they are to remain active and useful. Janet Finch (1983) shows that supportive activity on the part of wives is not restricted to professional families; there is a wide variety of occupations which men can only pursue if there is a cooperative input on the part of their wives. An obvious example is that of a doctor's wife who takes and relays telephone calls from patients. Here the wife must make a contribution which is additional to the conventional reference of 'housework'. Maila Stivens (1978) has drawn attention to the role of women in an Australian suburb as mediators of kinship aid networks. Such aid, 'contributes to physical maintenance, and the extensive "moral support" contributes to "psychological maintenance" ' (1978: 179). The activities of women in servicing these relationships were therefore important for the success of the household and in a more general sense, Stivens argues, for the reproduction of labour power.

These accounts refer predominantly to middle-class women in industrial societies. Does this mean that this kind of household servicing is more important in those households which have a special status to maintain? One might expect the opposite, in that working-class households surely need more of the concrete aid and moral support obtainable through well-serviced networks, given their lesser security. Certainly the poor black women studied by Carol Stack (1975) in America devoted a good deal of energy to cultivating relations of mutual aid which they could fall back on when times were really bad. Or is it that such work must be performed in all households whose resources (social and material) are not totally exempt from short-term fluctuation, that is, all but a few households hopelessly stuck at the very bottom of the class hierarchy and the few firmly ensconced at the top?

We might well expect that these activities would be more prominent when household status is insecure (the negative case) or when there is much to be gained in terms of social mobility by active efforts to husband social and material resources efficiently (the positive case). The mobile and expanding commercial class of Victorian Britain provides a good example of the latter. Leonore Davidoff's (1973) research has shown how middle- and upper-class women of this period, who wished to maintain their family's claim to participate in 'Society', had to spend much time in social ritual, entertaining husbands' friends and colleagues, helping establish advantageous contacts for their families, and maintaining these contacts through the correct performance of the ceremonial of visiting. Associated with this effort was a variety of minute domestic tasks, for example, knowing and being able to produce the exactly correct dress for a particular occasion, supervising servants to ensure that they provide the appropriate dishes when entertaining. Household management was far from being simply a matter of ministering to the physical needs of the family in a manner appropriate to their economic means, since it involved also the ability to minister to an elaborate social life which status demanded and which was largely constructed and maintained by married women. All this effort was characteristic of a particular period when the new bourgeoisie sought access to the real and symbolic privileges of elite status and, according to Davidoff, it contracted as the class system stabilized in the twentieth century.

As far as I know, the only attempt to classify and theorize this type of work and to relate it to a consideration of class and status in general is that of Hannah Papanek (1979). Her ideas have been of especial interest to me since they were developed in the context of research on South Asian society.

In an article written in 1979 she states that:

'Women, as members of families and households, produce many goods and services that benefit other family members, whether their work is paid or unpaid. Their work also affects the family's relation with others in the community or reference group. Particular kinds of work that I call *family status production* maintain and enhance the family's social standing, although they do not necessarily enhance the women's status within that unit.'

(Papanek 1979: 775)

Women perform work which contributes to the household's joint effort to maintain its status – all kinds of work, ranging from the public observance of religious ritual to the provision of secretarial services to a professional breadwinner, and the other kinds of occupational support described by Finch (1983), and the training of children in duties relevant to their status. Rather a rag-bag category, one might think, and in some instances hard to distinguish from housework as conventionally understood. But the common element is that all these activities are performed by women in and around the home and contribute to the long-term project of sustaining or enhancing the household's collective standing.

There are several features of family status production work which should be noted here. First, Papanek considers the concept to have cross-cultural validity, though she does not claim universal validity. Second, she considers it to be a feature of households which either have or expect to have some status to maintain, rather than of those who have no status nor any hope of upward mobility. Third, in so far as family status production work actually consumes time there is an opportunity cost involved if the women in high status households undertake paid work outside the home; therefore Papanek tends to regard these two kinds of work as mutually exclusive alternatives for women.

This is not the place to embark upon an academic discussion of Papanek's concept, since it will be clear in the course of this book in what respects I concur with, and in what respects I differ from, her formulation of this kind of work. Here, I will do no more than register the following notes; that I like her appreciation of the fact that status is something which is *produced* and has to be constantly recreated; that I think she has made an original revelation of the links between the household and the status system in complex societies via a hitherto invisible category of work; that she is correct in stating that this work is usually, although not necessarily, done by women; that, however, not only high status is reproduced but also low status, therefore family status production work is surely not the prerogative of women in high status households only. From the point of view of the people who do it, family status production work is done to ensure the security, or at any rate, survival, of the individual members of the domestic group. If housework, as some Marxists have suggested, contributes to the reproduction of the labour power of individual workers (or future workers) then family status production work can be said to do the same, albeit less directly. But from the point of view of the sociologist it needs to be distinguished from housework (as that term is conventionally understood) since it contributes to the continuity of the very *unit* within which the welfare of individuals is catered for and house-work is carried out. And since the resources of the domestic community which family status production work helps to maintain may include quite concrete forms of aid, property, and privilege, we should think of it as reproducing class position as well as household status or prestige. For 'family' therefore read 'household', and for 'status' read 'class'?

'Household class production work' is not a very happy term though, and we need a concept that extends Papanek's idea rather than denies it. There is no need to prejudge whether it is *class* or *status* that work of this kind (re-)creates, nor whether it *produces* such relationships in the first place or *reproduces* them once they are established. As my data will show, the kind of work thus catego-rized may help to maintain the class position of a household but also further the formation of status groups within a class. In a situation of rapid change, such as I studied in Shimla, it may contribute to the actual *production* of class and status positions; in a more stable situation it might more appropriately be seen as contributing to their *reproduction*. I propose to use the term 'household service work', the term 'service' having the appropriate connotations of being connected with distribution, communication, maintenance. Perhaps this term is still rather bland and unspecific, but I think it will do, since it enables us to identify and re-aggregate many activities which had previously been either ignored or trivialized as a genuine category of household *work*. I therefore decided to take it as the starting point for my research project on women and the household in an Indian city.

Women, class, and the household in India

The data for this monograph were gathered in Shimla, an administrative city in North India. Most of the women who participated in the study had migrated from somewhere else, as had their husbands. Many retained important links with their own and their husbands' places of origin. The women in the households most recently committed to urban living usually maintained the most active connection with their villages.

In general, while a good deal has been written on women in Indian cities, little attention has been paid to their role in the process of urbanization itself. Women's part in managing the transfer of people from villages and their reconstitution into urban households has been ignored. In the first place, the migration of women to cities has frequently been regarded as secondary, that is, they migrate in consequence of the migration of male relatives, not in order to take up economic opportunities themselves (a view which I criticize in Chapter 4). Second, links between urban households and their rural areas of origin are generally considered in terms of the continuity of relationships among men. Joint interests in land may persist among dispersed male kinsmen and related men separated by the migration process may continue to cooperate financially (e.g. in funding the education or marriages of younger members of the family). If migrant women revisit their villages it is likely to be attributed to their nostalgia for rural life or difficulty in adapting to urban ways (Majumdar and Majumdar 1978: 121) although, as I shall subsequently show, it is just as likely that practical household business occasions such visits. I hope to be able to use my data to question this view of women as passive participants in the process of urbanization and the maintenance of rural–urban links.

Even the role of women in established urban households has been little researched. That is, there have been plenty of studies of urban women in India, but many of these have treated them as individual subjects and have not primarily been designed to reveal their position in the political economy of the household. New research is remedying this situation and suggests the following points of comparison with urban women in the west:

1 If working women in the industrial west have less complete control over their earnings than men, waged work is even less likely to prove a source of independence or autonomy for more than a few women in Indian cities. Their earnings are likely to be appropriated by parents, parents-in-law, or husbands (Kapur 1970:141; Standing 1985:37). And since public ideologies place little value upon the paid work of women, they are unlikely to derive much social esteem from selling their labour unless they can command very prestigious jobs.

2 On the other hand, considering urban women as housewives and domestic workers, they perform domestic work under social conditions that are in some respects less isolating than those suffered by many housewives in Britain. The urban neighbourhood in India is as likely as the village to provide forms of sociality and cooperation available to all but the most secluded women; relations of ritual exchange and quasi-kinship establish themselves in stable suburbs, and urban localities develop their own ceremonial life (Vatuk 1972:178ff.).

These generalizations must remain very tentative since there are so few studies which allow direct comparisons among different groups of women (most concentrate on particular occupational or income groups) and therefore it is hard to gain a comprehensive idea of how class differentiates the experience of urban women in the household, except in the most crude and obvious ways.

The descriptive project of this book is to convey both the common content of household service work in India and also the ways in which such work varies with class position and other relevant factors. At a more theoretical level, gender and class (considered as structural lines of division in society) interact in a way that is not fortuitous. Defining their relationship more precisely is the next task of feminist scholarship, and I hope that the present study will suggest some new ways in which this task might be approached.

Notes

1 See Caplan and Bujra (1978). Most of the papers in this volume deal directly with this problem.

2 Shimla: city of migrants

Approaching Shimla, one still feels the sense of excitement described by the journalist William Russell in 1859:

'At the turn of the road, I catch sight of a conical hill, covered with a deluge of white bungalows, dominated by a church behind, and above which again rises a steep sugar-loaf of fir trees. "This is Simla! There is Mount Jakko!" I replied with pleasure and thankfulness.'

(Quoted in Barr and Desmond 1978:18)

Even today, when the long climb from Kalka in the plains can be accomplished in under four hours by a fast bus service, the sense of pleasure is still great. One may also share the amusement expressed by a later visitor, Lady Curzon: 'The first view of Simla amused me so, the houses slipping off the hills and clinging like barnacles to the hill-tops' (quoted in Kincaid 1973:257). Indeed, the houses really do slip off the hill-tops occasionally when their foundations are loosened by the torrential monsoon rains which fall in the summer. One asks oneself why anyone should seriously have tried to maintain the capital of a state, let alone the capital of an empire, on such an awkward site; a narrow twisting ridge about 7,000 feet above sea level, steep to precipitous in most places and pitted with inconvenient ravines.

Shimla was nothing but a village until the 1830s when the British began to use it as a hill station where British officers and civilians might take their families to pass the summer months away from the hot plains. It provided an environment which reminded them of England, at least so far as climate was concerned (the summer temperature seldom rises above 75°F and there is snow in winter). The expansion of Shimla's political and military functions was also informed by the idea that the hill people of the area were 'innocent' and would provide a subservient workforce, unlikely to pose any political problems.

In 1864 Shimla became the official summer capital of British India and thereafter its bureaucratic functions grew rapidly, as well as the services needed to maintain the bureaucrats and summer visitors. This growth was to be maintained throughout the British period. After India became independent in 1947 Shimla remained the administrative capital of Punjab (as that state was then constituted) until 1953. In 1966, after prolonged political pressure on the part of the Sikh political groups, the state was partitioned into the two present-day states of Haryana and Punjab, separating the Sikh-dominated from the Hindu-dominated regions of the original state. This reorganization provided the opportunity for detaching the Himalayan districts, whose incorporation in the old Punjab had been the outcome of political conquest in the past rather than any strong cultural or social affinity with Punjabis. These districts were then joined to the existing Union Territory of Himachal Pradesh, with the hearty approval of most of their inhabitants. In 1971, Himachal Pradesh ceased to be a Union Territory governed from the centre and became a fully-fledged state with its own government, ministers, and legislative assembly, and with Shimla as its capital. The city has therefore had a long though not entirely continuous history as a political and administrative centre.

While its imperial past is evident in the architecture of the older buildings and in some well-known institutions and landmarks (the Gaiety Theatre, the municipal library, Christchurch) it is not this which distinguishes Shimla from other Indian cities of comparable size today. Shimla is after all, a Himachali city now, as the official revision of the spelling of its name proclaims: 'Shimla' was how Himachalis always pronounced the name, 'Simla' being a purely British version.

Anthony King (1980) reminds us that the colonial city (of which Shimla must surely represent the epitome), was, as a consequence of its dependence on the metropolitan society,

'primarily devoted to political, military and administrative functions. Their inhabitants keep order, administer justice, control aspects of the economy but not, as is the case in the industrial city, generate production.'

(King 1980: 14)

Production took place elsewhere. Himachal Pradesh being industrially backward, Shimla still does not generate production and its functions are still for the most part administrative, political, and military, with the important distinction that a completely different elite has control. There is therefore both continuity and discontinuity in Shimla's history. Had more accounts of Shimla been written from the point of view of the armies of minor officials, servants, soldiers, shopkeepers, and rickshaw pullers whose labour enabled the British to live as they did, the continuities might be more evident.[1] This is not to pretend that the discontinuities do not exist, but the current British fashion for fond and, I think, self-indulgent nostalgia for the days of the Raj makes it necessary to point out that Shimla today is a bureaucratic and administrative centre of an underdeveloped region and, as such, may be compared with many others of its kind in India and the Third World in general.

The formation of the new state of Himachal Pradesh in 1971 was an event of profound significance for the people of the Shimla hills and adjoining mountain areas. Paharis (Himalayan hill people) have always felt themselves to be distinct from plains people, and in this part of the Himalayas the people of the plains with whom they contrast themselves are those of neighbouring Punjab. The Pahari attitude of muted distrust towards Punjabis has its roots in the political, social, and economic relations between the two regions. Substantial parts of what is now Himachal Pradesh were originally annexed to Punjab by the Sikh ruler Ranjit Singh in the nineteenth century. These parts continued to be administered as part of Punjab under the British and from 1947–66 as part of the post-Independence state of Punjab. Paharis in general welcomed the formation of new Himachal Pradesh as a political expression of their sense of cultural distinctness and their desire for greater autonomy.

On the other hand, there is no getting away from the fact that while there is more urban employment available within Himachal than there was twenty years ago when I first conducted fieldwork there, many Himachalis continue to be obliged to seek work in the cities of Punjab and other neighbouring states, whose industrial expansion is immeasurably advanced compared with that of Himachal. Himachal will continue to depend on specialized labour imported from these neighbouring states until it has built up a substantial educated class of its own. Most of the highest level administrators in

Shimla are of Himachali origin now, but there is still a number of 'technocrats' (portmanteau word meaning workers with a technical or professional training, such as engineers and scientists, employed in the government bureaucracy) and professional people who are Punjabi or of Punjabi origin.

Nor should it be thought that a sense of common Himachali identity overrides other Pahari attachments. Identities are relative to the situation in question, so that while a Himachali from Kangra and one from Sirmur will feel a strong sense of identity as hill people distinct from Punjabis, Haryanvis, or Bengalis, in other contexts their local identities or caste loyalties may come to the fore. Some migrants in Shimla, for instance, belong to associations which cater for the needs of Himachalis from a particular area, celebrating festivals together and furthering their mutual welfare. The 'politics of scarcity' mean that Himachalis from different regions are in competition with each other for scarce resources, in particular government funds and employment, and there is the expectation that those who have influence will use it to help their own. However, the idea of a Himachali identity has greater political currency than it did twenty years ago, and the fact that I am married to a Himachali proved to be a great advantage to me in conducting this research.

Shimla is by far the largest city in Himachal Pradesh, being the only town with a population of over 30,000. The expansion in its population has been particularly dramatic in the post-war period, as *Table 1* demonstrates. Paradoxically, Shimla has grown greater

Table 1 *Population of Shimla Municipal Corporation area since 1911*

	total population	males	females
1911	22,605	15,739	6,866
1921	31,461	23,077	8,384
1931	22,804	16,255	6,549
1941	23,320	16,315	7,005
1951	46,150	29,735	16,415
1961	54,185	34,199	19,986
1971	69,132	40,460	28,672
1981	70,604	42,254	28,350

and faster as the centre of a small and rather backward hill area than it did during its period as the summer capital of an empire, a growth which has been almost entirely attributable to migration from rural areas of Himachal Pradesh.

This rapid expansion has brought about a great pressure on municipal services and resources. The problem of supplying water to a large city built on a mountain ridge has always been a difficult one, and the question of refuse disposal has not been adequately confronted. There is an acute shortage of housing, and indeed of suitable sites on which to build new houses, so steep and rugged is the terrain. This has meant that, always a sprawling city, Shimla is now more sprawling than ever. The colonization of suitable scraps of level land in distant suburbs has often taken place in advance of the development of local facilities such as shopping precincts, schools, and adequate bus services. As most of Shimla's thorough-fares are not suitable for wheeled traffic anyway, Shimla-ites are very used to walking long distances to work, to school, for shopping, or visiting their friends. If one sees an obese person strolling on the Mall he or she is almost sure to be a visitor and not a resident.

In spite of its growth in size, however, Shimla has not lost its intimacy and sense of small-town sociability. Long-term residents know a great deal about each other's affairs and the activities of the political and bureaucratic elite are as publicly known as they ever were in British times. Indeed the very geographical structure of the city is such as to facilitate the circulation of information. Shimla's city centre is where it was in British times, that central stretch of the Mall (the main street and 'spinal column' of Shimla) flanked by high-class stores and used as a rendezvous for clerks leaving the office after work, well-to-do housewives meeting for window shopping, families strolling up and down in the evening and on holidays, not to mention Shimla's resident *bandar-log*, the hordes of yellow monkeys. Below this dignified thoroughfare runs the crowded lower bazar, less fashionable but possibly more interes-ting, the centre of a warren of tiny alleyways and staircases climbing the steep hillside. The government offices, schools, hospitals, and colleges where the majority of workers are employed are not grouped together in the centre of the town but scattered among the trees and bungalows on either side of the Mall: there is little segregation of residential from other types of land use in Shimla outside the central bazar (commercial and shopping) area. To reach a given point in Shimla from almost any other point one is obliged to walk along some stretch of the Mall, that very public promenade, so that while it is easy enough to mind one's own business, it is difficult to ensure that no one else knows what it is.

Shimla is essentially a white collar and service city with a tiny industrial sector, as the census figures for 1981 reveal very clearly (see *Table 2*). The problem with the occupational categories used in the 1981 census of India is that while they are logical enough for a country which is mainly agricultural, they do not allow us to disaggregate the service sector. The domestic servants, bureaucrats, teachers, bus drivers, porters, and clerks, etc. who make up the greater part of Shimla's working population are simply lumped together as 'other workers'. The 1971 census used a slightly more detailed set of categories as shown in *Table 3*. Assuming that the actual proportions of workers in each category will not have changed greatly during the decade, this may give us a more specific picture of Shimla's occupational structure. It shows for instance, the dimensions of the commercial sector, and demonstrates that sizeable minorities of the working population are engaged in construction (as one would expect in a rapidly expanding urban area) and in transport and communications. Both *Tables 2* and *3*, however, show a fairly low proportion of non-workers to workers (i.e. low in the context of the dependency rates which

Table 2 *Occupational structure of the population of Shimla Municipal Corporation Area, 1981*

	total	males	females
cultivators	449	297	152
agricultural labourers	80	58	22
household industry, manufacturing, processing, servicing, and repairs	73	50	23
other workers	28,551	25,345	3,206
marginal workers	681	365	316
total workers	29,834	26,115	3,719
non workers	40,770	16,139	24,631
totals	70,604	42,254	28,350

Table 3   *Occupational structure of the population of Shimla Municipal Corporation Area, 1971*

	total	males	females
cultivators	164	135	29
agricultural labourers	95	83	12
livestock, forestry, fishing, hunting, and plantation, orchard and allied industries	755	716	39
mining and quarrying	—	—	—
manufacturing, processing, servicing, and repairs (household industry)	359	345	14
manufacturing, processing, servicing, and repairs (other than household industry)	1,899	1,881	18
construction	1,350	1,278	72
trade and commerce	4,179	4,094	85
transport, storage, and communications	2,538	2,485	53
other services	13,972	12,230	1,742
total workers	25,311	23,247	2,064
non workers	43,821	17,213	26,608
totals	69,132	40,460	28,672

obtain in India in general). This is almost certainly due to the fact that so many migrant workers in Shimla have left their dependents in their places of origin, a point which will be discussed in more detail in the next section.

Shimla and its hinterland

Himachal Pradesh is an area of low population density, which is not surprising when one considers that it is entirely mountainous. Its population of around 4.25 million people is mainly rural: indeed it has the lowest rate of urbanization of all Indian states. Its urban population was only 7.72 per cent in 1981, although this represents an increase over previous decades.

Himachal is a backward area by any standard, having for long been treated as a labour reserve. British patronage of Shimla and other hill stations had few economic consequences for the region as a whole other than providing increased employment for cooks and porters. The British treated these hill areas mainly as a good source of 'loyal' house servants and foot soldiers, fine territory for shooting game, and a picturesque back-drop for their own picnics and parades. Its agriculture is almost entirely of a subsistence type, various cereal crops being grown on terraced hill sides and in the valleys. There has been no 'green revolution' here since the kind of mechanization and irrigation which so dramatically increased productivity in neighbouring Punjab and Haryana could not so easily be practised in such mountainous terrain, even were the capital for such development available. The Himachal Government has tried to stimulate agricultural production through extension schemes at the village level, designed to inform farmers of new crops and methods and there have been some local success stories in recent years. However most villagers see 'service', i.e. waged employment, as a quicker route out of poverty than agricultural innovation. The exception has been in those areas where certain cash crops have proved profitable, mainly apples and other fruit. The Government has operated a programme designed to increase fruit production by developing a marketing infrastructure and establishing processing plants to manufacture jams, canned fruit, concentrates, and other products. This has led to an enormous increase in the value of land in what is popularly known as the 'apple belt', but elsewhere subsistence production is the norm.

The pressure on land for subsistence farming, due to increased population, has led to the cultivation of more and more marginal land. This, as well as the commercial despoliation of Himachal's forest resources, has led to deforestation and consequent soil erosion in many areas. Stricter government control over the use of and access to forest land has been of help here, but it has been much more difficult for successive governments to solve Himachal's more fundamental problem – that of providing local opportunities for enterprise and employment.

As might be expected of a region that has straddled some important trade routes, Himachal has its commercial castes – Suds, and Khatris of Punjabi origin. The bazar in Shimla was from the outset dominated by Indian rather than British business. But the entrepreneurship of these groups was commercial rather than industrial and Himachal has never had much industry other than manufacturing of a strictly domestic or small-scale nature. This situation may well change in future with the development of several major hydroelectric power schemes and the establishment of an industrial estate at Parwanu (about thirty miles from Shimla, near the broad-gauge rail head at Kalka). The Himachal Government is also developing state enterprises in appropriate areas – agro-industries, fruit processing, brewing, tourism, and craft goods. As things stand at the moment, however, it would be correct to say that industrial enterprise, whether of the state or private capitalist kind, has scarcely established itself in Himachal as yet. The region remains peripheral to what is already regarded by many as a peripheral form of capitalism.

Patterns of migration

As this study very largely concerns migrant households, it may be useful here to discuss the nature of rural–urban migration in Himachal Pradesh.

Migration was for long discussed in terms of 'push/pull' factors. This rather mechanistic view treated migration as a response to rural unemployment, landlessness, or famine (push) or to urban attractions (pull). Criticizing the 'push/pull' analysis, Bose (1971) points out that this method does not yield useful generalizations at the macro level. The groups who ought to be the most miserable in terms of low income, landlessness, etc. are not invariably the ones to migrate in largest numbers, and the migration which does take place is not always to the places one would expect in terms of the 'urban attraction' hypothesis. Sociologists find themselves obliged to appeal to cultural factors like the well-known 'adventurousness' of Punjabis, or to find other *ad hoc* means of compensating for the deficiencies of the model.[2]

Another long-standing intellectual fashion was to see migration as primarily a cultural process by which rural emigrants become assimilated to a new way of life, involving new values and assumptions. In the rural–urban continuum the migrant was potentially or actually a cultural mediator between rural and urban values and practice. Migrants certainly do play this role (see Sharma 1977) but the process of transformation and diffusion of values is better understood if the socio-economic context of rural–urban movement is also examined. What other resources are being transformed, for instance? How do migrants perceive their villages

Central Shimla, showing the main commercial area

of origin? As a base to return to on retirement? As an area for investment in further resources, power, or prestige? As a place where wife and children can generate additional earnings and live relatively cheaply? For this understanding a more structural approach is needed.

One formulation which has received critical attention has been that of Meillasoux (1981), who sees the relationship between city and countryside in a situation of nascent capitalism in terms of capitalism feeding on the subsistence economy. The rural domestic community provides labour power (realized in the form of migrant labour) which presents itself for use by capital. Capital does not have to take into account the cost of reproducing labour power and can therefore pay lower wages than would be otherwise necessary. These low wages ensure in turn that migrants will not transfer their social and family life to the towns; their households still need the goods and food produced by the parasitized domestic community in the village. Push and pull (if we must use this kind of language) do not exist independently of each other in this model.

Although Meillasoux's formulation is not without its problems, it does throw some light on the situation in Himachal, provided always that we remember that when Himachali migrants move to Shimla it is rarely private capital to whom they sell their labour direct, but more usually the state.

In the Himachali villages where I conducted fieldwork in 1966 and 1977 (see Sharma 1969, 1980a) it was common for a father and his sons to farm land together (or occasionally a group of married brothers whose father had died), the household exporting its currently most employable members to work in the army, Punjabi industry, or wherever else they could find waged work. The time spent by the migrating member in the city would usually be limited and he would eventually return to resume fulltime farming, making way for a younger member who replaced him, and perhaps helping the latter to find a job. Women almost always remained in the village to care for young children and farm any land the family might own or rent. Money earned in the city might be spent on houses, wedding expenses, jewellery and where possible, invested in the purchase of land to increase holdings diminished by the joint effects of population expansion and a system of partible inheritance.

In 1966 few women abandoned the family home to join their

husband in the city apart from a handful of military wives whose husbands obtained married quarters and could be spared from agricultural work. I have the impression that there is now a greater tendency for women to transfer their residence to the cities where their husbands work and for retirement to the village in old age to be less automatic, but the general pattern still persists. An army of wage workers (mostly male, but nowadays including some women as well) is being reared in Himachali villages, ready in future to sell their labour to the state or private companies, according to the kind of opportunities that present themselves and the qualifications they are able to obtain through the rural education system. This structural relationship between city and hinterland has not had any very dynamic effect on agricultural production except in a few areas of Himachal, since the possibilities for investing money earned in the city in new farming methods or types of crops are limited in this region.

It is also true that at the moment the households from which migration has been longest established have, on the whole, not been the poorest. In both the villages I studied it was members of the dominant land-owning caste (Brahmans in Ghanyari, Rajputs in Chaili) who had been the earliest and most successful migrants, although migration is not confined to these groups nowadays. The reason for this is fairly simple; they had been the groups able to take the quickest advantage of the expansion of primary and secondary education in the rural areas and therefore their children were the best equipped in the competition for jobs in the urban sector. Having obtained this advantage, they tended to keep it, since to find a job in the city one needs not only qualifications but contacts. A Ghanyari Brahman was always in a better position to find work outside the village than a Ghanyari untouchable, since there were already other Ghanyari Brahmans (mostly related to him in some way) who might look for openings, accommodate him while he sought employment, provide contacts, and so on.

The particulars of the social commerce which takes place between village and city will vary according to the type of rural production and the different modes of urbanization, but the general truth remains; it does not make sense to see the rural social structure as a kind of historical residuum. Hoselitz wrote in 1960 that,

'the urban structure is the result of the outflow of the moderniz-ation and industrialization process. The rural structure is largely

a survival of what might have been called a "traditional" society
had the last decades not substantially destroyed many features of
rural society which could genuinely be attributed to tradition.'
(Hoselitz 1960:151)

However one characterizes the agrarian modes of production that
presently exist alongside capitalist industry in India (and there are
great problems attendant upon this characterization, see Patnaik
1978), in an area like Himachal they cannot be seen as forms which
just 'happen' to have survived, but as forms which have entered into
a relationship with the capitalist mode of production. The nature of
this relationship may be described as a parasitism of capitalist
industry upon the subsistence sector (as in Meillasoux's (1981)
theory), or we may decide that petty rural elites are parasitizing the
capitalist sector by selling labour to capital and acquiring resources
which boost their threatened position in the rural economic
structure. The situation in Himachal can be seen from both these
points of view. What we cannot do is represent the city and its
hinterland as structurally discontinuous.

In concrete terms this means that many of the migrants we
encounter in Himachali cities retain a stake in their villages of origin
for some time, even if they do not return to them on retirement. As
we shall see, the nature of this stake may vary and need not be a
material one; it could consist of kin links and a residual fund of
'social credit' as well as land holdings or other property. Migrants'
orientation to their rural interests will also vary; some leave wives
and children in the village and do not regard themselves as other
than temporary sojourners in the town, while others are already
consolidating their resources in the urban environment. Of the
latter group, some have lost interest in farming altogether while
others are busy investing their earnings in more profitable land
which will yield income to support their urban life-style.

This dual participation in urban and agrarian class systems may
or may not be permanent so far as individual households are
concerned, but the situation in which urban workers retain rural
interests is not necessarily a transitory phase in the process of
urbanization, a brief and incidental stage in the transfer of
households from village to city, from subsistence farming to
industry and other urban occupations. The value of Meillasoux's
approach is that he sees this dual participation as an integral and
persistent feature of a certain type of capitalist development.

Class and the household

In India one cannot identify a simple class structure such as Marx expected to become increasingly evident in European capitalist societies. The expanding capitalist mode of industrial production has begun to penetrate and transform the rural sector, but genuinely capitalist forms of agriculture have a very limited extent as yet, and in Himachal are scarcely present at all. The coexistence of a number of modes of production yields a situation in which a simple polarized class structure cannot develop. However I do not think that this poses any greater intellectual difficulty to the student of Indian society than that of any other, since in any social formation the historical and functional groupings that overlay the structural relationships postulated by a Marxist conception of class are bound to be complex and various.

In Shimla, if one could ignore the rural affiliations of its inhabitants, one is dealing with a population that is largely composed of wage labourers of one kind and another (manual, clerical, managerial, technical), a few self-employed professionals, and a small, but locally important, petty bourgeoisie (shopkeepers and traders of various sorts). Strictly speaking, the wage labourers cannot be said to have entered into capitalist relations of production; most of them sell their labour to the state and not to private capital, of which there is little in Himachal Pradesh as yet. A better way of describing the situation would be to say that the state is the agent in this peripheral region by which the empirical social forms which are characteristic of capitalist production, such as bureaucracy and waged labour, are disseminated in advance of capitalism itself.

For some theorists the fact of depending upon the sale of one's labour on the market is the crucial feature which distinguishes a 'working class' from other groups, and the divisions in the labour market which undoubtedly exist are 'ideologically determined' (Allen 1977: 78). Other writers would find this insufficient, claiming that one must distinguish between different kinds of labour (productive /unproductive, manual /managerial, etc.). Historically, of course, the creation of a class of wage labourers from existing groups who either performed family labour on their own land, various forms of unfree labour for landowners, specialized work within *jajmani* relations, or any of the various other forms of work which obtained in Indian agrarian society, has profound significance. Indians recognize this in their use of the term *nokri*, generally translated as 'service'. *Nokri* has the connotation of not being one's own master (as the translation implies) but it also suggests the security of a wage paid under some kind of regular contract. At least, it has this security if it is *pakki nokri* – proper service, as opposed to *kacchi nokri*, i.e. temporary or casual labour.

We could say, then, that in Shimla we are witnessing the emergence of a 'working class' in advance of capitalism itself, from a collection of peasants, share croppers, unfree labourers, and other agrarian classes. Yet the conception of a working class which includes both domestic servants and highly paid bureaucrats seems a rather raw and clumsy concept. What further distinctions will be useful, or are any further distinctions merely 'bourgeois categories' (Allen 1977: 76)? Certainly once we begin to differentiate the class composed of those who live primarily by selling their labour power, there is almost no end to the distinctions we may make which might prove relevant to the explanation of political and economic behaviour. The concept of class would then seem to have little more intellectual clout than concepts like 'status groups' or 'interest group' – terms which can often be useful for the purposes of description but which lack theoretical rigour.

In the present context (and probably the same will apply in many other 'underdeveloped' regions) I think that it is useful to distinguish those who sell their labour to the state bureaucracy. This is not because of the bureaucratic nature of their employment; capitalism, where it achieves a sufficient scale, uses bureaucratic means of recruitment and organization in India as elsewhere. The more important point is that in analytical terms, their relationship to the means of production is mediated by the state itself, and a state which plays a somewhat different role from that which it plays in advanced industrial societies. In Himachal Pradesh, and no doubt the same is true of many other peripheral regions, a local bourgeoisie is absent or underdeveloped. The state plays (or tries to play, according to how one judges its success) an entrepreneurial role. It seeks not merely to direct production but to undertake production and marketing itself, as the best means of stimulating growth. The various state corporations that exist in Himachal do not represent industries or concerns which have been 'taken over' and nationalized, but the state's own attempts to generate produc-

tion and employment. The situation in Himachal is only different
from that obtaining in its more developed neighbours in that this
form of state socialism exists in isolation rather than alongside a
local form of capitalism.

There are good grounds for suggesting that the functions of the
state in India are not the same as those characteristic of the state in
advanced capitalist societies. Anupam Sen, for instance, has argued
that it is not useful to see the Indian state as a tool of the capitalist
class (or indeed of any other class in a crude and literal sense). In
India, the state represents a force which is to some extent
autonomous, and may even act in opposition to the emerging
bourgeoisie. He writes of 'the struggle', of the bourgeoisie to bring
the state apparatus under its control, yet neither is the state the tool
of the old agrarian ruling class. The type of state socialism we find
in India is one which is

> 'really in the interests of a bureaucratic state which, through the
> monopolization of basic productive forces and state control
> measures, has kept the bourgeoisie in check and has maintained
> its own independence from class hegemony.'
>
> (Sen 1982:220)

Regarding class structure, Sen writes that

> 'in terms of output, it would be very difficult to locate the state in
> any class because, as it appears, its policies were (and are)
> principally directed towards the augmentation of its own power
> and not the power of any social class.'
>
> (Sen 1982:105)

If the state cannot be located in any other class, then those who
work for it and promote its policies and interests may surely be
treated as a separate and identifiable class of workers, although this
is my own conclusion, not Sen's.

This situation has parallels in the post-colonial history of other
'developing' countries. Roxborough, writing on the social structure
of underdeveloped countries, notes that there is often an

> 'indistinct class which forms around the political roles and
> managerial positions in the nationalized industry. This one may
> call the state petty bourgeoisie, or even the state bourgeoisie.'
>
> (Roxborough 1979:78)

In Shimla this class is not so very 'indistinct' and can be identified as an important and separable class of wage labourers. This class has, moreover, in spite of internal differentiations of rank and remuneration, a degree of self-consciousness which stems from the fact that it enjoys special privileges; permanent government servants are entitled to perquisites which few private employees enjoy – access to special government housing, liberal arrangements for maternity leave, 'dearness allowances', and pension rights. Indeed, members of different grades of the bureaucracy often form associations to protect and extend these benefits.

This class of state employees is not undifferentiated, of course, and it would be foolish to ignore the effects of gradations within it according to the type and status of work performed, levels of remuneration, and consequent differences in consumption and life-style. More importantly, workers who have in common the fact that they sell their labour power to the state are distinguished from one another by the fact that they may simultaneously occupy various positions in the agrarian mode of production. As we have seen, many households unite urban and agrarian interests. These diverse rural interests might be expected to fragment the urban based class I have been discussing, but in fact they appear to have the effect of pegging certain households the more firmly into that class. A clerk with a little land in the village he came from may use the income he receives from it to obtain a better education for his children and thereby obtain a better position for them than is possible for a clerk who has no such additional source of income. A bureaucrat who receives a high salary may save to acquire orchard land in the apple belt; with the proceeds of his fruit crops he may then acquire land for a house in Shimla itself, which may be rented to tenants, providing income to finance a much higher level of consumption or more prestigious life-style. My argument in this book is that such factors tend both to the differentiation of urban wage workers according to their rural interests, but also to the more secure establishment of some households in this class as a result of their participation in coexisting modes of production.

Exactly how this happens and the role which the work of women plays in this process will be described subsequently (see Chapters 4 and 5). The only further point I wish to raise here is that in this context it becomes evident that it is quite inappropriate to see the household as a kind of elementary building block from which social classes are constructed. A class need not be composed of equivalent household groups; households within it may vary greatly in the different combinations of class interests which they present. Where members of the same household have different class positions or share diverse class interests it is more useful to see the household as the arena in which these different interests or positions are mediated than to insist that the household has a unitary class position.[3] It provides the means by which resources in one structure may be mobilized to create resources in another. In some cases rural resources are mobilized to produce advantage in the urban bureaucratic system, in others the reverse may be true.

This theoretical preamble has been quite long enough, though necessary in order to specify what sort of class structure I believe to be emerging in Shimla. It is time now to consider the particular role and activities of women in the urban milieu.

Women in the urban milieu

We can see from *Table 1* (p. 15) that the proportion of women in the population of Shimla is low and has been low throughout the present century. There were 672 females to every 1,000 males in Shimla in 1981. In terms of sex ratio, therefore, Shimla's population is more unbalanced than other towns with which we might reasonably compare it either in terms of size or function. In Dehra Dun, for instance, the 1981 ratio was 799 females to 1,000 males, in Hoshiarpur it was 862, and in Phagwara it was 803. The next largest Himachali city, Sundernagar, has a ratio of 806.

The ratio in Shimla is also low in relation to that of Himachal as a whole, which was 988 females per 1,000 males in 1981. Indeed, Himachal is second only to Kerala among all Indian states in terms of the 'femaleness' of its population, even though it is flanked by states whose sex ratios are among the lowest of all Indian states (Punjab, Haryana, and Uttar Pradesh). There is the rather odd phenomenon, therefore, of a city with a very low sex ratio situated in a region with one of the highest sex ratios in India. How can this be explained?

Basically there are two kinds of explanation which are used to account for imbalances in the sex ratio in the Indian context. One source of imbalance may be differential rates of migration among men and women. Thus, if Punjab has a low sex ratio this can be explained by appealing to the fact that Punjab is an area of high economic growth which has attracted large numbers of (mostly male) migrants. Himachal, on the other hand, is an area of out-migration from which migrants (mostly male) have left to seek work elsewhere. This is the kind of explanation favoured in the census reports.

Alternatively, we may prefer to see sex ratios as the outcome of the differential survival rates of males and females. In an area where sons are preferred for ideological or economic reasons, the distribution of food, medical care, etc. in the household will favour the survival of sons (see Miller (1981) for a detailed exploration of this argument). On this account it is not surprising to find that Himachal is an area with a high sex ratio, since it is a region where women play an important part in agriculture and where women's marriage expenses have traditionally not been high (indeed in many communities bride price was more usual than dowry).

In the present case, I think that both kinds of explanation are relevant. The high ratio of women to men in Himachal as a whole may be in part due to out-migration but, all other things being equal, one would then expect an excess of women over men rather than a situation of near parity, given that Himachal is a major exporter of male labour. An explanation in terms of a relatively low preference for sons and a narrow differential between the survival rates for boy children and girl children seems more appropriate. But when we come to the local level, Shimla's low sex ratio is best explained in terms of differential migration rates. I experienced nothing during my period of fieldwork in Shimla that suggested a desire for sons in exaggerated excess over that which might be found in, say, Punjabi cities. In fact many couples expressed a relatively low level of concern on this issue. Some women who had no sons told me that they had been sterilized because the cost of bringing up a child of *either* sex in Shimla was so high, and the household resources were fully stretched after the birth of two or three daughters. Some quite explicitly argued that as there were good opportunities for girls to receive training and find work before they married, the problem of marriage expenses did not loom so large. Such statements should not, perhaps, be taken at face value; most couples still strongly desire at least one son. But the strength of this preference can hardly explain such a gross imbalance, especially when we consider that in Phagwara, a Punjabi city in an area where there is known to be a very strong preference for sons, the ratio is 803, far less unbalanced. That fewer women than men migrate to Shimla from the countryside seems a far more plausible explanation at the local level.

If women are in the minority, they are none the less highly visible in Shimla. There are female shopkeepers and shop assistants on the Mall, and a couple of policewomen are sometimes seen pacing through the bazar. The army of clerks that trudges towards the office in the morning and homewards in the evening includes women of all ages. A few of my informants attributed this visibility of women and their involvement in civic and social life to the influence of the British. Certainly when Shimla was a British town, British women were as active in its public life as they were in equivalent social circles at home. But nowadays Shimla is a Himachali town and most of its inhabitants come from other Himachali towns or villages. In general, there is little seclusion of women in this state and their mobility outside the home is little restricted. In Himachali villages we find the same segregation of space into areas where women may go and areas which they are expected to avoid as we find in other parts of North India (see Sharma 1980b) but this segregation is weaker and less restrictive. Indeed, the work which Himachali women commonly do could not be accomplished if there were rigid restrictions as to where they might move about, since most Himachali households rely on women to perform farm labour, fetch water from the well or spring, and cut fodder for the cattle from the hillsides and firewood from the forests. There has been no sizeable class of leisured women such as might provide a model for secluded gentility. The practice in Shimla is therefore continuous with the practice in the countryside around and we need no 'special' explanation.

We may summarize this section and anticipate the argument of future chapters by suggesting that the social visibility of women is congruent with the importance of the work they do, both in the household and elsewhere.

Notes

1 According to Buck, in 1904 Shimla's summer population averaged about 38,000 of whom only 7,000 were Europeans and Eurasians. (Buck 1904: 76). For a social historical account of Shimla's development to

1947, which takes into consideration both Indian and British views, see Kanwar (1983).

2 See Bose (1971) for a critique of the push-pull approach as applied in the Indian context.

3 British sociologists have created artificial problems for themselves by assuming that the household must have a single identifiable class position in spite of the diverse activities or interests of its members. One then has to assume that all the members of the household really share the position of its head, or try to work out some kind of average position calculated from the occupations of different members. The frequently discrepant positions of men and women in the same household has been the focus of much current debate (see Heath and Britten (1983 and 1984), Goldthorpe (1983 and 1984), Erikson (1984)).

3 How the study was conducted

The first anthropologists found their scientific imagination most stimulated by societies that were from the western point of view exotic – isolated tribal groups, usually in remote locations. Later generations of anthropologists widened their conception of how they might properly study mankind to include both the rural fringe of western society and urban communities of all kinds, but especially those of the 'developing' Third World. However, in shifting their attention to the urban milieu they continued to adhere to their favoured method of data collection – participant observation.

Participant observation involves living with, or in as close proximity as possible to, the community or group that is to be studied and, as far as the anthropologist can manage to do so, joining in their activities and social life. In this way, anthropologists believe, one can gain access to case material (genealogies, details of disputes, or whatever kinds of concrete data are needed for the study in hand) and also gain an empathic grasp of the people's cultural values and assumptions. This method is a useful scientific tool, albeit one which makes heavy demands of the observer's emotional, intellectual, and social resources. However, it is also problematic in that it has tended to foster the illusion that the total social process has been observed when nothing of the sort has taken place.

For a start, there is one vital respect in which participant observation is seldom complete; the anthropologist cannot participate fully in a rural society since he or she never relies entirely on agricultural production for a living as most villagers do. The anthropologist may become ritual sister to the headman and be invited to feasts and domestic ceremonial, but will never participate more than superficially in the productive process which sustains all these other activities, and so has to study a central institution from the outside.

Furthermore, however happy and intimate the relationships which the anthropologist is able to create with some of the villagers, there will always be others from whom he or she is divided by barriers of class, sex, caste, or ethnic origin. Female anthropologists have accused male anthropologists of ignoring features of community life which would be evident to anyone with access to the world of women. Others have accused colleagues of identification with a high caste view of life. It is certainly impossible to live in an Indian village and have equal intimacy with members of all castes. The totality of rural life is fractured, whatever ideological image of cosy solidarity the villagers may manage to project, and immersion in it is as likely to intensify the effects of these divisions in the anthropologist's own perception as it is to overcome them.

Few, if any, would now defend the illusion that one can ever apprehend the totality of an agrarian society through participation, and I do not think anyone ever seriously entertained this illusion where urban society was concerned. If one can live in even quite a small village where everyone's business is everyone else's and still overlook important processes or ideas, how could one ever study more than the finest slice of urban life, with its greater scale and faster pace? Yet there may be respects in which participant observation in the city is both more honest and more effective. The method I used in Shimla was more genuinely *participant* observation than was living in Chaili or Harbassi, the villages studied in my previous research on women and the household. In Shimla I had an occupation – social science researcher – which, if not familiar to most people, was at least a credible urban trade. People in cities do not expect to know about or understand the precise way in which all their neighbours gain their livelihood, and therefore the researcher does not stick out like the proverbial sore thumb, as he or she must do in the village.

More than this, in Shimla my family did actually experience many of the concrete problems faced by our informants – finding accommodation, obtaining admission to schools for our children, finding time to visit my husband's village where he still has family and land, helping kin and fellow villagers find jobs or deal with officialdom in Shimla. These were all concerns we shared with many of the people we studied. I suppose I did my share of the household service work that is required in middle-class households in Shimla and I certainly found out for myself the need for well-maintained information networks.

As well as being more 'authentic' in the sense just described, fieldwork is also in many ways easier to do in a city like Shimla. In so far as city air really 'makes men free' it facilitates communication with informants, since barriers of caste or religion may be more easily penetrated or circumvented in a large town than in a village. There is little residential segregation in Shimla and one can get to know families of widely differing means and origins with rather little social or physical exertion. As a research team, we had between us a number of prior links with Shimla which gave us entry into a variety of social circles. My husband, Om Prakasha Sharma, who was employed as one of the research assistants on the project, comes from a village in Himachal Pradesh; we could meet the families of clerks and petty employees hailing from the area around his village on a friendly footing as quasi-kin or fellow villagers. I had previously conducted fieldwork in areas of Punjab and Himachal which also send migrants to Shimla and I managed to meet several families related to my friends and informants in those areas. We already had acquaintances among senior government officials, including one who had studied at the university where I teach. Balvinder Gill, the other research assistant working on the project, was brought up in Britain but quickly located some of her parents' friends, who were able to introduce her to families from the business community. Through their college-going children she was also able to make contact with students and young working women. Looking back, I feel that my relationships with friends and neighbours in Shimla were less intense than some of those I formed in Chaili and Harbassi, generated by the intimacy of village life. But they were based on more solidly common experience.

The problem with conducting this kind of fieldwork in the urban setting, however, is that one has little idea of the range of possible variations in the process or institution one wishes to study. The sample of households represented by personal acquaintance in Shimla was no doubt a fairly wide one, but I had no means of knowing how representative it might be of the total field, or of what important types or instances might have been omitted. For one thing I needed to be able to compare the kind of household work performed by women who were in paid employment with those who were not employed, and most of the women whom I came to know through our personal networks were not employed. Second, I needed to be able to compare the organization of work in households of different income groups in order to discover whether household service work is an important category of work in all households, or only those above a certain level of wealth and prestige. Although, as I have indicated, the families of whom we had direct knowledge were fairly varied in this respect, the greater number were probably clustered around the middle of Shimla's income hierarchy. I therefore planned to extend the range of ethnographic data which I would expect to gather through the means of participant observation by conducting interviews among a sample of women from a variety of occupations and income groups with the help of a research assistant.

Ideally I would have wished to have constructed a sample representative of the pattern of income distribution in Shimla, with appropriate percentages of respondents from different income groups. This was not possible since the necessary information on income distribution was not available. Another possibility would have been to select a sample representative of the occupational structure of the city, but here again the relevant information was not available at the time (the 1981 Census of India had been completed but the data were still being processed during 1982 while I was staying in Shimla).

In the end I decided to operate with a simple set of four broad income bands (household income of less than Rs750, Rs750–1,500, Rs1,500–3,000, more than Rs3,000)[1] and to interview roughly equal numbers of married women in each income band. Within each band I hoped to locate similar numbers of employed and non-employed women. This would not produce a *representative* sample – of course, the population of Shimla is not divided equally among the four income groups I used, and the married women who live there are not equally divided into employed and non-employed. But this method would yield a sample which would enable me to make the comparisons I was interested in.

One quite serious drawback of this method of sampling was that it did not take into account the domestic cycle. The household work of a recently married woman will be different from that of one who has several school-age children. As her sons and daughters grow up, some tasks which she formerly performed may be delegated to

them; on the other hand, she may have to undertake new work connected with their marriages or education or with the care of elderly relatives. When her children are married and her husband has retired (her own retirement may be an important factor in the situation if she has previously been in employment) then the organization and distribution of household tasks will be trans-formed again.

I felt that if the interview data was to be used for comparisons between working and non-employed women and between women of different income groups, then using it for comparisons between different stages of the household cycle as well would grossly overload a small sample. I therefore decided to select women for the interview sample who had either borne or adopted one or more children, and who had at least one child still unmarried and living at home. Most of the interviewees were therefore within the age range of 20 to about 55. Their households would thus represent certain phases in the domestic cycle, those at which women are most active in household service work. Comparative data on women's work at different stages in this cycle would be obtained through other means than sampling – mainly through detailed case studies. Much could also be learned from what interviewees had to say about their experience at other stages in their lives.

Locating respondents was the next problem. Sampling frames such as electoral registers are not very useful for this kind of purpose since they give no indication as to the income of the households or individuals listed. As there is so little residential segregation according to income or occupation in Shimla, to take four different neighbourhoods as representative of my four income groups would not have been useful. The informal 'snowball' method seemed to be the best procedure; that is, an initial group of interviewees was obtained through personal contacts, and they in turn introduced us to other likely candidates. This worked very well since most women lived in very mixed localities and housing clusters and most of the initial contacts had friends, neighbours, or colleagues in different income groups from their own. For instance, a lecturer's wife put us in touch with a domestic servant who lived in the outbuildings of the tenement where she herself rented rooms. The instructress of a tailoring school introduced us to some of her students. A sweeper woman introduced us to the washerwoman and the clerk's wife who lived in the same quarters as herself. This rather personal mode of operation is appreciated in Indian society where much else is effected through personal contact and recommendation, and there were only two refusals as against seventy-two completed interviews. The main problem was in locating a sufficient number of non-employed women in the under Rs750 household income band and I concluded that women in this category are probably not to be found in Shimla in large numbers; most very poor men who go there to work leave their wives behind in the village if the latter are unwilling or unqualified to seek work, on account of the high cost of family living.

Most of the interviewees were not only willing but seemed to enjoy their part in the survey. Interviewing was done as far as possible in the respondent's home without the presence of others but in some cases the workplace provided a quieter and more convenient venue. Some women preferred to be interviewed in the company of female friends or neighbours who were also to be interviewed and we indulged this preference where it was strongly expressed. Sometimes a group of interviewees would embark upon a lively discussion of the issues raised by our questions after the interview session had ended (What are the problems of working women? How is the domestic budget best organized?) and these unstructured sessions were as worth recording as the actual interviews. One woman remarked, 'We liked being interviewed, we thought it would be hard, but it was easy because the things you asked us about were just the sort of things we chat about amongst ourselves.'

The interviews were of a fairly informal nature; that is, a schedule of questions and topics was adhered to, but if the respondent wished to digress or expand upon an answer, if it seemed sensible to vary the order of the questions or to ask supplementary questions, then there was latitude to do so. The interviews with the main sample of women were conducted by myself and the research assistant, Balvinder Gill. Respondents were interviewed in Hindi, Punjabi, or English according to their choice, and most of the interviews were tape recorded.

As well as the main sample just described, additional interviews were conducted with a sample of male migrants and with a group of unmarried women. If many conventional studies of Indian society have ignored women because they were conducted by men, feminist researchers sometimes assume that there is no need to make a special study of men since their views and activities in the field of social life under study have already been recorded. This is not always true and certainly is not the case where studies of household activity are concerned. These interviews were conducted by the other research assistant, Om Prakasha Sharma, and provided valuable data on how the household activities of women are perceived and evaluated by men.

The interviews with unmarried women conducted by Balvinder Gill were intended to illuminate the process by which women's employment careers are shaped, the means by which they make decisions about education and training, what kinds of job to apply for, etc. They also provided useful data on the household activities of daughters and supplemented the main focus of the study, which was on women's activities as wives.

I have given this rather detailed account of how the interview sample was conducted because I want to make it clear that it was designed essentially as a quantitative adjunct to a qualitative ethnography of urban life. This may not always be clear in the text; combining qualitative and quantitative methods is not particularly difficult in the field – anthropologists routinely combine such methods in one way or another. Problems enter at the stage of writing up where quantitative data which can be presented in tabulated form is liable to upstage the descriptive data gathered from personal observation. In the following account I frequently move in a way that I realize may be confusing at times, from the consideration of one kind of data to another, so I have tried to signal to the reader when I am using data from the interview sample and when I am using information conveyed by other informants or derived from direct observation (for instance by distinguishing between 'respondents' and 'informants'). I have felt freer in citing the words of respondents from the interview sample, who after all were much more conscious that they were participating in social science research and that their words were being recorded. In the case of both interview data and the data gathered from personal observation I have carefully disguised the identity of the individuals. There is no way in which I could have disguised the identity of the place I studied, and in spite of its size Shimla still has something of a small-town atmosphere so that much of the case material based on observation which I could have cited might have led to the identification of individuals.

In the study of large-scale societies (are there any small-scale societies left?) both the ethnographic method, based on personal observation by an individual or small team of individuals, and the large-scale survey, based on positivist assumptions about the equivalence and objectivity of data, have their limitations. My own training and intellectual background as an anthropologist incline me to attempt to adapt the former to the requirements of studying urban life rather than to abandon the qualitative approach. I hope that what I have produced is not too uneasy a compromise between the dual requirements of range and depth.

Note

1 During the period of fieldwork the value of the rupee was approximately Rs15 to the pound sterling.

4 Urban households

Is there such a thing as the urban household? In a crude and obvious sense there must be; any household located within the limits of a city is urban – even if its members are engaged in agriculture, they are presumably exposed to urban values and institutions. How far such households differ from rural households in their composition and behaviour is a matter which can only be decided on the basis of comparative studies. What we can usefully discuss here is the process by which migrant households manage the transition from rural to urban living, or (in some cases) the transition from one city to another. My purpose in this chapter is to use data from the study to illustrate these processes, and to indicate the context within which women's household work is performed.

Women, men, and migration

Most people who live in Shimla at the moment are either migrants themselves or had parents who were migrants. Only 14 of the 72 women in the interview sample had been born in Shimla. Not all migrants have moved to Shimla directly from a village, although many who have previously lived in another city were born in a rural area or have parents who were of rural origins. In some households there is a history of repeated migration – sometimes related to upward social mobility, but often to quite other factors. A woman whose husband is in the army or who is employed in certain kinds of government service may have to move many times during the span of her husband's career, in response to his various postings. Some informants came from Punjabi families who had to leave West Punjab at the time of the Partition of India in 1947 and who had moved several times subsequently before becoming settled.

Generally speaking, distance of migration is crudely related to socio-economic status in Shimla. Unlike many industrial cities in

India, it does not attract many unskilled labourers from very far afield (a notable exception being the Nepali families who are employed in road construction).

Migrants from such distant places as Kerala or Bengal are mostly to be found in the upper ranks of the bureaucracy or professions, although migrants from Punjab (for reasons discussed in Chapter 2) are to be found at all levels of Shimla society.[1]

Very few women with rural backgrounds seem at all likely to return to the villages from which they came. As the majority of them came to Shimla at or soon after their marriages, they have brought their children up in the city, and these children for the most part have only the most tenuous links with village life. The wife of a shop assistant told me,

> 'I found it difficult living in Shimla when I came here as a new bride. I had never been out much because in the village girls do not travel about much without their parents. We have lived in Shimla for more than twenty years now and we think about the future a lot. We could go back to the village, but then we shall have to live as farmers and do agricultural work. We have not done this work for so many years and I do not think I could do it now as I have a heart condition, nor do my children know how to do it. I do not know how we shall pay the rent when my husband cannot work any more, but I suppose we shall stay here in the end.'

For another woman, a generation removed from her grandfather's village and employed as a university lecturer in Shimla for several years, her family's rural background provided no more than pleasant vacations for the family.

> 'It is a nice village and the house we have there is nice and large. If everyone is there it is fun. If the rest of the family are not there it is not so much fun. We go for a very short trip sometimes, say ten days. Last year the children went, but they did not like it much. There is nothing much for them to do there. They can play as much as they want, but there is no television to keep them busy in the holidays and they don't want to read all the time.'

In fact few informants of either rural or urban background saw themselves settling anywhere else but Shimla. Only 11 per cent of the interview sample expected to move on, and these were mostly married to professional men of non-Himachali origin for whom Shimla was only one stopping place in a lifetime of transfers and mobility.

Under what circumstances do women migrate to Shimla in the first place and for what reasons? Data from the interview sample suggest that most come either at the time of their marriage to join a husband already living there or after marriage, accompanying the husband on his transfer from another place, or after spending some time living with parents-in-law in their village (see *Table 4*). On the face of it, these data seem to show precisely what anyone who has read the recent literature on migration in India would be led to expect, namely that women's urban migration is primarily related to their husbands' employment. They do not migrate independently. This kind of migration has sometimes been termed 'social' as opposed to the 'economic' migration of men, who migrate primarily to take up a job or some other economic opportunity. However my research leads me to question these categories, as the situation in Shimla (and probably in many other large cities in India) is much more complex.

Recently sociologists interested in urbanization in the Third World have drawn attention to the fact that female migration has wrongly been treated as secondary, as entirely consequent upon the migration of men. This oversight has had implications for the formulation of social policy. Andrea Menefee Singh notes that the assumption that women come to cities as dependents of men means that 'their earnings when they do work, are thus regarded as marginal and only supplementary to those of male earners in the household' (Singh 1984:99). Yet as far as India generally is concerned there has been insufficient study as yet of the economics of female migration. Where North India in particular is concerned, female migration has largely been ignored or treated as uninteresting since with village exogamy as a very general practice much of this movement is 'marriage migration' between villages. Majumdar and Majumdar (1978), for example, are content to start a discussion of streams of migration by eliminating female migration 'much of which results from marriage and other non-economic factors' (1978: 119). In other words, the rural–rural migration of most of the adult female population remains unanalysed because it is seen as belonging to the domestic sphere rather than to the sphere of production and the economy. On similar grounds sociologists are

Table 4 Interview sample: circumstances of respondents' original move to Shimla

household income		in infancy	to study, take up job or for higher salary	on marriage (from parents' home)	after marriage			always lived in Shimla	total
					from parents-in-law's home	with husband on his transfer	after husband's death, to take up job		
<Rs750	employed			3	1		4	2	10
	non-employed			3		1			4
Rs750– Rs1,500	employed			4		2	1	2	9
	non-employed	1		4	2	1		1	9
Rs1,500– Rs3,000	employed		3	5				4	12
	non-employed			3		6			9
>Rs3,000	employed		3	2				4	9
	non-employed	1	2	2		5		1	10
total		1	8	26	3	15	5	14	72

prepared to give only scanty attention to the migration of women to cities – the women are seen as migrating to join their husbands and not in order to take up jobs. Certainly in the Majumdars' study, most of the families in the squatters' settlements which they researched had indeed followed the pattern of the husband migrating to the city first, with the wife and children following later (1978:118). But the fact that the wife comes to town ostensibly to join her husband may be a fact of profound economic significance, especially if (as in the case of many of the poor families studied by the Majumdars), she has joined her husband precisely because there are better opportunities for her employment in the town than there were in the village. If this is the case, then the 'social' migration of women is 'economic' as well, or rather it demonstrates the obfuscating nature of this dichotomy.[2] (Studies of rural–urban migration among men have shown that men usually migrate to a particular city because they have kin or friends there, but this does not lead sociologists to term their migration 'social'.)[3]

Of the interview sample as many as 13 of the 58 women who had come to live in Shimla from elsewhere had originally come to the city to study, to train for a job, or to take up a job. Those who had come to study or train came before marriage and those who came to take up a job were for the most part widows who had come to work in Shimla to maintain their families after their husbands had died. All these could be said to have come for predominantly 'economic' reasons, if we are bound to use this terminology, even if a few of those who came to study did not in the end take up jobs, or took up jobs unrelated to the subject which they studied.

It is true that many more respondents (44 in all) had come to Shimla at or after marriage because their husbands worked there. Most of these women had come to Shimla at marriage but some had accompanied their husbands from other areas where the husband had been formerly employed. But looking at the matter in this way obscures the fact that a number of these women took up employment after coming to Shimla, never having undertaken paid work before. Nine immigrant women fell into this category, although not all of them were still employed at the time of the study. One more had arranged to begin paid work in the month after I interviewed her and there were a further two immigrant women who appeared to be very likely to take up paid work in the near future. Therefore we could say that for about a third of the women in the sample who were immigrants, arriving in Shimla had represented a real opening up of economic opportunities. (Only one woman gave up paid work as an immediate result of moving to Shimla, although several others gave up work subsequent to their move for reasons not connected with residence.)

It would be dangerous, of course, to generalize from a sample in which employed women were deliberately overrepresented but these data certainly entitle us to question existing approaches to female migration.

For a substantial category of immigrant women, therefore, the immediate and obvious motive for moving to Shimla might be 'domestic' or, to be with husbands and children, but this does not mean that the move does not have important 'economic' consequences in the sense of representing increased scope for economic activities. In the lowest income groups many migrant men keep their illiterate or poorly educated wives in the villages precisely because such employment opportunities for them are lacking. They are better employed looking after the family land and their transfer to the city would represent a drain on family resources rather than any kind of economic gain. Both the migration and the non-migration of women married to town-employed men has 'economic' as well as 'domestic' significance.

Household composition: who lives with whom?

Doing social science research is like shining a torch around a darkened room. As one object is illuminated, shadows are cast on others. The focus of light shifts and so do the shadows. Focusing studies of the household on wage earning males means that certain important areas remain unilluminated – especially the area of domestic work, relations between women in the household, the productive activities of women in the home. Feminist research exists in these areas which conventional research has put into the shadows. On the other hand, contacting households through their female members also casts a 'research shadow' especially on the many migrant men in Shimla whose wives have remained behind in their villages, for there is no way in which these households can enter the study. These men have little family life while they are in Shimla, although in some cases their wives spend part of the year with them – during the school holidays, for instance, or during the slack periods of the agricultural year.

Many male migrants live (officially or unofficially) at their place of work. Gyanu, for instance, an unmarried boy of about twenty, works as the *chowkidar* (caretaker) in a government office. His work is to look after the suite of offices he serves, locking them at night and unlocking them in the morning. During the day he makes tea for the office staff and runs errands. At night he sleeps on a table in the main office, spreading a few blankets to make it more comfortable. He usually eats his food in a tea shop in the bazar.

Prem Chand is a domestic servant who works for a family living in the same building where Gyanu is employed. He is married, but his wife and family live in a village twenty miles from Shimla where they have a little land. Prem Chand sleeps on the floor of his employer's sitting room and eats what food is left over from the meals he cooks for them. He visits his wife whenever he can take leave from work, but she cannot visit him as there is nowhere for her or the children to stay. He has managed to save enough to buy a small plot of land in a suburb of Shimla and is trying to build a house there so that his family can join him. But his wages are low and the price of building materials rises daily and one cannot help wondering whether he will win this battle with inflation.

Chotu Ram is an elderly man of sweeper caste who has been employed for many years in a smart hotel. His work is to clean the bedrooms and the toilets. He has sons and grandsons in his home village, who have asked him to leave this work and return to live with them. But he is happy enough in Shimla and has lived there so long that he would, he says, be bored staying in the village. He has his own room in the servants' quarters of the hotel, a tiny cubicle just large enough to take one string cot and his tin trunk.

Other migrants lodge with friends or relatives. For example, Sri Ram is from a farming family, earning about Rs1,200 per month as a shorthand-typist. His wife lives with his mother in their village and manages the family land. He lives as a lodger in the house of a friend and returns home to his village every two or three months. Sometimes his wife visits him in Shimla for a short time, but he definitely intends to return to his village eventually since, as he says 'I have my roots there'.

Tej Singh is a *peon* (office messenger) earning Rs700 per month. He is also from an agricultural family, and he owns some good irrigated land as well as several head of cattle. His wife remains in the village with his mother to farm this land, and they produce enough to feed themselves and the children quite adequately. This means that Tej Singh does not need to send regular remittances from his pay but can save a good deal every month. His main problem is that accommodation for single people is hard to find and expensive.

'People give you a room on rent for a short time and then they ask you to vacate. They are afraid that the government will find out (that they are sub-letting government quarters). Now I have found a room with someone from Mandi, the district I came from myself.'

These cases illustrate the kinds of living arrangements experienced by male migrants who do not have wives and children living with them in Shimla. Many of these arrangements involve a degree of privation and some are clearly seen as temporary. Tej Singh, for instance, does not intend to sleep on a table all his life, but is hoping that a clerical job will come his way eventually. He will then be in a position to marry and perhaps bring his wife to Shimla. Others, such as Prem Chand, are clearly bound to be living under such conditions for long periods, having little choice. Some, such as Sri Ram, put up with cramped conditions and separation from their family since they do not regard Shimla as their 'real' home. Their work in Shimla is seen as a contribution to the advancement and improvement of the household in the village, not as a means of bringing the family to the town.

There is therefore a considerable population of men who are either single or living away from their families and who must find accommodation where they can. Many of them, especially the domestic servants, cannot be said to have much home life of their own. I have devoted some space to them here because, since they lie within the 'methodological shadow' cast by this study, they might otherwise be overlooked or forgotten.

In fact the domestic arrangements of men who migrate alone has generally been neglected in studies of the household, even those that focus on men. Sociologists have been much more fascinated by the problem of why some urban people live in 'joint' households and others in nuclear family households than in the (possibly more relevant) question of why some people apparently have to live alone or in sub-nuclear households.

The hypothesis that nuclear family households will become the predominant form as urbanization progresses is informed by the idea that individual wages and occupational interests are likely to prove divisive factors whereas community of property interests and /or joint agricultural activity make the joint household a more viable form in villages, at least among landed families.

Much of the work on household form shows such varying proportions of nuclear and non-nuclear households in towns that it is difficult to perceive any pattern at all. Yet the data on rural households are just as variable. Vatuk concludes a cogent summary of some work done in this area by saying,

'Despite the varying conclusions of these and similar studies, all report from one-third to one-half nuclear households in their urban samples, figures clearly within the range of variation of rural Indian samples. However we wish to interpret these data, they certainly show no very clear tendency toward increasing "nuclearization" of the household in urban areas, as determined by household composition alone. Some of the data in fact indicate the reverse process for given regions.'

(Vatuk 1972:57)

Rao's (1972) study of a village on the fringe of the Delhi conurbation has shown that cash incomes and wage labour may even favour the persistence of joint living, since a man who is working in the city may well find it more economical to leave his wife at home with his parents or brothers, especially if he wishes to retain a stake in the family land. And from the point of view of the group rather than the individual, a situation where household members can migrate in turn leaving whoever is left behind (male or female) to organize the farm work, is advantageous for many reasons. We have seen the urban consequences of this rural practice in the discussion of lone male workers who have migrated to Shimla without their wives.

In Shimla we find a similar range of household types to that found by sociologists in other North Indian cities. So far as the interview sample data is concerned, I have summarized the situation in *Table 5* using a threefold classification of household types:

1 *sub-nuclear households* i.e. households that do not include a married couple. So far as this study is concerned, this means households where the respondent is a widow or divorcee but it

Table 5   *Interview sample: structure of respondents' household*

household income		'sub-nuclear'	'nuclear'	'complex'	total
<Rs750	employed	5	3	2	10
	non-employed	1	3	0	4
Rs750– Rs1,500	employed	2	3	4	9
	non-employed	0	8	1	9
Rs1,500– Rs3,000	employed	2	6	4	12
	non-employed	0	9	0	9
>Rs3,000	employed	0	4	5	9
	non-employed	0	8	2	10
total		10 (14%)	44 (61%)	18 (25%)	72

could equally apply to the household of a widower or divorced man, or one consisting of a group of unmarried siblings.

2 *nuclear family households* composed of a married couple and their children.

3 *complex households* I use this term (both in relation to the interview sample and elsewhere in this book) in a broad sense to include any household which comprises more than one married couple or which consists of a nuclear family plus other adult relatives of either husband or wife. This groups under one head all those types described variously in the literature as 'joint' family, 'extended' family, 'supplemented nuclear family household', etc. and avoids the problem of inventing terms for all the different possible kinds of complex family. However, it is relevant to ask how the complex households came to be complex, so I have indicated in *Table 6* the various kinds of arrangement

Table 6   *Interview sample: composition of complex households*

household consists of respondent's nuclear family

+ husband's parents (with or without husband's siblings)	5
+ own married sons and their wives and children	3
+ husband's widowed mother (all or part of time)	5
+ other relatives of husband	2
+ own parents and siblings	3
total	18

found in the complex households in the interview sample. These data are not aggregated according to income band since the total number of complex households was small and showed no sign of concentration in any one income group. Judging by the households I studied in detail it seems more probable that 'complexity' is associated with length of residence in Shimla rather than income or class, but a larger sample would be needed to establish which, if any, of these variables is important.

The categories I have used were devised so as to correspond broadly to three different kinds of domestic situation in which a woman can find herself:

1 *as sole wage earner*, also responsible for domestic arrangements,
2 *as sole organizer of domestic arrangements*, in some cases also contributing part of the household income,
3 *as one of a larger team of people* among whom the responsibilities for domestic work and for bringing in income may be divided in a number of ways.

If we are interested in the household as an economic unit which depends heavily on the input (domestic, financial, social) of women, then this seems to me the most relevant kind of classification to use, although for another kind of study a different classification might be relevant. Also, it should be quite clear that this classification is not exhaustive of all the possible types of household composition which may be found in Shimla. There are some types of household which will not appear in a sample based on married women selected at a certain stage in the domestic cycle. One of these types is, as has already been mentioned, the household composed of a single male migrant. Less commonly one finds households consisting of several male migrants, usually related in some way, who share accommodation. Another type of household, which is not very common at present but which may become more common in future, is that consisting of a group of unmarried siblings. In Shimla such households are generally formed by single men or women migrating to join an older brother or sister already settled in work in the city.

It seems to me that there are two general observations which can be made about these data. First, focusing on married women irrespective of their husbands reveals an important minority of female headed households, a category generally neglected in the literature on the domestic sphere in India. In such households the female 'head' is usually also the main breadwinner, but I did encounter cases where the 'head' was not employed and the household relied on pensions or on the earnings of grown sons or daughters. Not surprisingly, most of these households were very poor.

Second, for reasons to be discussed shortly, I am not prepared to generalize about the incidence of complex households in Shimla from this particular sample. This type of household is obviously an important minority form. As *Table 6* shows, most of the complex households in the interview sample are complex because of the presence of the parents or the parents-in-law of the women contacted, though a sample using a wide age range such as this one also 'catches' women who live in complex households as members of the senior generation.

These data illustrate certain processes of household formation found in a city like Shimla. What they do not entitle us to do is draw conclusions about the 'prevalence' or otherwise of the nuclear family in urban India, or about typical household structures in cities. Indeed there are immense methodological problems which sociologists wishing to evolve such generalizations need to over-come. Almost any method of sampling will introduce sources of bias which will complicate attempts to demonstrate the true proportions in which different kinds of household are represented in the urban population. For example, the gender composition of the sample is obviously important. My own, wholly female, sample reveals a number of female headed sub-nuclear households but fails to include households composed of single male migrants. Kapadia and Pillai used an urban sample taken from the industrial workforce of Atul colony (presumably mostly male) and discovered no households headed by women but a large number of lone men – 'singletons' as the authors aptly call them (Kapadia and Pillai 1972. 144). Samples based on locality will be affected by the nature of that locality. Comparing Singh's (1977: 71) study of families in a Delhi squatter colony with Vatuk's (1972: 54) study of a settled white collar area in Meerut, it is not surprising that the latter shows a far larger proportion of joint family and supplemented nuclear family households. Third, as the more perceptive commentators have noted, we need to take account of the way in which households evolve over time (see Ross 1961: 36 and Desai 1964: 45). From certain points of view, the joint family household can be seen as one phase in a developmental cycle, rather than as a distinct type of household. Most individuals will spend part of their lives living in a joint family household and some part in a nuclear family household. What incidence of complex households is revealed by a particular sample will depend very much on the age structure of the individuals chosen, or of the population of the locality.

Rather than attempt such generalization, it seems to me a more useful exercise to discuss the data in relation to such local conditions as might be expected to affect patterns of residence and household composition, such as housing, property, and the geographical mobility or dispersal of families.

Housing presents an acute problem in Shimla at the moment. There is a shortage of good building land and land prices are high. Building has not kept pace with the influx of new immigrants all needing accommodation to rent, and most of the new apartments coming on to the market are very expensive.[4] Old buildings are being divided into tinier and tinier flats and many hotels which used to cater for summer visitors are being converted into tenements. Many of the elegant old bungalows which used to house British families resting from the heat of the plains are now divided into two- and three-roomed flats for middle-class tenants, while individual rooms in the old servants' quarters are let out to the families of clerks, servants, and *peons*.

Few people live in houses owned by their families, and the 13 respondents who did were mainly born into or married into families which have been established in Shimla for some time. However, bank loans for building are more easily come by than was formerly the case, especially for government servants in permanent jobs. Four more of the respondents had already bought plots in Shimla where they and their families would eventually build houses, and a number of others were expecting to be able to place a deposit on a building plot in the near future. In the long run this is the best option for a family that intends to settle in Shimla and is a realistic investment for even a fairly poor family, provided the wage earners are in permanent jobs and in a position to set aside a little every month. Those families who definitely do not intend to settle (like many of the Punjabi technocrats) must opt for rented accommodation which will take a major slice out of their income every month and which may be far from the offices where they work. *Table 7* summarizes information on respondents' housing situations.

Table 7 Housing situation of households in sample

household income	own house (or share of house)	rented (private sector)	rented: government accommodation provided with		rented: private employer provides accommodation with		service given lieu of rent	total
			husband's job	wife's job	husband's job	wife's job		
<Rs750	0	8	0	2	0	2	2	14
Rs750–Rs1,500	1	13	1	1	2	0	0	18
Rs1,500–Rs3,000	3	15	3	0	0	0	0	21
>Rs3,000	9	5	5	0	0	0	0	19
total	13	41	9	3	2	2	2	72
			12		4			

In most parts of North India the concept of the joint family household constitutes a powerful ideal which is respected even by those who for personal reasons prefer to live separately from their relatives. Conventionally a bride joins her husband's household at marriage: if he is living with his parents, as would be common for a boy who is employed in his home town, then the young couple will continue to reside with the husband's parents, for the moment at least. The idea of the community of sons and daughters-in-law obediently serving thir elders and caring for each other's children in harmonious cooperation is an attractive one. Even if, as many recognize, it often generates quarrels and tensions in practice, it is still looked upon as essentially an admirable way to live. Given this cultural ethos, and given the difficulties of finding reasonably priced accommodation one would expect a young married couple in Shimla who have the opportunity to do so to stay under the parental roof for as long as possible. Of sixteen households in which members enjoy the possibility of living in the conventional type of joint family household (i.e. where the husband's parents or the married sons are alive and living in Shimla) only three have chosen not to do so. On the other hand, if we take the eight households where the husband's parents were dead or living elsewhere but where the husband's brother was living in Shimla, we find only one case where brothers opted for joint living.[5] So it seems that considerations such as high rents and the housing shortage do not have the force to sustain the 'collateral' joint family household where the parents are dead or absent.

For a couple to live with the wife's mother is culturally less acceptable in terms of the North Indian kinship ethos, unless perhaps the wife is sole heiress to agricultural land owned by her parents. This has not prevented three women in the sample from living with their own parents, although two of these are separated from their husbands and unlikely to ever rejoin them. The third is a professional woman whose husband works outside Shimla for much of the time. She stays with her parents who help care for her little son while she is out at work, but this arrangement will cease when the couple manage to get jobs in the same place. In fact in as many as five of the households in the sample the husband was employed outside Shimla and spent long periods away from his wife and children. In compiling *Table 5*, I did not treat these men as belonging to separate households from their wives although there were varying degrees of division in budgeting, decision making, etc. consequent upon their absence. In all cases the husband had a job which involved frequent transfer or extensive touring in country areas and in several the wife had a good job in Shimla which she did not wish to relinquish. All five respondents mentioned that the continuity and quality of the children's education was a major reason for putting up with the inconvenience of prolonged separation. If some households are retaining a rural base (where the wife works the land and the husband earns in the city) a few are establishing urban ones, enjoying the educational, medical, and other facilities of a large town while the husband is posted up country.

A few families live jointly because the husband and his father or his brothers are jointly engaged in running a shop or some other business and it is convenient for them and their families to live together. Urmila, a university lecturer, is married to a man who runs the family wholesale business with his father and they live in a large joint household. Suman's husband does not come from Shimla but has built up a dry cleaning business in cooperation with his brother who lives with the couple. On the other hand, in some families the parents (or the surviving parent) live separately from the son and wife precisely because the property they jointly own is situated elsewhere and needs one member of the family on the spot to supervise it. Thus Satish's widowed mother could quite easily (and a lot more comfortably) live with her son and daughter-in-law in their flat in Shimla and have the company of her grandchildren, instead of living in much rougher conditions in her village. But the family have valuable land which they are developing for commercial crops and she is the one member of the family who is free at the moment to supervise this property. Saroja's mother-in-law lives separately from her son and his wife for the same reason, although the couple would like to sell the land they own in Punjab and buy some orchard land nearer to Shimla, so that the members of the family can live closer together. In the light of these cases, we might say that it is the *work* associated with holding property that seems to be the important factor in shaping residential arrangements, as much as the simple fact of owning it jointly.

There is another respect in which work and its organization may be related to household composition. When I examined the households in which the husband's or wife's parents are present, I found that in only two of the thirteen is the respondent not employed outside the home. Could it be that the rationalization of domestic work is the key factor here? Where a woman with children is working, her mother or mother-in-law can look after her children for her more conveniently if they live under the same roof. Therefore there is less incentive for couples where the wife is at work to establish a separate household. (This is not easy to prove but I shall be presenting material in Chapter 8 which adds to its strength as a hypothesis.) On the other hand, this could not possibly be the only reason for the persistence of joint living arrangements. After all, the material on married women's employment also shows that there are many women in Shimla who are not living with either mother or mother-in-law but who nevertheless rely on these relatives to care for their children while they are at work. Evidently this rationalization of child care can be achieved without co-residence.

But a positivistic quest for single 'causes', as though any one factor determined the form the household takes, cannot be appropriate in any case. In those families where a married couple has the option of living with other relatives there need not be only one, or even only one *main* cause for the pattern they actually adopt, merely a number of reasons for favouring or disfavouring a certain arrangement. Putting it another way, there may be as many reasons for living jointly as there are members of the joint family household. Different members may benefit in different ways and advantages which strike one member might not be important for another, although one would expect joint living arrangements to last longer when the greatest number of members find their practical or emotional needs satisfied in this way. The rationalization of household work and child care that can be achieved when a couple live jointly is something which has been regarded as a felicitous by-product of the joint family household system rather than as something that positively supports its persistence, and the joint family household in general has been seen (not entirely without reason) as something which offers more obvious satisfactions for the male members than for the women, especially the younger women. This view may be a sound one so far as rural communities are concerned, but the potential satisfactions offered to women may increase where their paid work outside the home becomes a real possibility.

Property and the household

Each respondent in the interview sample was asked whether she or anyone else in her household owned any houses or land outside Shimla and I summarize the data which this question yielded in *Table 8*.[6] I would not place a high degree of reliability on these data since it became obvious in some of the interviews that when the respondent said, 'We own such and such property' she was identifying herself with her parents, her parents-in-law, or with her brothers and their families. It was not always easy to disentangle what the members of a particular household owned separately from some wider kin group. Some women did make the distinction between what they or their husbands owned and controlled now, and that which they stood to inherit on the death of parents and parents-in-law, but the question was further complicated by the fact that in different families there were different degrees of separation of control consequent upon separate residence. In some families, parents-in-law might administer the property themselves, but on behalf of the group which included both themselves and their sons, and any income would be divided among the households in this group. In other families the parents-in-law administered the property and enjoyed the income themselves, on the understanding

Table 8   *Property situation of households in the interview sample*

household income	member(s) of household own(s) land or houses		member(s) of household stand(s) to inherit land or houses		no property	total
	rural	urban	rural	urban		
< Rs750	3	0	1	0	10	14
Rs750–Rs1,500	3	3	2	1	9	18
Rs1,500–Rs3,000	3	4	3	3	8	21
> Rs3,000	6	9	3	1	0	19
total	15	16	9	5	27	72

that their sons and daughters-in-law would inherit and divide it among themselves after their death. Also many respondents were very vague about the precise amount of land owned. In many cases this was obviously due to genuine ignorance – women were often talking about land in a village they had scarcely visited in years. Others may have been chary of revealing such detailed information to a stranger in case the information might find its way to the tax authorities.

But if these data must be regarded as rather rough and ready they do show certain broad patterns. As we should expect, the households which apparently own no property whatsoever become more numerous as we travel down the income ladder (although there are a few households with very high incomes which have not yet acquired any house or land). This does not mean that all low income workers are without property. As I have already emphasized, many men in the lower income groups do not bring their wives to Shimla precisely because they own property in their home villages and it is more economical for the wife to stay in the village and live off the produce of the land rather than come to Shimla and rent the land for poor returns. But as these wives could not enter my sample this tendency is not reflected in my data.

I have already discussed living accommodation, so I shall concentrate here on property held outside Shimla. Most of this property is held in the village or town from which the respondent or her husband originally came. What is interesting is that so few households claim to derive any substantial income from such property. Again, this information may have been withheld deliberately as a matter of caution, and some respondents may not have had a very clear idea of the amount of income anyway if it was collected and handled by another member of the household.

Many couples would appear to own property which is unproductive in the sense of providing little or no income at the moment. But such property may have a meaning which is not really communicated by these crude figures, yet which becomes very clear when we look at the total circumstances of some of these households. This is best summarized by saying that some of these families are in the process of investing in property while others are in the process of abandoning it. In many cases the couple owns land in the husband or the wife's ancestral village which they themselves will never farm again or houses which they will never live in again.

The land presently is being farmed by relatives or by tenants. The current land legislation facilitates the reversion of land to a cultivating tenant after a long period of unbroken tenancy, and several respondents talked in a resigned manner of their land reverting to a tenant as though it were something that they could not prevent or were unlikely to resist.

In such cases a family which is now based in Shimla is coming to terms with the fact that their ancestral land is no longer very useful to them, even if they retain a sentimental attachment to it. If the children are being educated in Shimla and the parents are unlikely to ever retire to the village, the family land does not even have the value of a security against old age and bad times. A house or apartment in town and a government pension are more useful in old age, and the income the land yields is not enough protection against difficult times. Where the family land is small in acreage and located far from Shimla it will be the more readily abandoned by a family whose income is low, for the rent or produce yielded by the land will hardly be great enough to justify the cost of collecting it.

Some property, however, obviously represents the urban household's attempt to better itself. Old unproductive property is sold and exchanged for new income-yielding property, and cash savings are invested in land which will, either now or in the future, bring income and security. Much of the rural property which is held by households in the higher income groups consists of orchard land situated in the 'apple belt'. Families whose original home was in this area do not abandon their land, but replace subsistence crops with commercial fruit production. The Thakur family, for instance have lived in Shimla since Mr Thakur obtained a permanent government post. His village land is all planted with orchards now and he has saved enough from the proceeds to build a large apartment block which he rents out to tenants. Others, whose origins are in other parts of Himachal, or even outside Himachal itself, invest their savings in plots of land in this area, which they then plant with apple trees. Trilok Nath comes from a farming family in a remote valley. He retains some farm land there but has recently invested in orchard land nearer Shimla as well as some urban land in Shimla itself. An orchard planted now will not yield a profitable crop for some years, but an urban family which is currently provided for by the wages of its working members can endure this period in expectation of future income more easily than a peasant farmer. A good deal of energy will be put into conserving this property diligently, attending to the needs of the orchard, hiring labour for pruning and harvesting, as will be described later. Rural property will be equally diligently attended if it is irrigated and capable of being planted with commercial cereal crops and a number of Punjabi families have land of this type in the plains.

We have already seen that those migrants who expect to stay in Shimla invest in urban plots when they can and build on them when they have saved enough to do so. Those whose income is low can only afford to build a few rooms for their own family's needs, but most aim to build accommodation which can be let out to tenants. Rents being high, this kind of investment is very worthwhile and means that very substantial assets can be passed on to children.

The patterns of property holding therefore represent a process, with some households being at one stage, others at another. The families in the lowest income groups are mostly either without property at the moment or have small plots of distant or unprofitable agricultural land which is not very useful to them. This land will be even less useful to their children who will have had little to do with it and have no knowledge of agriculture. These households are busy striving to improve their employment prospects where this is possible and to ensure those of children, mainly through investment in education. They are principally 'service' families for the moment. However, there comes a time when the service family has managed to save enough to secure a loan on building land in Shimla or to invest in other kinds of property (commercial farm land, urban property in some other town where they eventually intend to settle). If at this point they come into property inherited from parents, then this will facilitate the process of accumulation. Eventually they will be in a position to derive income from the property they have acquired. They will pass on a valuable patrimony to their children who will then presumably be less entirely reliant on their service income to enjoy a good standard of living.

I am not suggesting that all households participate in this cycle, or that having embarked upon this process they all necessarily succeed in the competition for urban resources. A few of the households in the sample seem to be in danger of falling into a definite downward spiral, especially those headed by divorcees or widows, or by men suffering from long-term ill health or unemployment.

I could also be criticized for depicting the process of accumul-ation as though it occurred within one generation. In many cases it clearly takes longer and the period of total dependence on service wages is extended. Some of those who are so hopeful for the future of their children, educated to a degree they could never dream of in their own village primary schools, will see their sons and daughters join the mass of unemployed graduates or obtain only mediocre jobs, unworthy of their qualifications. For what we are actually witnessing is, of course, not a purely private and familial cycle of development, but the formation of an urban class who are wage earners, but who hope to derive extra security from house rents or agricultural rents and produce. The army of government servants does not aspire to become merely some sort of bureaucratic proletariat, but to consolidate and diversify its interests. This is not a new phenomenon in modern India, of course. In late nineteenth-century Punjab, for instance, successful members of the commer-cial classes began to invest in agricultural land, often through the extension of mortgages to the increasingly indebted peasantry. The British rulers regarded this development with some alarm as one which might undermine the position of that class of peasant proprietors which they saw as most loyal to the Raj, and as an excellent source of army recruits. But once a market in land had been established the trend could only be limited, not reversed. In contemporary Punjab there continues to be an interweaving of urban and rural interests. The new capitalist farmers often have kin who are industrialists, professionals, or administrators; urban capitalists still invest in valuable irrigated land. In Shimla, clearly it is not only the members of the urban elite who are seeking to spread their interests but also groups much lower down in the social scale. (Had the sample included 'singleton' households where the wife is still engaged in full-time agricultural production this would have been even more evident.) This could be the effect of the over-whelmingly rural character of Himachal Pradesh and the fact that as yet it has no developed capitalist or commercial sector in which either rural or urban households can invest surplus income or energies. For the farming household the only extra scope is to send a member into 'service', and for the government servant the only extra source of security is land. This has implications for the class structure of the area which are pursued elsewhere in this book. For the purposes of this chapter it is enough to note that if we pitch our interest at the level of the household then the interests of this group are diverse and evolving.

In this chapter I have not set out to provide a comprehensive survey of household forms in Shimla. As I have been at pains to point out, the nature of the sample described is not such that one could draw from it conclusions about the distribution of household types or behaviour in the entire urban population. What it can do, as I hope I have shown, is demonstrate some of the issues relating to the urban household which are raised when the study is focused on *women*.

Notes

1 One woman from a shopkeeping family which has been settled in Shimla for several generations said: 'I still feel Punjabi, and I would like my daughters to marry Punjabis, though I don't mind whether my sons-in-law live in Punjab itself or in Himachal.'

2 This dichotomy has its origins in the tendency of sociologists to overlook the economic dimensions of the urban household on the grounds that it is no longer a unit of production. E. Bruner, in a useful critique of the way in which sociologists have treated urban kinship in the Third World, notes that 'in the urbanization literature, family and kinship are often seen as purely "social", whereas the economic and political are seen as located elsewhere, in other domains' (Bruner 1982: 107).

3 See Bose (1971: 101) for a discussion of this point.

4 It would not be unusual for a household to spend as much as 40 per cent of its income on rent in the private sector. Subsidized government quarters are available for some government servants, but such accommodation is in short supply.

5 In fact several of these complex households are in one sense not the conventional type, i.e. parent(s) plus those married sons and their wives who have not yet made separate homes for themselves. In four cases the parents or widowed mother of the husband had come to join the couple in Shimla in their old age or retirement after a prolonged period of separate residence. In this respect these 'complex' households correspond to a cycle found in western societies where joint living is chosen as a solution to the problems of the elderly rather than to those of the younger couple.

6 In most cases this property was legally owned by male members of the household, being registered in their names.

Lower Bazar, one of the main shopping thoroughfares

Women and children enjoying late afternoon sunshine
outside their apartment block

A tenement block, formerly part of a hotel dating from British times

Migrant construction workers, who cook and sleep on the building site

5 Housework and housewifery

All married women in Shimla do housework, whether or not they have a proper house to live in. Even the Nepali labouring women, who come down with their families to work on the roads, can be seen outside their makeshift shacks scouring dishes or washing their shabby clothes. Housework is scarcely separable from the female role, a division of labour which is little questioned. A few educated women were aware that the possibility of men helping with housework was an issue being discussed by feminists in India and the west, but most regarded this idea as too unrealistic to be worth serious reflection. This was not because the women regarded Indian men as by nature unfitted for housework, simply that they saw men's disinclination to do domestic work as having such deep roots in their upbringing and early experience that it would be a waste of time for them to try to combat it themselves. 'Our Indian men are not ready for this kind of thing', or 'Indian men have not been trained by their mothers to do housework, they have always had it done for them. How can you change them now?' were typical attitudes. A few educated professional women did say that they intended to see that their own sons were capable of basic cooking and the like but if they were serious about this, their efforts would receive little institutional support or recognition. Home science is still a subject taught in girls' schools only and several women were rather sceptical when I said that my two-year-old boy enjoyed playing with a toy stove and cooking pots.

For a few women, domestic work was so much a part of their very being as females that they could not even detach themselves from it sufficiently to see it as a job of work from which they might snatch intervals of leisure, however short. Typically, one woman said, 'If I am free, there is always something to be done at home, sewing or mending or things like that. I am never at a loose end.' Others, when asked to name any recreational pursuits they enjoyed in their spare time would name such activities as designing clothes for their children, trying out new dishes, or equally domestic 'hobbies'.

In a study of British housewives and their work, Ann Oakley found that there was not a lot of difference between working-class and middle-class women as far as the experience of housework was concerned. They might not all describe this experience in the same language, but 'these linguistic distinctions do not necessarily denote a diversity of experience' (Oakley 1976:94). As far as the way they evaluated housework was concerned, some differences did emerge. The working-class women were more likely to hold what Oakley terms a 'traditional' view of housework, that is, as something to be done for its own sake, as part of women's self-concept. Middle-class women were more likely to take an 'instrumental' view of housework, as something which must be got through as quickly and efficiently as possible so that time can be made for more intrinsically satisfying activities, especially for their relationships with husbands or children. In Shimla the situation was rather different. Common to almost all the women was the 'traditional' attitude that housework is part of the female role and that efficiency as a housewife is an important measure of success as a woman. But beyond this common orientation the women showed wide differences as to how they experienced domestic work, which is what we should expect where the material conditions in which housework is performed are so various.

Conditions of work

One important variable affecting the way in which the housewife experiences her work is the amount of space available in which to do it. At the minimal level, the housewife in a poor family has only one room which is the scene of all her activities, and indeed of all those of everyone else in the family. She has less to clean, it is true, but a greater degree of patience and organization is needed if there is not to be mutual interference between her housework and every other kind of activity going on in the household. Leela, for instance, is a sweeper woman and lives in one room with her husband and three small children. The room is on the first floor of a tenement inhabited by about a dozen other sweeper families. There are no bathrooms in the block, only a common toilet shared by all the residents. At supper time Leela has to spread her utensils to cook the meal while her two older sons are doing their homework and the little one is running about at play. If her husband brings a few friends home for a cup of tea, there is hardly room to move. The same cement-lined sluice has to be used both for washing the clothes and scouring the dishes. As Leela has no private courtyard or balcony space she has to hang her laundry to dry on the railings beside the public footpath (if they are not already occupied by her neighbours' washing). If it rains while they are drying, then the damp cloths just have to be draped over the curtain rails. Ironing is out of the question while the rest of the family are at home as it can only be done on a blanket spread on the limited floor space between the beds.

Devaki, wife of an office worker, is a little better off. She lives in a large upstairs room in a building which was once a private hotel for holiday-makers and is now divided into one- and two-room sets for permanent tenants. She has a tiny kitchen, hardly more than a pokey cupboard, and a damp and dingy bathroom, but laundry and cooking activities can be kept quite separate. Also she has a little more storage space than Leela, since the one living room is quite large and accommodates a number of tin boxes piled against one wall. The furniture is positioned so as to form an alcove where members of the family can change their clothes without being seen by a visitor in the sitting area by the door. However there is still really only one living space – meals must be served in the room where the family sleeps, children do homework, her husband studies for his exams or entertains his friends. Like Leela, Devaki has no private outdoor space other than part of the balcony immediately outside her door.

Going up the scale, Prabha has a suite of rooms in a crumbling mansion dating from British times. It is in an appalling state of disrepair but its wood panelled walls and spacious sun lounge have a certain charm. The toilet is ancient and primitive and the kitchen is dark and gloomy, but she and her daughters have three other rooms between them, so that their various activities need not interfere with each other much, although they do not have any yard, garden, or balcony for their exclusive use.

Sarita is the wife of a high ranking civil servant and lives in a house provided with her husband's job. This house is detached and stands in a pleasant garden of its own. In appearance and design it is much like a British suburban villa of the early twentieth century (which is probably when it was built) with three bedrooms upstairs and two reception rooms downstairs. The only difference is that there is rather more kitchen space and an extra room behind the kitchen which can be used as servants' quarters. The downstairs is clearly divided into an area where housework is carried out (where Sarita goes to issue orders to her servants and to help them cook) and a reception area where the family can relax or entertain friends. The members of the household and their guests need not even be aware of the domestic work which serves their needs unless they choose to. When visiting in a house like this, the guest can enjoy refreshments which appear from 'behind the scenes' without having any idea of what effort went into making them, or being confronted with the mess involved – the vegetable parings and the dirty dishes. The division of domestic space into 'front stage' and 'back stage' (cf. Goffman 1959: 106ff.), with all that this implies for the manipulation of impressions and status messages, is a possibility at this income level.

These very different kinds of domestic environment must surely differentiate the experience of being a housewife for these women. So also must the different kinds of domestic equipment which they can afford. Wealthy women in a city like Shimla have access to much of the kitchen gadgetry and labour saving devices which are available in the west. Electric toasters, refrigerators, steam irons, and even washing machines are now on the market in Shimla, even if the range in style and price is not as great as it is elsewhere. In Europe, however, the development of these devices coincided with, and was largely stimulated by, the disappearance of cheap domestic labour. In Shimla domestic labour has not vanished and is financially within the reach of many housewives in the upper and middle income bracket. This means that these women have a choice of strategy. They may invest in machinery to save their own time and energy, or they may employ servants; whether they prefer to have machinery at their command or people is determined by personal and practical considerations which I shall discuss later. For a fortunate minority, a third option is open; they can buy domestic machinery and then hire servants to operate it for them.

Some domestic devices have been on the market for almost as long in India as in the industrialized west and have penetrated far down the income scale. Many poor women own an electric iron, so that their children can go to school with freshly pressed clothes and their husbands can look smart at work.[1] The sewing machine has long been a fixture in many rural households and is one of the most widespread pieces of domestic machinery in the cities too, and pressure cookers are popular because they save fuel. While middle-class women cook on a stove fuelled by gas or electricity, most poor women cook over a brazier fuelled by charcoal or round balls made from a mixture of coal dust and sawdust, bound with a little cow dung and dried in the sun. Some cheap electric stoves are now on the market at around Rs40 each. They are rather crude and the elements are liable to break easily but they are not beyond the budget of some lower-class families and may well become more widespread. Cooking equipment such as electric toasters, sandwich makers, blenders, and small electric ovens are very popular in middle-class households. So also is the refrigerator, although the cooler climate of Shimla makes this less of a necessity than in the plains. Working wives like to make food for several days and store it in the refrigerator to be taken out and heated as needed. Washing machines are available, but very few of the women interviewed had one or even thought the investment in one at all attractive, which is interesting since washing was one of the most disliked chores. However it is worth mentioning that there are a number of products available now which were not found a few years ago and which enable washing clothes and dishes to be done more efficiently, for example, new kinds of detergents and scouring pads. Most Indian households do not have running hot water but some middle-class families in Shimla have bought immersion heaters so that, for a few, hot water is available for laundering and washing up.

Why have some areas of domestic work been mechanized more readily than others? Why are the pop-up toaster and the blender widespread whereas the washing machine is a rarity and the vacuum cleaner almost unknown? One obvious explanation is that there is less demand for labour saving devices where work like washing clothes or cleaning the house are concerned because these are tasks which are commonly off-loaded onto servants. The housewife will not invest in machinery which consumes expensive fuel when she can hire a full-time servant for under Rs150 a month. Food preparation is the area of domestic work, however, which women are least likely to delegate to servants. This is sometimes a matter of preference; many women enjoy cooking and do not want to leave all of it to a servant. Or it may be that they cannot afford a full-time servant, only part-time help. It is easier to find a maid who will come in for a few hours in the morning to wash dishes and clean the kitchen than it is to find a part-time cook for mealtimes only, so in these circumstances cooking will remain the housewife's own responsibility. In either case the housewife will be more willing to spend money on labour saving devices in the kitchen since it will be her own labour which is being saved. However, I think that there is more to it than this.

Among the middle class and upper class, eating habits have changed somewhat, though this change has not been radical. Indian families, that is, have not given up their daily fare of curried vegetables with chappatis or rice for British style 'meat and two veg.' or other western fare. Their concept of what constitutes a well balanced and satisfying main meal has not changed fundamentally. But there is an increased preference for cake, ice cream, soup, or sandwiches which are enjoyed as snacks or trimmings to a traditional Indian meal, especially when guests come to the house. Some of the investment in kitchen gadgetry is a response to such changes in taste and eating patterns rather than to the need to save time or labour. The Shimla housewife who gets herself a sandwich toaster is behaving in the same way as the Englishwoman who buys herself a Chinese wok or a griddle for making chapattis. It is a little ironic that just as the middle-class Indian housewife is turning to the electric blender, her English counterpart is looking for a genuine stone pestle and mortar to grind her spices, so that her curries have a more authentic flavour.

This discussion of labour saving devices is perhaps out of proportion to the amount of time actually saved by such devices in households in Shimla. For the average woman, cooking, cleaning, and laundering for the family will consume most of the time available to her and will involve considerable expenditure of energy. If the housewife also takes on paid work outside the home her double burden is great indeed.

Housework and social relationships

Much has been written about the isolated and isolating nature of the housewife role in western society. It is isolated because it is privatized. Each housewife performs the same routines at much the same times of day as other housewives but in her own separate workplace, without interacting with others as she does her work. It is isolating because the notion that this work must be privately done – both a premise and an ideal – has effectively prevented women from working out ways of doing housework cooperatively or from rationalizing it by dividing tasks among women in different households. Its private organization means that it consumes an excessive number of woman hours and few housewives have much leisure time to go out and meet other people during the day. One might add that in most western cities the nature of neighbourhood planning and domestic architecture mean that few women are likely to interact with each other or even to observe each other in the course of their housework, although there is always the chance of a chat in the launderette or a casual word with a neighbour as the clothes are hung out. As joint family living is not the norm in most western societies, most women will have sole responsibility for domestic work in the households where they live. Even when the children are small it is lonely work, relieved only a little by tuning in to the radio or TV while doing the ironing. This at least is the predominant picture,[2] although there is also a strand of research which shows that there are some communities at any rate (mostly stable working-class communities) where, if housework is not done in company, than being a housewife does not preclude a good deal of informal interaction with other housewives: the casual encounter at the corner shop and the dropping in for cups of tea in the afternoon (Willmott and Young 1962: 107).

How far is this also the case in Indian cities? We might well expect the situation in Shimla to resemble the more unsociable patterns reported in Britain. Unlike most Indian urban areas Shimla is not densely settled (except the old bazar area), so few housewives will be forced to interact through concentration of residence. The houses are not built with quarters facing onto a common courtyard for instance, or along pedestrian alleyways which can be used as meeting places for neighbours. There are few shared neighbourhood amenities (for instance, a well, tap, or group of shops) such as might provide a meeting point for housewives in the community. Since the climate in Shimla is so much cooler than on the plains, the housewife is likely to spend less time sitting out in her yard or on her balcony, visible and accessible to her neighbours. So climate, terrain, and style of architecture would appear to conspire to isolate the Shimla housewife quite as much as her British counterpart.

Yet the Shimla housewives I met evidently did not experience their situation as isolated. Some reported that they had felt lonely when they first moved to Shimla but in no cases had this feeling lasted more than a month or so. Most considered that they had as much social life as they wanted, although as we shall see later, their ideas of what constituted a satisfactory social life and how this social life was organized might vary. Those who expressed regret that they did not do paid work outside the home would mention a desire for economic independence, mental stimulation or a better standard of living as reasons, but seldom a wish for more companionship. Housewives living in the same quarters or block of flats usually seemed to know each other well and very few of my interviews were conducted without interruption from some neighbour or friend calling for a chat. In the late morning or afternoon when the main chores were done, women would find a sunny spot on the hillside to sit together with their mending or knitting until it was time to start preparing the next meal. Potentially, therefore, privatized housework is always isolating for the woman who does it full-time, but if it actually creates loneliness, then this says as much about patterns of community life and local conventions of neighbourly behaviour as it does about the nature of housework. Interestingly, of the very few respondents who did feel that their social lives were impoverished, the majority were working women who found that the housework which they had to do on their return from work in the evening and at weekends left them insufficient time to mix with friends and neighbours.

There is one other respect in which housework in a city like Shimla is less of a lonely occupation than in most western societies. The responsibility for housework is definitely a female one, but the woman who organizes the material servicing of the household is not always doing it alone. She may belong to a household in which there are other women – a mother-in-law or sister-in-law to help her – or she may be able to afford to employ a part-time or full-time servant. At the very least a sweeper will come and call once a day to clean the toilets and empty rubbish cans (as in other Indian cities, there are few households which are without this facility). *Table 9* shows the pattern of domestic teamwork in the households represented in the interview sample, and we see from this that 33, i.e. fewer than half

Table 9 Interview sample: household structure and the employment of servants

household income		complex households		nuclear family households		sub-nuclear family households		total
		employ servant(s)	no servant	employ servant(s)	no servant	employ servant(s)	no servant	
<Rs750	employed		2		3		5	10
	non-employed				3		1	4
Rs750–Rs1,500	employed		1		8		1	9
	non-employed		4		3	1		9
Rs1,500–Rs3,000	employed		4	5	1	1	1	12
	non-employed			4	5			9
>Rs3,000	employed	3	2	3	1			9
	non-employed	1	1	7	1			10
total		4	14	19	25*	2	8*	72

* These figures represent women having sole responsibility for housework.

of the women in the sample, had sole responsibility for the housework in their household and some of these probably received help from teenage daughters. All the rest either belonged to a household where there were other adult women or could employ a servant (sometimes both), i.e. they were part of a team of people among whom domestic tasks and responsibilities could be allocated. This sounds rather grand when in some cases all that the 'teamwork' consists of is the help of a part-time maidservant who comes to wash the dishes and sweep the kitchen out every morning. However in a few households the domestic work team was quite large. For instance, in one complex household whose menfolk were employed in the family wholesale business, the mother-in-law was the main person responsible for organizing the housework. Her unmarried daughter did a good deal, and the daughter-in-law did a certain amount when she was not out at work. In addition the household employed a full-time male servant and were currently looking for a suitable *ayah* (nurse maid) for the daughter-in-law's little girl. In another household, that of a senior civil servant whose wife was also an administrative officer, there were two full-time servants, a cook and an *ayah*, who also did a certain amount of waiting at table, answering the door, and so on. Both these women lived in the servants' quarters attached to the house and both had relatives whose services could be called upon occasionally if, for instance, the couple wished to give a large party.

In households where no servants were employed, it was really only adult women who counted as far as domestic work teams were concerned. Other members of the household were not likely to contribute much to getting the housework done. Husbands, as we have seen, were not regarded as being either capable or willing to do much in the house, and many women found the idea of them doing so rather amusing.[3]

A few working women praised their husbands as being very 'helpful' in the house, but it often transpired that the husband did not do anything very concrete towards the actual housework. It usually meant that he would entertain or supervise the children so as to enable the wife to get on with her cooking or washing without interruption – a very useful service but not the kind of contribution to housework which I am considering here. A few working wives mentioned that their husbands would help out with cooking or cleaning if there was an unusual accumulation of work at the weekend, but this was uncommon. Several of the working women made the point that it was not what the husband actually did or did not do that mattered to them, rather his attitude to their workload. A husband could help more by making time for a working wife to get through her chores by attending to the children, by not making demands for inessential small services (endless cups of tea, for instance) and by not grumbling if meals were occasionally late or shirts not ironed in time.

The services of young children were not as important as I had expected them to be, even in the poorest families. In a few low income households a boy might be asked occasionally to fetch small items from the shops or a girl to mind the baby for a short while, but few women depended on the regular performance of these tasks. This is interesting when we consider the volume of evidence from other cities showing that the contribution of small children to the poor urban household can be crucial, e.g. in a study of women in a South Indian city, Manohar, Shobha, and Rao found that, 'A large number of respondents felt that education of children was not necessary because they could not afford to do without their assistance both at home and at work' (Manohar, Shobha, and Rao 1983:80).

It is likely, of course, that much of the work done by girls was not mentioned because it was taken for granted. Most women of all classes did consider the training of daughters in domestic skills to be an important part of a mother's duties, so presumably the daughters of these women did spend some time in the kitchen. But this work seems to have been counted as a course of necessary training rather than as an indispensable contribution to the household economy.

Having said this, I still think that young girls from poor families in Shimla are less likely to have a regular round of domestic chores than their counterparts in the villages or comparable communities The most probable reason for this is suggested by the words of one informant, a poor widow employed as a *peon* in a government office. She told us:

'I do all the housework myself – all the cooking, cleaning, washing, fetching the rations, everything. My children help a little in whatever way they can, but only a little because they are also busy with their school work . . . I would like my children to study and do well and be able to get good jobs. I want my daughters to study as well, because if they have to work they will need good qualifications too.'

Since one of the main attractions of Shimla is the good educational facilities it provides, poor families will endure the exorbitant rents and high cost of living there if they feel their children will benefit in future from the schooling they can obtain here. It would make no sense for them to then interfere with their children's studies by loading them with household chores when they should be doing their homework. Many of the women of rural origin regretted their own scanty education, casually snatched in the intervals between fetching water from the well and feeding the cattle. Unmarried daughters past school age were clearly expected to do more, especially if the mother was out at work. But even here, there was an unwillingness to impose anything that would interfere with success at college if they were studying and a general feeling that they would have their share of domestic work anyway once they were married.

In households where there were several adult women present, a common pattern was for the eldest to take the main responsibility for organizing the housework. If the mother-in-law still controlled the finances of the household, she usually controlled the allocation of housework also. But in many households the mother-in-law had evidently taken a back seat and relinquished this key role. Where this had happened, the daughter-in-law usually described the older woman as 'helping' her. This seemed to be a more usual pattern in the smaller complex households, consisting of husband, wife, and the husband's mother. The mother-in-law was more likely to act as team organizer in a large household where several of her sons and unmarried daughters were also present. It would be interesting to know whether the division of household duties was ever the subject of tension in families, although I did not ask specifically about this. Certainly few women brought the issue up spontaneously. Those working women who lived with their mothers or mothers-in-law usually spoke appreciatively of the simple fact that they did not have to do all the housework themselves on coming home at night. Some women were obviously aware of a potential problem but found ways of avoiding disputes or confrontation. Gauri, who works all day as a cleaner, has a newly married daughter-in-law who is not employed outside the home, and who does a lot of the household work. The daughter-in-law can sew well and Gauri would like it if she could save the family money by making more garments at home. But, as she said, 'She does not have the time, so I do not press her. She is only young, why to quarrel for nothing?'

Hiring servants

From the point of view of household economics, it would seem that Rs1,000 approximately represents the income threshold below which few families would feel able to afford to hire a servant. Three of the women in the interview sample belonging to households with incomes lower than this actually earned their living as domestic servants themselves, and several others provided domestic service to a landlord in lieu of rent. Above this level of income, whether or not a servant is hired depends on several kinds of consideration. Surprisingly, the wife's employment outside the home does not seem to be the most important factor. Some of the working wives who could have hired a full-time servant stated that they preferred to hire part-time help or none at all because they did not wish to leave a servant alone in the house all day unsupervised. There was a widespread feeling among all the women who were actual or potential hirers of domestic labour, that servants cannot be trusted, they cannot be left to get on with things. A major fear is that the servant will purloin the family's food. One domestic servant told me how she had once had a job where her duty was to look after two toddlers all day while the mother was out at work, as well as doing the housework. Her mistress was so convinced that the servant would steal the food while she was gone that in the morning she would put out the precise quantity that would be needed for the children's lunch in the morning, and lock the rest away. This servant left the job in disgust after a short while, thereby no doubt fuelling the widespread idea that 'servants are unreliable'.

Another consideration for working wives was that they did not feel they would have the time to train a servant to their own satisfaction, and that they would not find an untrained servant useful. There was a widespread feeling that even an experienced servant will not adhere to the mistress's standards and preferred way of doing things unless taught to do so, and working women did not see how they could take time off work to supervise the servant during this necessary period of induction. These considerations help to explain why more working women, who theoretically can afford to do so, do not hire servants in spite of the fact that they clearly find their double load of housework and paid work burdensome.

If anything, the employment of servants may be more closely related to household structure than to the employment of the wife. In the interview sample only 4 of the 11 complex households in the two upper income bands hired servants, whereas 20 of the 29 nuclear and sub-nuclear households did so. It looks as though in households where a mother or mother-in-law is present the existing team of female household members is adequate, even if one of the women is in full-time work outside the home.

I think we shall understand the economics of hiring domestic help much better if we consider the nature of the relationship between the servant and the mistress. I shall discuss this in more detail in another chapter, but it is clear from their statements that women do not regard servants as simply human alternatives to the vacuum cleaner or other labour saving devices, nor as simple substitutes for their own elbow grease. They have a meaning over and above the work they do. For a start, servants bring a particular kind of kudos in any society where prestige is derived not solely from what material goods are owned but from what (or whose) services can be commanded. Women who had come down in the world looked back with nostalgia to their parents' establishments of servants as evidence of past good living, rather than to the quality of the clothes they wore or the food they ate. To be able to provide guests with milkshakes or toasted sandwiches made with the latest gadgets tells of one's comfortable income, but to be able to tell the maidservant to 'bring some tea and biscuits' conveys a social message that is not just about money, but about one's power to command others. This power cannot of course be obtained without money, but hints at a feudal ambience which even the shiniest and most up-to-date electric blenders or coffee percolators cannot communicate. Those who did not employ servants often gave as their reason the fact that servants could not be trusted to stay with a family nowadays and left their service without compunction if even a slightly better paid job came along. There is no satisfaction to be derived from employing people as adjuncts to an illusion of social power if they spoil the game by not appearing loyal and grateful.

In some cases a servant, especially one who had been with the household for a long time, provided discreet moral support and unobtrusive company more important than the material services paid for. One retired professional woman who lived alone admitted that she kept her manservant on more for these reasons than because she could not cook her own modest supper or clean her rented room. She had been used to having a house full of servants in the past and would feel odd not having one now her circumstances were straitened. Besides, the man had been with the family for a very long time, knew her preferences, and had the discretion of a Jeeves.

In some households, hiring a servant is not done in order to save work as such, but to save the housewife from having to do particular kinds of dirty or demeaning work. I have already mentioned that the majority of households pay a monthly sum for the services of a sweeper who will clean the toilets, the most polluting task of all. To a lesser extent, scouring dirty dishes and washing dirty clothes have generally been regarded as if not actually polluting, then the most degrading and unpleasant of domestic chores. The wife of a minor bureaucrat may employ a part-time maidservant to do this work where she could scarcely afford to get a full-time servant. Even a part-time dishwasher gives a newly arrived housewife the sense of belonging somewhere in the urban hierarchy, even if her position is still very far from the top.

Enough has been said by now to make it clear that the decision to hire a servant is much more than a matter of simply saving time. If women in nuclear family households are more likely to employ domestic help, it is not solely because they have a greater workload than other women. A servant adds an extra dimension to their lives at home. The ideal servant does much more than simply perform domestic work which the mistress would otherwise have had to do herself, but provides a delicate kind of social support. Some women, having tried many servants and failed to find one who could fulfil this ideal and was prepared to stay, gave up and abandoned the idea of employing a servant at all. Others were prepared to put in a good deal of time training a raw country girl or boy in the hope that she or he would eventually provide the desired mixture of hard labour, tact, and constancy. To be fair, many of these women were prepared to offer quite a lot in return – sympathy, practical help in family crises, affection, and training in useful and marketable skills (although the one thing they were not usually prepared to offer was high pay). They would work quite hard at developing the relationship, and if it broke down or the servant left for a better job they would feel considerable disillusion at this wasted expense of effort. A few women honestly admitted that they never kept a servant because they did not feel prepared to put in this effort in the first place, although this was not quite the way in which they expressed it. As one woman, employed in the university administration, said: 'It would save me a lot of trouble to have a servant to do the cooking instead of doing it myself. But with the servants you have to put up with their whims and then you get dependent on them.' Other women frankly wanted a more business-like relationship with the servant they hired and were likely to be the cause of disappointment themselves if the servant was looking for a more committed long-term relationship. The happiest households were those in which the needs and expectations of servants and mistresses were most nearly matched.

In the case of some households in the upper income groups there was a strong preference for well-trained servants who were looking for long-term employment (rather than as a stop-gap before getting married or getting a better job). In these households there might be a good deal of entertaining in connection with the husband's job, and the role of servants in providing and preparing for such hospitality is crucial. The guests must be greeted in proper style with due awareness of their various ranks and positions, the food must be of a certain style and quality, and the service must be discreet yet sophisticated. Where this kind of service is needed there is a preference for live-in servants who make domestic service their career (these are usually male) rather than for locally resident servants (usually female), who are likely to withdraw from this kind of work if their household circumstances improve slightly, or if they find alternative work.

Models of the good housewife and the meaning of housewifery

Housework and the female role were so inseparable for most of the women I met that they did not often feel they could stand back and declare that they either liked or disliked housework as a general category of activity, although many felt able to specify like or dislike of some particular tasks. Washing clothes, for instance, was universally disliked. At many times of year in Shimla it is difficult to dry the laundry unless it is hung out very early so as to catch every last ray of sunshine, so washing has to be done as soon as possible after rising and giving the family breakfast. At this time the water in the tap will be freezing and the air cold. The housewife must squat in the cold damp bathroom and beat her laundry with a *thapi* (a flat piece of wood shaped rather like a small cricket bat) until it is clean. After a while the hands become numb and wrinkled from immersion in cold water.

Cooking was the task more frequently mentioned with approval and even women from quite poor families enjoyed planning interesting meals and new dishes when guests were expected. Many women also mentioned designing garments to be stitched for their children, or knitting. In Shimla, with its mountain climate, warm sweaters are a necessity for all the family and although ready-made knitwear in acrylic and pure wool is becoming more available in the shops, many women still find it cheaper to make most of their family's knitwear themselves. Knitting is the constant accompaniment to most feminine activities in Shimla. Shorthand-typists and teachers take their needles and wool to work in the morning, ready to make up a few rows whenever the opportunity presents itself, and one sees housewives strolling down the Mall with their children, knitting as they walk. Knitting patterns are unknown, so each woman has to design her own garments and judge the measurements correctly. Paper patterns for sewing are also rarely used, so that knitting and sewing are genuinely creative tasks, involving a sense of design as well as accurate work and a neat finish.

If there was any general complaint about housework expressed by women of all classes it was simply that there was too much of it and that it was difficult to get through it in the time available without some lowering of standards. Of course, as must be clear from the preceding discussion, the women were not all equally burdened. Some had to tackle the demands of a large household single handed while others had to cater for only a small family with the help of other women in the household or of servants. Some worked long hours at a paid job, others were at home all day. But irrespective of these differences, all but a few of the women felt themselves to be everlastingly busy, never able to withdraw their attention from the machinery of the household without causing what one woman aptly described as a 'pile-up'.

If there were differences in the way in which women experienced housework, these were expressed in terms of their models of what housewifery involves and of what it takes to be a competent housewife. Crudely speaking, one can perceive two models of the good housewife here, and these models were approximately related to differences in income.

For the poorer women, good housewifery was basically a matter of actually managing to get through all the work involved without leaving anything out. As we have seen, housework for these women is time consuming and often physically wearing. Good housewifery was also a matter of being able to feed and clothe one's family within one's means, skilfully cutting corners without the family suffering, saving money by not buying what you can make yourself, always being on the lookout for a bargain. This was not only a model which the poor held for themselves, it was a model which others held for them. Thus, a comfortably off professional woman commended her poor neighbour saying, 'She is a very clever woman indeed, she is always stitching or knitting something for her family and she never wastes anything at all.' Poor women were not much given to expressing judgements of each other's standards of housewifery so it was not very easy to find out what standards applied here, but clever management of resources seemed to be paramount. (As we shall see in a subsequent chapter, women of all classes tended to have important responsibilities for the management of money and other resources; poor women only differed in singling out economy and budgeting skills as a criterion for judging the housewife.) One woman who had moved to Shimla to join her husband only a couple of years ago from their village expressed disgust with the whole business of urban housewifery, just because it seemed to be more to do with managing money than with producing things:

> 'We are village people, we feel constricted in the city. In the village we produce everything ourselves – we grow it and then eat it. Here, if you have money then you can get things. Everything has to be got from the bazar. The city is nice only if you have cash. In the village, the harder you work, the more you eat.'

Most of the poor women from rural backgrounds were only too glad to have put this endless agricultural toil behind them and did not share this woman's desire to return to the village. But many would understand the problem she is referring to, namely, that being a housewife in a poor urban household is largely a matter of juggling demands so as not to exceed the household budget, while having little or no control over the size of that budget.

Women in the higher income groups saw being a good housewife much more in terms of developing skill and originality in performing tasks like sewing, cooking, and home making. A good housewife, for them, meant one who could cook interesting and varied dishes for her family, who could knit attractive garments for her children, or could sew and embroider imaginatively. At the highest income levels it meant also having good taste in matters of home decoration – an eye for colour schemes and the skill and patience to find just the right fabric for the curtains, just the right style for the dining room furniture.[4] Good housewifery might also mean being a thoughtful and imaginative hostess – being able to organize a satisfying spread of dishes for guests at a supper party, ensuring their comfort and enjoyment.

The distinction I have made between these two models of housewifery is not intended as a rigid dichotomy. I am not suggesting that poor women do not think it important to try to make their homes as attractive as they can; the little embroidered covers placed over the radio set, the choice of religious pictures or arrangement of family photographs on the walls bear witness to the fact that their idea of housewifery is not purely utilitarian. Similarly it would be unrealistic to suggest that middle-class women are all out to impress the neighbours with their good taste and domestic imagination without thought for careful budgeting. The two models I have presented reflect the ways in which women judge their own efforts rather than strict differences in practice. They indicate differences in emphasis on the various aspects of housework and housewifery.

There is in any case a good deal of overlap. Some women were obviously striving towards a situation where they would be able to give priority to considerations other than sheer economy and thrifty use of resources. These were the women who looked most eagerly to women's magazines, radio and television programmes for new ideas in cooking and homecraft, and who looked forward to 'kitty parties' as opportunities to learn new recipes or gather new ideas for entertaining.[5] Putting the same thing in another way, we could say that the more elaborate notion of housewifery expressed by the middle- and upper-class women was in the process of filtering down the hierarchy, pressurizing poorer women into more and more

exacting ideas of what competence as a housewife should mean.
Caplan notes that this process seems to be invading the urban scene
in India. Where there should have been a reduction in the amount
of housework a woman had to do (with the drop in the average
number of children and the increased availability of labour saving
devices) there has actually been an increased burden.

> 'The women's magazines and the mass media also help to foster a
> desire for a house that is nicely decorated, perhaps ornamented
> with the wife's handiwork. Cookery, complicated and time
> consuming in its traditional form, now extends to making
> western style jams, juices, and so on. In short, fewer children and
> modern homes need more time and attention from women than
> that required a generation ago to cope with many children and
> old fashioned kitchens.'
>
> (Caplan 1978:113)

There are various ways of viewing this process, which is not
peculiar to India. We can see it simply as another application of
Parkinson's law; housework, like all other kinds of work, increases
to fill the time available. So if, for whatever reasons, housework
looks as though it can be reduced to only a matter of a few hours'
effort every day, the art of making the correct kind of bread roll or
the fashionable kind of lampshade present themselves to fill the
time made free by the dishwasher or vacuum cleaner. Or we could
see it as something more sinister, a process which conspires to keep
women at home, or at least out of the most interesting and best paid
jobs, by ensuring that they are fully occupied with ever greater
domestic detail, just when they were in a position to liberate
themselves from the worst aspects of housework altogether.

There is something in both these views. The organization of
consumption in the household is certainly not rational, in spite of
attempts to rationalize it. However I think that these views are often
motivated by an idea that production is the really serious business
of social life, while consumption, over and above the level necessary
to refuel human beings for yet further productive efforts, is a rather
trivial affair. Striving for a particular style of consumption, the
search for taste, style, fashion, or quality in domestic matters are
seen as means by which women (in their capacity of housewives) are
distracted from the more important pursuits open to them and
forced to immerse themselves in petty competition for meaningless
forms of status.

So far as western women are concerned, there is certainly some substance in these views. But I think that the role of women in organizing domestic consumption in Shimla and many comparable Third World cities has concrete, if indirect, consequences beyond the domestic sphere, and that therefore this process of differentiation and detail in the business of housewifery should be taken seriously. The distinctions in style and taste which the middle- and upper-class women reach for are not mere symptoms of an obsession with triviality. They should be seen as indications of a serious intention to *invest* in status, not just to *display* it.

Perhaps this point will be made clearer if I take one example of domestic activity, entertainment in the home. The way in which guests are entertained is an important criterion by which a household is judged in any society. The kind of food you offer to a prospective bridegroom or a prospective client who visits the home may communicate the degree of seriousness with which you view the deal to be discussed. In Shimla, the class structure is very fluid. Many families are in the process of rising in the urban class system and a few are in danger of sinking. By entertaining a husband's guests in the right way, by skilfully creating the right impression, a wife can help to extend his network of contacts and to impress his superiors – a point developed in more detail in Chapter 10. The more cosmopolitan the milieu in which he works, the more the wife has to be aware of the fine distinctions of rank and ethnic background among her visitors, and the more she has to be sensitive to the different degrees of formality required by various kinds of social occasion. She must be aware of these things both when entertaining and when attending functions organized by others. If she is to create the best impression, her style of presenting herself and her home must be neither too rustic and unsophisticated nor too showy, a combination of a desire for the comfort of others with a discreetly confident assertion of her own worth and standing. Seen from this point of view, the time she spends in choosing the precise shade of fabric for her table linen or the exact blend of spices for a new dish do not represent trivial preoccupations at all.

These women, then, are right to take these aspects of their housework seriously. It is true that no son will fail his examination because his mother has chosen the wrong brand of washing powder for his shirts, and that no husband will lose his job because his wife has chosen the wrong shade of darning wool to mend his sweater, contrary to what a certain style of advertising would have the housewife believe. But the *total* effort which the housewife puts into her management of the home will bear fruit in the way in which the entire household is perceived by others and affect its worthiness to compete in what is likely to become a very tough struggle for advantage in the urban class system.

Notes

1 In Shimla there are a few *dhobis* (laundrymen who collect the clothes from customers and deliver them washed and pressed the next day) but not as many as in other Indian cities of a similar size. And one does not find a 'press man' at the end of each suburban street as one does in Delhi, with his table and his charcoal heated iron.

2 See Hobson (1978:87), Hunt (1980:79), or Oakley (1976:101).

3 Some men almost certainly had a greater capability in this area than their wives gave them credit for. Many husbands, after all, had spent a period working in Shimla while their wives were elsewhere, or living alone in the city before their marriage, during which time they presumably had done a certain amount of cooking, cleaning and laundering for themselves. (However, doing one's personal housework when living alone is not seen as doing 'women's work' for a man, whereas doing, say, the washing, when a wife or some other female member of the household is available to do it has a quite different connotation.)

   Male servants are not regarded as less efficient than female ones – where there is a preference for the latter it has nothing to do with ability to do the work involved. So if women feel that it is laughable to expect husbands to do housework, this has as much to do with the effects of norms of proper male behaviour as with men's incapacity to acquire domestic skills.

4 This can be contrasted with the situation I noted in a rural area where even the prosperity of the rich women did not enable them to exercise much choice in styles of cooking, dress, etc. since the kind of goods that would enable a rich household to distinguish itself from a poor household in style and quality, as opposed to mere quantity, of consumption were hard to obtain locally (Sharma 1980a:127).

5 A kitty party is a regular social gathering among a group of women who have agreed to put a certain sum of money into a common pool each month. Each draws the money thus collected in turn. Whoever draws the money must entertain the others in her home that month and provide a tasty spread of refreshments. The kitty party nicely symbolizes the juxtaposition of thrift and style as considerations for the urban housewife.

6 Household management: material resources

In this chapter I shall consider the work which women do in managing the material resources of the household – cash and property. Most studies of the household recognize the importance of financial planning and decision making as a household function which must be performed by someone among its members, but few have treated resource management as *work*, that is, as a set of tasks that consume energy and time. One might expect that, on the whole, the more resources a household has at its disposal the more work must be devoted to managing them; given the greater scale of operation it ought to take more time to plan the budget and get in goods and supplies for a rich household than for a poor one. It certainly takes longer to decide how to spend Rs3,000 and to tot up the outgoings when it has been spent than it does Rs300. As several of my poor informants pointed out, one does not have to ponder long as to how to spend a monthly wage of Rs300, nor does it take long to spend it.

However, this is to look at resource management in a very narrow sense. The recipient of Rs300 may well need to organize credit to deal with shortfalls at the end of the month and will then have to spend time locating shopkeepers prepared to give goods on 'tick', or raising funds from well disposed neighbours or kin. The housewife with Rs3,000 to spend will probably have a car to take her to the bazar, or a servant to whom routine purchases can be entrusted, if indeed she does not make her orders over the telephone. On the other hand, a favourite mode of planning small savings among middle- and upper-class Shimla women is to participate in 'kitty parties' (see p. 84) – enjoyable engagements no doubt, but time consuming when considered as a means of resource management. It appears then, that at all income levels the management of income and property must be considered as *work* which consumes variable quantities of that other important resource – time. As I hope to show, it is the labour and time of the female members of the household that are most continuously deployed on this work.

Most writers who have tackled the subject of budgeting and the allocation of household resources have considered these activities less as a form of work than as an expression of power relations. A considerable body of literature and research developed from the 'resource' theory proposed by writers such as Blood and Wolfe (1960) according to which members of a household are likely to exercise power in the household in proportion to the resources they bring to it. Subsequent work has demonstrated that the matter is far more complicated. For one thing, the household is not an impervious unit: pervasive ideologies or broader structural forces may interfere with or reinforce the 'internal' power dynamics of the household. For instance, Pauline Hunt's (1980) study of working-class families in Britain shows that while the housewife bears the main responsibility for making the housekeeping money cover all the family's needs, she receives it from her husband who has the power to determine what portion of his total earnings she shall receive for this purpose and to whom she must turn if she cannot manage on the sum allowed. This material dependency is reinforced by an ideology according to which the housewife has no independent claim on the housekeeping money for the fulfilment of her personal needs and which makes it difficult for her to spend money on herself without feeling guilty (Hunt 1980:47). Similarly, Edwards reminds us that the inequality of men and women in relation to the labour market outside the household is bound to affect their exercise of control and resources within the household (Edwards 1981:133).

A distinction needs to be drawn between the 'work' dimension of resource management and the 'decision-making' dimension if we are to develop a sound methodology for its study. Safilios-Rothschild has made the useful distinction between 'orchestration power' and 'implementation power':

> 'Spouses who have "orchestration power" have, in fact, the power to make only the important and infrequent decisions that do not infringe upon their time, but that determine the family life style and the major characteristics of their family. They also have the power to relegate unimportant and time-consuming decisions

to their spouse who can thus derive a "feeling of power" by implementing these decisions within the limitations set by crucial and pervasive decisions made by the powerful spouse.'

(Safilios-Rothschild 1976: 359)

More straightforwardly, Edwards makes the distinction between 'management' and 'control' of domestic finances. 'Control' refers to decision making while the spouse who 'manages' carries out decisions already made (Edwards 1981: 4). In short, she who pays the bills does not necessarily decide what shall be bought. Empirically, these functions may not be as clearly separable as these conceptual distinctions imply, but they do enable us to perceive that the power dimension and the work dimension of resource management need not be vested in the same person.

However this distinction does not get rid of the problem of whether ability to make budgeting decisions means the same thing in terms of household power at all income levels. Any discretion which a poor housewife enjoys in deciding how to spend the money to which she has access seems a dubious privilege when the choices open to her are strictly limited and the very survival of other members of the household may depend on her capacity to economize and keep her eyes open for a bargain. A middle-class housewife with an allocation of Rs700 in her pocket is in a position to decide whether, say, to put by Rs50 towards new bed covers or to spend the same amount on hiring a part-time servant to save herself the chore of scouring greasy dishes. In a limited way her budgeting function gives her some real control over matters that affect her life, even if she is still ultimately dependent on her husband's approval and willingness to 'let' her have this 'allowance'. On the other hand, one could just as well say that it is the very critical nature of the decisions which the poor housewife has to make which must give them some weight. The discretion to decide whether to buy two kilos of flour and one kilo of fresh vegetables or three kilos of flour and a handful of chillies seem trivial but it might be crucial if it affects the diet of individuals who may be already living on the threshold of malnutrition.[1]

The distinction between management and control may therefore have different meanings at different income levels. There are many other methodological problems both practical[2] and conceptual[3] attendant upon the study of the relationship between power and resources in the household which researchers have not yet been able to resolve satisfactorily. In the following discussion I propose to concentrate on resource management activities considered as a form of work, but I will try not to beg the question of power entirely, and will return to it later.

Income management work: the division of labour

The work of managing the household's cash income (property will be dealt with on p. 95) involves a number of tasks. Some degree of planning is usually necessary, whether this consists of simply reflecting on the month's commitments on the way to the bus stop or sitting down with pencil and paper and drawing up a detailed budget. Bills have to be paid and as cheques are little used even among the wealthy, a personal visit to the electricity board office, the landlord's house, the children's school has to be made by somebody. If savings are made they may have to be deposited; if credit is required it must be raised by some means. Shopping for daily requirements is a time consuming task that someone must perform and requires energy, given that Shimla has few local shopping centres for a town of its size and most people have to walk a considerable distance to get their groceries and other necessities.

The respondents in the interview sample were asked how and by whom these tasks were performed in their own households and the replies they gave show that a wide variety of arrangements exist. However, if we separate out the female headed households (in which there could be no division of labour between husband and wife since the husband was dead or absent), three broad patterns emerge. These types are summarized in *Table 10*. This is only a very rough and ready classification of women's descriptions of the division of labour in their own households and each group conflates a range of combinations of work and responsibility. What can be said fairly confidently is that the extreme cases were absent, i.e. there were no households in which the total responsibility for income management fell upon either the husband or the wife to the exclusion of the other partner. It would be interesting to know more about the relationship between income management practices and variables such as level of income since researchers elsewhere have found these to be important. For instance, Meredith Edwards finds

Table 10   *Interview sample: household income management*

households in which the wife does most of the income management work	20
households in which the husband does most of the income management work	9
households in which the income management is divided fairly equally	30
female headed households	13
total	72

that in an Australian sample, income management on the part of the wife is more common where household income is low or where the wife is employed outside the home (Edwards 1981:132). Certainly I found no cases of household income being managed entirely by the husband in the lowest income band though the employment of the wife seemed a less relevant variable in Shimla (see p. 100). However I think it would require a larger sample than this to demonstrate such associations clearly.

If we take the first category, the group of households in which the wife claimed that she had the prime responsibility for income management work, a typical response was that of Jayashree, wife of an engineer employed by the government:

'He hands me over all his pay. It is my responsibility to manage the household and give him what he needs. I take a pencil each month and add up the rent, the children's school fees and the other expenses. If there is anything left after the routine purchases are made then I put it in the bank or use it for entertainment or clothes for the children. If we have to make some major purchase, for instance a wedding present for someone, then of course we plan it together. We do not keep financial secrets from each other. I tell him how much I have got left each month.'

In some households circumstances were such that it was inevitable that income management should be mainly the work of the wife. If the husband was absent from Shimla for much or all of the time, being posted elsewhere or having to make frequent trips outside in connection with his work, he was not in a position to take on the routine tasks. Veena, for instance, is married to an affluent contractor whose business takes him away from Shimla for long periods. She said:

> 'I do most of the paying of bills, trips to the bank and the shopping because my husband is not here most of the time. He gives me the money when he comes and I spend it – he is not concerned at all and does not even ask me about it.'

In such households the husband could not be involved in routine planning and expenditure and in several the wife had gradually taken over responsibility for the less routine matters also.

In some cases the situation was affected by the economic inactivity of the husband, as in the case of a domestic servant whose husband had been out of work for many months because of ill health. The only income in the household was hers and she did not give any to her husband. Frequently she had run into debt as her wages were pitifully low. On some occasions she had been able to borrow from her employers, and good relations with the more amenable shopkeepers in the bazar had yielded some groceries and other essentials on credit. When she did receive any money she was obliged to put a good deal of energy into balancing the demands of her various creditors and putting off the most pressing so that she could spend the cash in hand on food and fuel. In more favourable circumstances the inactivity of the husband might lead him to play a greater part in the management of income in as much as he had more time available. A university lecturer whose civil servant husband had retired early noted that her husband was more prepared to do the shopping and took a greater interest in the day-to-day running of the household than he had been during his busy professional life.

The households in which the wife undertook fewer of the tasks associated with income management than the husband were few in number, as *Table 10* shows, and even some of these have perhaps been inappropriately classified, being joint family households in which it was in fact the husband's mother who did most of the spending and saving. In such cases the husband's tasks were delegated to him by his mother and, being last in the line of responsibility, the wife took small part in this kind of work. Rama, for instance, is a teacher married to a police officer, presently stationed outside Shimla. She said:

'I give my pay to my mother-in-law who lives with us and my husband usually keeps his pay and spends from it himself while he is away. My mother-in-law manages the finances at home. I don't save any money separately. I do any shopping that needs to be done with my mother-in-law's advice as to what to get.'

Such divisions of responsibility shift over time, however, and Shanta, an administrator married to a businessman, described a curious transitional situation:

'I live with my parents-in-law and my husband's sisters. We have a common budget. The money which we spend on our children, their fees, clothes, etc., I get from my husband. But this is only recently. Before he did not get a wage from the family business himself, but my father-in-law used to give us pocket money. It was quite funny, getting pocket money like a child again. Even my husband got pocket money. My father-in-law is still really head of the family and my mother-in-law arranges most things from money taken from the business. Gradually things are changing and I take a bit more part in things and they recognize me. But my husband and mother-in-law still provide for day-to-day expenses and see to the shopping. I keep most of my salary – actually I don't know what to do with it. Usually I put it in the bank for holidays and things like that.'

At present Shanta is excluded from decision making and control of the family fund (the income from the business). Her own income is still treated as 'pocket money' (a situation only possible because the household is an affluent one). However she is beginning to emerge from the role of junior daughter-in-law; she expects that her mother-in-law will give up more of the responsibility to her as she grows older, in which case she will no doubt be expected to put a greater portion of her personal income into the common fund and to take a more active part in its management.

In another group of households the husband was obliged to play the greater part in income management as the wife was either unable or unwilling to do this herself. One woman had a handicapped son and found shopping, or indeed any kind of expedition beyond the immediate locality, very difficult. Shopping in Shimla generally involves a long trudge up hill or down hill as the nearest bazar is seldom very near and for this reason it is a problem for anyone with small children. Several women in this phase of family life preferred their husband to take the entire responsibility for income management work, handing over only a small sum to deal with minor expenses. Another situation in which most of the responsibility falls to the husband is where the marriage is relatively recent and the wife has moved to Shimla from elsewhere. The wife is perhaps unwilling to show unnecessary eagerness for independent responsibility until she has gained the trust and esteem of her husband and in any case may still be getting used to an unfamiliar environment. This was the case with a stenographer who had lived in Delhi until her marriage, eighteen months ago, and who was now pregnant with her first child. She simply handed her salary over to her husband and he paid the rent of their flat and did the shopping just as he had done when he was a bachelor, although she was insistent that he would not make any major outlay without consulting her. Another respondent, a 35-year-old wife of a college lecturer, told me that she left the 'shopping and everything like that' to her husband because she came from a very 'traditional' Punjabi family where the women had not been expected to visit the bazar if the menfolk were free to do the shopping for them. She saw no reason to abandon her family's notions of the proper domestic roles for men and women. Hers was an interesting case as she was the only respondent who gave explicitly ideological reasons for the division of labour in her household.

The households in which husband and wife divided the income management work fairly equally also showed great diversity in the details of their arrangements. Sometimes the couple planned expenditure or drew up a budget together and then split the work of executing the budget between them. Manjit Kaur, a government engineer's wife, described arrangements in her household:

'We both organize the expenses. It is not the sort of family where we keep things secret from each other. When he gets his pay we both sit down and make a list of expenses for the month. We see what we need that month and what the priorities are. If there is any big item of expenditure we discuss it then. Then he gives me the sum we have decided upon for shopping for the household. I get in the groceries and pay the children's fees. He does things like pay the rent and the electricity bill.'

Gita is married to a man who runs a small wayside stall, whose income fluctuates according to the fortunes of his trade. Because of this, she said, a regular allowance system was not practical. She and her husband would plan the monthly budget on the basis of his profits from the previous month and she would simply ask him to make the sums they had decided upon available as and when she did the shopping.

Routine shopping was a women's task in all but a few of the households studied. The shopping areas in central Shimla and its suburbs are not in the least male preserves and women of all classes can be seen at any time of day in the bazars, searching for a bargain among the vegetable stalls, chatting with friends or neighbours encountered in the steep and crazy lanes where one can buy anything from a mousetrap to an electric coffee grinder. The more affluent may meet their friends and eat snacks together in one of the local tea houses and the very affluent indeed enjoy coffee and gateaux in the smart restaurants of the Mall. This may seem a curious point to have to emphasize, since in the west shopping is almost invariably the wife's task, even if she uses her husband's services as chauffeur to get her to the supermarket. It must be remembered that in many parts of South Asia, especially in communities where women are expected to observe some degree of seclusion, or at least limit their appearances in public territory to the bare minimum, it is quite common for the men of the household to do at least some of the buying. Yet of the interview respondents with co-resident husbands, 67 per cent said that they themselves usually did the shopping, 15 per cent said that this task was divided between husband and wife, whilst only 13 per cent said that all the shopping was done exclusively by the husband. The remaining 5 per cent relied on other members of the household (e.g. adult sons or daughters or mothers-in-law). Shopping for groceries was not a job that commanded very much enthusiasm though, except among a minority of women rich enough to own a car or to employ a servant to help carry the goods. It was usually regarded as a time consuming chore involving a long walk to the bazar and a long walk back laden with heavy bags of flour, lentils, or tins of cooking oil. Shopping for occasional items such as could not be bought in the local shopping parade was more of a treat, involving an expedition to the Mall or lower bazar. Except in the depths of winter, it seems that all Shimla is out and about in the Mall in the evenings, strolling up and down, meeting friends between assignments or just window shopping among the brightly lit stores.

What generalities can be extracted from this diversity of arrangements? Income management work is by its very nature weighty work for whoever does it. Men and women in Shimla stressed that with high rates of inflation, budgeting and the management of expenditure requires more skill and watchfulness than ever. Constant adjustments to the pattern of expenditure have to be made as the price of one or another essential commodity goes up, school fees are raised, or rents increase, though the revised budget can be revised yet again if one or other partner is lucky enough to gain promotion or an adult son or daughter obtains a job and starts to contribute to the domestic fund. It is not surprising that so many women described this work as 'sitting down and drawing up a budget', a recurrent and time consuming chore.

I consider that my data confirm that women do indeed play a crucial role in the work of managing household income. In only a minority of households did the husband do most of the tasks included in this class of work and where the work was divided it was generally the wife who did the more time consuming tasks. In working out a division of labour, husbands and wives seemed to respond to circumstances and the stage of the household cycle rather than to preconceived ideals as to the appropriate pattern of roles for men and women in the household. So the fact that a particular division of labour obtained in a household at the time of the study could not be taken to mean that this pattern would always obtain, and some respondents explicitly described changes which they remembered or anticipated. A wife might leave the main tasks to her husband in the early years of their marriage and while their children were small, and then take a greater part when the children are past infancy and she can more easily move about outside the home. Or the responsibility might shift from husband to wife when the former takes a job outside Shimla, and perhaps back again when he returns. The husband's temporary unemployment or sickness might occasion a shift of responsibility to the wife which might or might not be reversed when he is in work again. As the children of the marriage grow up and can be entrusted with more complex tasks, they might relieve their parents of some of the routine shopping and paying of bills, though it was unusual for small children to be sent to the bazar other than for trivial purchases or errands.

Perhaps the most unexpected conclusion which can be drawn from these data is that once we look at income management as a form of work, rather than in terms of power to affect household decision making, there seems to be little difference in the situation of employed and non-employed women. It is true that there were only four employed women who played little part in their households' income management work but then there were five non-employed women in this category also. Among the households where the work was divided between husband and wife, there seemed to be no consistent tendencies in the division of labour which could be related to the employment or otherwise of the wife. Women who were not employed outside the home tended to rationalize their greater contribution to the time-consuming aspects of income management work by saying that as their husbands were at work all day and were therefore not free to visit the bazar, schools, municipal offices, or banks, it made more sense that they (the wives) should pay the bills and do the shopping. Yet in the households where the wife was out at work it was just as likely to be she who did this routine work in spite of her extra burden of housework. (In only a few cases was the wife in a job which had shorter or more flexible working hours than that of her husband). The employed wife may in fact carry a *triple* burden of responsibility.

The management of property

Many households in Shimla own some property, although it is not always property that is particularly valuable or useful to them. This property might take the form of agricultural land, a house or building plot, a share in a family business or shop. Sixty-three per cent of the respondents in the interview sample claimed that they or other members of their household either owned property individually or stood to inherit property at present administered by parents.

Often this property brought no current benefit to the household. Some of the poorer women reported that their husbands (or occasionally they themselves) still held land in the villages from

which they had migrated. But often the holdings were very small,
quite unable to sustain a household at even the minimum level for
survival. Repeated subdivision of already tiny scraps of unpromis-
ing mountain land had led to a situation in which the husband was
forced to migrate to find work and it was hardly worthwhile for the
wife to stay behind to cultivate the family plot. In such cases the
land was usually farmed by relatives who kept the produce for
themselves. The returns from leasing such tiny plots to tenants or
sharecroppers would hardly be worth the trouble and expense
involved in collecting the rent, given that many of these migrants
came from villages a whole day's bus ride from Shimla. Quite
obviously some of the families were likely to abandon such land in
the future, allowing their rights to revert to relatives still living in
the village. A few poor income families held land which was
substantial enough to warrant the effort needed to supervise its
cultivation. Bholli, for instance, had inherited a little land from her
parents in her own right (she was an only child)[4] and her shop
assistant husband had inherited a few acres himself. The villages in
which these separate plots were held were not far apart and now
that Bholli's children were grown up she could find time to travel to
the distant valley where she and her husband had grown up to make
or renew tenancy agreements with sharecroppers, collect produce,
sell it locally, and bring the proceeds back to Shimla. Since her
husband earned only Rs300 from his work all this effort was
considered worthwhile; the few hundred rupees it added to the
household fund annually would make a lot of difference at that
income level.

A few women who had migrated to Shimla recently would return
to their husbands' villages to help their parents-in-law at harvest
time, keeping alive their involvement in land which their husbands
would eventually inherit. But this was less usual; most women were
quite prepared to make the tedious journey back to the village from
time to time in order to carry out tasks associated with the
management of land. Such a trip was usually also a social visit
during which ties of kinship and affection could be renewed. Actual
farm labour however was an unpleasant and arduous form of toil
from which, on migrating to the city, they had thought to escape.

At the upper end of the income scale there were families who had
perhaps abandoned small unprofitable plots in subsistence farming
areas long ago but who were now reinvesting in land of a different

kind which could be farmed commercially. Himachali families, and families from outside Himachal who now regarded themselves as permanently settled in that state, usually preferred to buy orchards in the 'apple belt', the region above Shimla where the Himachal Government has lately encouraged fruit production. Some families of Punjabi origin held irrigated land in the 'green revolution' areas of Punjab or Haryana on which cereal crops brought in good returns. In a few cases this renewed involvement in agriculture did not arise from a reinvestment but from a revival of interest in inherited property which otherwise might have been abandoned. Jatinder, a government servant, for instance, came from a family of landowners in a fertile district of Punjab. They had not cultivated their land personally for a couple of generations, preferring to earn their livings in the professions, the civil service, or business. Now that modern agricultural methods and high yield varieties of wheat and maize made farming in that area very profitable, they had called in the land from the sharecroppers who had cultivated it and begun to farm it on a commercial basis. Jatinder and his brother took turns to visit the farm and supervise its cultivation taking leave from their employment as and when possible. Jatinder's wife took no interest in the management of this land, and indeed was ill equipped to do so, being an urban woman who found her husband's village dull and primitive. Otherwise a wife with a rural back-ground might well be expected to play her part in managing the land in a situation like this, since it is not always possible for the male members of the family to obtain leave from their employment at the time when attention to the farm is most needed. Rani, for instance was married to a government servant in a fairly senior position who found it difficult to be absent from the office during the whole period of the apple harvest. Rani herself would usually have to spend some time in the village where they owned orchards at this time of year, supervising the recruitment of temporary labour, making arrangements for the workers' accommodation and food, seeing to the packing and despatch of the fruit to market. Indeed, her sons and daughter sometimes took time off from their colleges to help with this work, and on one occasion even the cook was sent along to accomplish some urgent task connected with the harvest.

In some cases it was not the wife but some other female member of the household who did such work. One respondent for instance was married to a rich businessman. For many years the family had owned orchards and farm land just outside Shimla and since the husband was fully occupied with the hotel business, it was his mother who spent most time in the village looking after the orchards on their behalf. Several women whose children were now very young anticipated the time when they too would be obliged to make frequent trips out of Shimla to attend to the household's agricultural interests.

The patterns I have just described seem to be fairly common among households who own rural land. Eleven of the fifteen interview respondents who stated that members of their household held rural property in their own right (as opposed to a share in ancestral land which they had yet to inherit) played an active role in its management. Women were less likely to be involved in the supervision of urban property; few households held urban land or houses outside Shimla and therefore it was not usually difficult for the husband to do whatever was necessary without taking leave from his work (although where the family acquired a plot to construct their own house the wife might be involved in the design, construction, fitting, and decoration of the house when it was built). Women are more important when it comes to maintaining links with rural property, whether these links derive from the family's past, as in the case with inherited land, or represent an investment for the future, as in commercial land.

Decision making: managerial work and managerial power

I now return to the question which I promised not to beg at the beginning of this chapter – that of control over household resources. To participate in resource management work is not necessarily to participate in decisions about how such resources shall be used. One might do all the shopping from a list of requirements drawn up by somebody else and from a sum calculated and provided by that person. One might supervise the harvesting of a crop others had already decided to grow and sell the produce at a price stipulated by them.

Where both husband and wife were involved in resource management work (the majority of households) it was common for the husband to be involved primarily in planning and accounting activities. If he was involved in routine transactions these were often those involving larger sums of money such as paying the rent and bank loans. There were no households in which the husband's role was confined solely to routine tasks involving little discretion; if he did the petty shopping he also played a part in all other levels of planning and accounting. And while there were a number of households in which income management was almost entirely the business of the wife, in none of these was the husband excluded totally from the 'orchestration work'. Indeed it was probably for this reason that so many of the women saw budgeting as work which consumed identifiable amounts of *time*. It does not take long to decide how to spend the month's income on your own – or if it does, one's reflections on the matter may take place alongside or interspersed with other tasks and therefore be harder to isolate as work. It was because planning a budget usually meant holding a discussion with the husband to work out priorities for that month, to calculate whether anything could be saved or how much might be needed for a relative's wedding, that women saw budgeting and planning as distinct tasks. And even those who claimed to have complete discretion over how the family income should be spent were obviously aware of the husband's potential power as chief or only breadwinner. An electrician's wife told me that her husband gave her money to spend very much as she thought fit. All the same, she would submit an account of what she had bought after any major shopping expedition. She said, 'I am a shopkeeper's daughter, so I am quite used to book-keeping and counting pennies. But the person who earns the money has control over it.' Another poor housewife felt that the discretion her husband allowed her in household spending did not mean much at their level of poverty.

'If there is any major expense, what difference does it make if he does it or I do it? There is nothing left from Rs350 once you have got the ration and paid the rent. But all the same I can only spend it if he gives it to me.'

Whether or not these husbands were really looking over their wives' shoulders all the time to see what they were doing with household funds one cannot tell, but the wives certainly felt that reference to their approval was necessary.

Of the women who were in employment all but a few kept and disposed of their own wages but this in itself cannot be taken to mean that they necessarily had greater decision making power than those who did not earn. Often a wife who had a job would be given no allowance by her husband but would be expected to meet all regular household expenses out of her wage, giving her little effective choice as to how to spend it. Or she would spend it according to a predetermined division of financial responsibility (e.g. he pays the rent, she buys the groceries) which, again, would give her little room for manoeuvre unless the couple were both very highly paid.

I have less detailed data on the way in which decisions about land and other property are made, but here again I would point out that doing the work and deciding what work shall be done are not the same thing. Women who helped manage land held by members of the household were very conscious of the fact that they did such work as representatives of the whole group and in the interests of that group. Some wives did claim to make decisions about the hiring of farm servants and labourers or allocating the tenancy of land that was not commercially farmed, but matters such as the purchase, sale, and registration of land were never dealt with by the wife alone.

In summary we might say that these data show that while few wives (if any) are altogether excluded from decisions about the use and disposal of household resources, their financial power is not necessarily in direct proportion to the amount of time they spend on resource management work. To have demonstrated that women make crucial contributions to this aspect of household mainten-ance, therefore, is in no way to negate the body of research which indicates that women's financial power is not of the same order as that of their husbands. On the other hand, the data do show that women have a fairly exact knowledge of household finances (except possibly where they are junior daughters-in-law in a joint family household). Most of the women demonstrated a detailed acquaint-ance with them regardless of whether they had much control over them. The only women who could not give an exact answer to the question 'How much does your husband earn?' were those married to self-employed professionals or traders whose incomes fluctuated from month to month. Most men in Shimla are employed by the government in one way or another, and are in jobs where there are known pay scales. Promotion from one grade to another is a matter that will usually be public knowledge among a man's friends and colleagues. The niceties of bureaucratic hierarchy are a common concern. As we shall see in Chapter 10, office colleagues often mix socially and their wives are quite likely to be known to each other. While I am not suggesting that people discuss the intimate details of their pay packets with all and sundry, it is not difficult to guess roughly what a man (or indeed woman) earns once his (or her) job and grade are known. As in any community where most of the members are engaged in the same trade or industry, a total separation of personal and occupational life is difficult to achieve. All these factors work in favour of wives being well informed about their husband's earnings. Where women are involved in the management of land it is likewise improbable that they will not gain a precise knowledge of the extent and value of household property. Those wives who are recent migrants from rural areas will probably have weeded and harvested every acre of the husband's land at some time or other. It would be hard therefore for husbands to throw a veil of mystery around the family finances in order to exercise control over their wives, and few men would regard this as desirable anyway, judging from what male respondents told us. Most households are in the process of establishing themselves in the urban hierarchy having recently migrated from elsewhere. Those who are already established seek to make their positions more secure by diversifying their assets. Acquiring building plots or orchard land gives the next generation a solid base from which to combat inflation and competition from below. This almost invariably entails work which a single individual (especially an individual tied to an office desk or a demanding superior for six days of the week) cannot manage alone. From this point of view a wife who is not a well informed and able organizer is a liability.

Notes

1 There is considerable evidence that the differential survival rate of boys and girls in parts of South Asia may be due to the differential allocation of household resources, especially food and medication. If 'valued' members of the household are given more or better food and more medication when they are ill, then the household power of whoever makes such budgeting decisions is critical in a situation of scarcity (see Miller 1981:83ff.).

2 For instance, can one collect reliable data on household decision making through interviews? One has only respondents' accounts of how

decisions are reached and no way of resolving conflicting versions. Observation may be more satisfactory but household decision making is by its nature difficult to observe, requiring intimate and long-term access to what goes on inside the household.

3 For instance, is power in the household uni-dimensional, akin to bureaucratic power as it is commonly characterized, so that one can decide which partner 'has the power' in a particular household? Or are there many types of resource which spouses have access to, leading to a highly complex and cross-cutting system of sanctions and controls?

4 Hindu daughters now have the right to equal shares of family property with their brothers, but for reasons which I have explained elsewhere, they seldom claim this right if they have brothers living at the time of the parents' death (Sharma 1980a: 56).

7 Women, education, and the household

In this chapter I shall discuss education as a household resource and the part which women play in the husbandry or, in view of the incongruence of this term let us say cultivation, of this resource.

Education is conventionally regarded as a resource from either of two perspectives. It can be seen as a *personal* resource; it trains the mind and provides skills of diverse kinds which can be used for cultural or material enrichment. Or it can be seen as a *national* resource; the education system creates community capital, a pool of trained personnel who can be deployed for the purpose of more efficient production and administration. To see education as a *household* resource is to take an intermediate view; education provides certain individuals with skills or qualifications from which the whole domestic community may benefit in a number of ways. The most obvious way in which household members benefit in a meritocratic society is from the increased earning power which education confers. But I hope to show that the household also benefits substantially from the education of its non-earning members, especially that of women. This helps to explain the ever increasing demand for female education in a country like India where the participation of women in the waged labour force is still limited.

Education, access to jobs, and recruitment to elites

Most people in Shimla are either wage earners or directly depend upon wage earners from the public sector. In this sector, and in most parts of the private sector also, access to work is obtained through education, although educational qualifications are not the only factors which determine a person's employment prospects. Considerations such as religious or caste affiliation, personal contacts, local origin, and a number of other individual and social characteristics may help or hinder those who compete for salaried posts. But without education no man or woman can enter the race in the first place. The illiterate may only compete among themselves for the privilege of working as domestic servants, porters, *peons*, or road menders.

The importance of educational qualifications is especially evident in a city like Shimla, which is dominated by a bureaucratic elite. This elite is of fairly heterogeneous origin, but its members have all gained entry to the highest ranks of the civil service through a selection process which requires a high degree of educational attainment. However, in all but the most menial forms of employment, education is increasingly important for urban work in general, and is likely to remain so as long as there are more competitors for urban employment than there are jobs; it is not unusual for a stenographer to have a master's degree. I consider, therefore, that the arguments about education and the household which are developed in this chapter have an application outside Shimla, and the situation in a predominantly industrial city will differ only in degree from that which I describe here.

Educational aspirations for children

It is evident that for any household in a town like Shimla, education is a vital but uninheritable resource – although the means of getting it may be inherited. Education must be got again in each generation by the efforts of the household members. All the women we interviewed were very conscious of this fact, even those who had received no education themselves, and took the education of their children very seriously. None of those who had children over the age of six had failed to register them at school (school attendance is not required by law in India) and as noted earlier, it seemed unusual for children in poor families to be withdrawn from school in order to provide services at home (as is common in rural areas). Several widows and divorcees clung to a life of unrewarding urban poverty in Shimla rather than claim the aid of village kinsmen or seek their fortunes in some less expensive city, because they saw Shimla as providing the best educational opportunities for their children. One widow, for instance, had lived on the tiny income she was able to earn from doing hand knitting for private customers since her husband died, but she never considered returning to the mountain village where she was born since, she said,

> 'even if my family could support me it would not be good for the children. They are used to Shimla and they could not study so well in the village as they can here. So for the sake of their future I must stay here, even though it is hard. I just want my sons to get their education and find good jobs.'

Further evidence of how seriously women of all classes take their children's education can be adduced from the answers the interview respondents gave to open questions about what they wished in life for their sons and daughters. These are summarized in *Table 11*.

It is possible that respondents, conscious of being interviewed by women who were themselves educated, stressed education because they thought it would be an acceptable response, but even so the convergence of their answers was striking. Many of the women elaborated upon their initial answer by stating that they wanted education for their children as a means of obtaining other good things in life (well-paid jobs, good marriage partners, the respect of others, self-respect) and many of those who cited education as a desideratum went on to specify different types or levels of education for sons and daughters. Some very poor respondents were dubious as to whether they would actually be able to afford much education for either sons or daughters, but none the less they were willing to indicate some minimum level of schooling they would aim for.

Those respondents who answered in terms of particular professions they hoped their children would follow invariably cited professions which demand a high level of education or specialized

Table 11   *Interview sample: respondents' aspirations for children*

answered in terms of education	43
answered in terms of jobs only	9
answered in terms of marriage only	1
children themselves must decide what they want	9
don't know	2
not applicable because sons and daughters all adult	8
total	72

training, and most of those whom I have classified as saying that they would leave it to their children to decide their own aims in life were very wealthy women. They took it for granted that their children would be educated but wanted to stress that they would not put pressure on them to specialize in one form of training or another. So the weight given to education was actually rather greater than *Table 11* indicates.

Women did not specify a great deal of difference in the respective importance of sons' and daughters' education. Many stated that when they were children, education for girls had not been thought important because girls were not going to seek employment and therefore did not need qualifications. This was especially true in rural areas, and in the villages it is still very largely true. Urban parents, however, even those who have no thought of their daughters ever needing to look for jobs, are emphatic that their education is crucial to their future since, apart from anything else, it helps to determine the kind of husband they can hope to attract. Having said this, it is still true that in households where resources are limited the girls will end up with less schooling than their brothers, just as my respondents generally had less education than their brothers or husbands (the differential tends to narrow as one ascends the income scale).

The parental contribution to education; the role of mothers

Taking education seriously does not on its own guarantee the children's success. The parents will have to put in a certain amount of work themselves if these aspirations are to be realized and my contention is that in practice most of this work falls to the mother.

Parental input probably mediates the efforts of the children themselves in any educational system. In Britain, for instance, middle-class children are held to have better chances of success in school because of rather intangible factors such as the following: they have already been socialized into the modes of speech, interaction, etc. which are dominant in the school itself; their parents are more likely to be able to communicate easily with teachers and to be well informed about the education system; their parents will have the means, interest, and necessary knowledge to provide them with books and equipment which stimulate and reinforce interest in school work. All these factors no doubt operate in Shimla; as everywhere, academic success in one generation tends to lead to academic success in the next. But in India there has to be a very active and conscious input on the part of the parents if the child is to get the best out of the system which is much less evident in the British context. This will be clear from a description of the way in which schooling is organized in urban India.

In Shimla, as elsewhere in India, education is organized according to the '10 + 2 + 3' system. That is, basic education spans ten years, at the end of which pupils may 'matriculate' by passing examinations in all the main subjects. Students may then proceed to a two-year pre-university course. Those fortunate enough to secure admission to a college or university may pursue a three-year degree course.

Needless to say many children never complete the basic ten years. At the end of each year the child must pass an examination on the year's work before he or she is allowed to progress to the next standard. Those who fail are obliged to repeat the year. In poor families a child who fails at the fourth or fifth grade may simply be withdrawn. Many children, especially in rural areas, are never sent to school at all. In 1974, 64 per cent of children in the age group 6–11 were enrolled in Grades I–V, and 36 per cent of the age group 11–14 were enrolled in Grades VI–VIII. A much smaller percentage continue to pursue an extra two years of pre-university or vocational education, or, eventually, the three-year undergraduate course.

In any Indian city there will be a variety of schools taking children from the first to tenth grades, some provided by the government and others by private foundations, as well as kindergartens for preschool children. There is no requirement that a child attend a particular school on account of residence in a catchment area and some private schools have their own buses to ferry children from distant suburbs. Obviously a poor family will have no choice but to send its children to the nearest government school since state schools charge the lowest fees. Above a certain level of poverty there may be a very wide choice, or at least potential choice of school, for the child must actually secure a place at the school of the parents' preference. How easy this will be depends on the popularity of that school, and on the child's ability if an entrance test is required for admission. Parents able to afford the private sector must be at pains to inform themselves of which are considered the 'best' schools in their area, the degree of ease with which their child can expect to gain admission and the relative cost of different schools. (Cost here includes not just fees but the price of uniforms, school books and equipment, fares, extra courses and tuition, and many other incidental expenses.)[1]

Shimla offers a better choice of schools than many other cities of comparable size, since during its ascendancy as the summer capital of the British India it attracted both Catholic and Protestant foundations who founded boarding schools to which wealthy Indians could send their children. These schools still exist and are still the most prestigious although they cater for a predominantly local and more heterogeneous clientele nowadays. A number of other private foundations, both religious and secular, have established schools, kindergartens, and colleges and there is also a variety of provision (both state and private) at the tertiary level. With the expansion of Shimla's population in the last decade the education system can only just keep up with the demand for education and consequently securing admission for one's child in a private school (or in any kind of degree college) is a time consuming business. Several applications may have to be made before the child is successful. This pressure on the school system in turn creates pressure at the nursery level, since aspiring parents hope that their children will acquire competence in the kindergarten which will help them pass the entrance tests demanded by the elite convent schools. Even the mother of a 3-year-old may have to expend a certain amount of time in the pursuit of scarce places.

To be well informed is to hold a critical advantage in the competition for places at good schools and conscientious mothers are ever alert for scraps of information about the relative merits of different schools, availability of places, and requirements for admission. Such matters are topics of conversation of consuming interest to women who have aspirations for their children. Meeting other mothers at the kindergarten gates, chatting while shopping together in the bazar, or more formally at coffee mornings and kitty parties, women busily compile mental dossiers of information from the gossip they hear.

In Shimla many schools conduct entrance tests and some even interview the parents so the mother herself may be scrutinized for her suitability. One of the women I arranged to interview declared that she was eager for the experience since the next week she and her husband were to visit a well-known convent school where they hoped their daughter would gain a place. She was apprehensive at the thought of being interviewed by the principal, since she herself had studied only a few grades at a country school. She hoped that taking part in my survey would give her some practice in the business of being interviewed. (I am glad to say that her daughter was successful, so perhaps social scientists are occasionally able to provide useful services to their subjects!)

Whether the child is admitted to a prestigious convent or simply to the nearest government school, the parental input must continue. Most schools require the child to wear some kind of uniform which the mother must buy or make, and even government schools require the parents to equip the pupil with stationery and text books. Before the school term begins the bookshops and stationery stores are crowded with mothers and school children checking over lists of requirements issued by the schools, seeing that they have the right kind of exercise books, pens, geometry sets, and text books. Organizing this expenditure and doing the actual shopping is usually the business of the mother and until the children are old enough to be entrusted with the task themselves she may have to visit the school or kindergarten monthly to hand in their fees.

But the most time consuming item of parental input is the supervision of homework. Government schools and private schools in India hold yearly examinations which each child must pass if he or she is to proceed to the next grade. The child who fails will have to repeat the year and will have the shame and chagrin of being separated from his or her erstwhile classmates as well as the displeasure of the parents at being obliged to lay out resources on an extra year's schooling. From the age of five or six the child is impressed with the importance of cramming for tests and learning by rote. In most schools the curriculum is overloaded, so that to ensure that the children cover the course on which they will be examined, massive assignments of homework are necessary. First graders will not be exempt from an hour or so of homework and at the higher grades much of the evening must be spent in schoolwork if the child is to keep up with the course. An important domestic function of women is to see that the victims of this sorry system do complete their assignments and, where possible, to help them in learning their lessons. At the very least this is a kind of policing exercise, ensuring that the boy or girl does not run out to play on the street or switch on the television until the evening's work is done, sternly ignoring tears, protests, and excuses until such time as the child can exercise the necessary self-discipline. At the most, the mother may assume the role of teacher herself, going through the problems set by the maths teacher, testing the child on dates and dynasties for history, checking spelling and grammar of Hindi exercises. As examinations approach the pedagogic and policing roles of the mother intensify. When I visited the home of one respondent to carry out an interview I found her devising a complicated revision schedule for her children which, she said, she was determined they should stick to in order to make sure they covered all the work on which they would be examined (the children in question were aged six and eight).

Of all the duties connected with their children's schooling this is the one which mothers resent most. Women who have no education resent the fact that their children depend on assistance, which, through no fault of their own, they are unable to provide. Those who have some education but little leisure resent the demands which this supervision makes on an already pressing round of domestic duties. Highly educated women resent the fact that school teachers who have less education than themselves rely on their unpaid labour to ensure success rates in examinations. As one woman put it, 'Either they do not know how to teach or they cannot get through the curriculum in the course of the term, so they rely on us to do the work for them.' Some of the women especially disliked the policing aspect of this work. They felt that it was a legitimate part of the teacher's role to be stern and demanding; their own job was to make up for the heavy demands made of the children at school by receiving them with relaxed affection at the end of the day. Instead they had to continue to reinforce the discipline of the school with nagging or punishments. From some points of view the mother's contribution to her children's education is regarded as an extension of her maternal role, a continuation of her intimate involvement with the children when they are small, and this was the argument most often put forward to explain why this kind of work is done by mothers rather than fathers. Yet some obviously found that in practice their children's academic success required behaviour that ran counter to their own conceptions of motherhood, and frequently restricted their own freedom also. One mother said,

'When your children come home you might like to take them out, visit neighbours or go shopping together. But you feel guilty about going anywhere until all the homework is finished, and by that time there is only time to eat and go to bed.'

Once they are in their teens boys and girls are expected to take more responsibility themselves for getting school work done and the mother's input becomes less burdensome. The work that is necessary to secure admission to a college or university is as likely to be done by the father as the mother, but for a number of years the main burden is hers.

This responsibility obviously places two categories of women at a particular disadvantage – those who are uneducated themselves and those who are in full-time employment. For married women employed outside the home, the children's homework has to be fitted in among the many other household chores that await her when she returns in the evening and she may have little mental energy to mark the children's arithmetic or test their Hindi. Indira, a low paid clerk, said,

'I have little spare time and no social life. When I get home in the evenings I sit for a while and do puja (prayers) to compose myself and then I spend some time with my son. I have to teach him because my mother-in-law, who lives with us, is illiterate and cannot help him with his studies. I like to go through his work and then read him some stories, but it is a strain to try to do this as well as all the mending, cleaning, and washing that waits for me when I come home.'

Lata, a trained lawyer who had taken over her husband's practice after his death, also managed to fit in these duties at the expense of her own leisure.

'I get up at five o'clock in the morning and teach my children for an hour before breakfast. I am in the courts from nine until about four thirty. Then I sit with my children for a while, helping them with their school work. After supper I usually do paper work for my practice. I like my work but the problem for working mothers is that they have no time to be with their children. Our educational system is such that parents must help their children with their school work. Often, just as I sit down with my children a client turns up and I have to break off to deal with the case. I feel guilty then because I feel that I have let the children down. It is an extra burden to bear.'

In some cases such regrets were tempered by an awareness that the children might not be able to attend such a good school if it were not for the mother's earnings. But women who were illiterate themselves suffered greater feelings of impotence and frustration since even if they were employed they were unlikely to be earning enough to afford more than the cheapest form of education available for their children. Nor were their husbands likely to be able to compensate, since husbands of illiterate women seldom had more than a few grades of schooling themselves. Most of the women in this category could do little more than see that their children turned up for school appropriately dressed and equipped in the morning, chivvy them into getting their homework done in the evening, and see that the fees were somehow squeezed out of the monthly budget. One poor widow, employed as a *peon*, said:

> 'All my daughters are studying. After being in my unfortunate position [i.e. an uneducated widow] I know that to get a decent job you must be educated. If I had been better qualified I might have been able to get a good job and look after my children better. I want them to have a better life than I did so I can't send any money home to the village. I spend it all on the girls' education.'

Women who had little or no education themselves tended to see their illiteracy as irremediable. Few saw residence in Shimla as an opportunity to improve their own qualifications, one of the main obstacles being that while there are some courses available for women who had not completed their schooling, there are none suitable for those who never had any schooling to start with. Those who had aspirations to acquire new skills thought in terms of learning practical skills like tailoring. There were some exceptions, such as one sweeper woman who had studied to matriculation level in school but had never passed the examination. She enrolled in a private college which ran day courses for women with a view to passing her matriculation and then getting an office job under the provisions which allocate a certain proportion of government jobs to members of the scheduled castes.[2] Although intelligent and hardworking, she did not find it easy to resume studying again:

> 'It is not easy to begin studying after such a long time. There is never space at home to work as we have only one room, and there

is never time. The children interrupt all the time and my husband does not have the inclination to help me. I shall finish the course somehow as I do not want to sweep toilets all my life, but it will not be easy.'

Teachers are well aware of the problems faced by children from homes where neither parent has much education. Nursery education is seen by many as a means of compensating children for such educational disadvantage, just as it has been in the west. In some parts of Shimla there are *balvaris*, centres for preschool children, which offer play facilities and some instruction preparatory to 'real' school. These are provided by the government and can be attended for a small fee, and to some extent represent a 'cut price' version of what the child from a richer household receives at the kindergarten. An experienced *balvari* teacher described her work thus:

'I do not try to teach them much in the way of Hindi or sums and it is not very formal. They have a little general knowledge, number work, building their vocabulary. The main thing is to get them used to the idea of school. They get accustomed to the discipline of working with other children, asking to go to the toilet, holding the pencil correctly, and things like that. By the time they reach school they will be prepared socially and will have developed good habits. Many of the parents are uneducated and cannot teach the children these things themselves. But it is important that they should be encouraged to take an interest in their children's education. When a child comes home and recites a little rhyme he has learnt here, his mother can listen and she will feel that he has indeed learnt something. Even illiterate women can do a lot to encourage their children and I try to impress upon them how important this is, and give them confidence.'

This teacher had a thoughtful approach in her dealings with uneducated women and a realistic notion of the kind of 'good habits' which the working class child must acquire if he or she is to run the educational gauntlet with any success. A number of poor and uneducated women in the interview sample had scraped the fees together to place their children in *balvaris* or nursery schools of some kind, implicitly concurring with my informant's view of the educational advantages they offer.

The demand for female education

It should by now be clear why a woman's education is an important resource for her household, even if she never converts it into earning power by taking a job. Her own schooling feeds that of her children, enables her to sift information relevant to their educational careers, to deal with teachers confidently, to help her children with their school work, and to monitor their progress. It is not surprising that the bride's education is an important consideration when a marriage is arranged, even though it is still unusual for men to seek wives who are educated to a higher level than themselves.

To some extent the demand for female education appears to exist for its own sake; men like educated brides because they in turn can educate their daughters who in turn will attract offers of marriage from men who like educated brides. But educated mothers also help produce educated sons who can compete for well-paid jobs and enhance the household's material resources, so female education can be converted into other kinds of social capital.

Yet besides these more obvious advantages there are more diffuse, though just as important ways in which a woman's education can be a resource for her household. To have matriculated implies a knowledge of science and Hindi, a bachelor's degree betokens an understanding of Sanskrit, political science, or whatever the discipline may be, knowledge which will soon be forgotten as is usual with the subject matter of examinations. More importantly it betokens the experience of having mixed with people of a certain class (even if not originating from that class oneself), familiarity with a certain style of manners and deportment (many girls' schools and colleges pay great attention to these aspects of their students' behaviour), fluency in Hindi and English (the media of instruction throughout the education system and the languages used by the educated elite in Shimla in preference to the Pahari dialects which most Himachalis use in their everyday life). Competence in household service work does not depend entirely on education. An illiterate woman can be a clever housekeeper, an energetic builder of networks, a thoughtful hostess, and an inspiration to her husband's and children's efforts to better themselves. But the educated woman has had a greater chance to acquire skills and social habits which will be helpful in this department of her life and hence assets to her whole household.[3]

Urban men increasingly realize this and some unmarried inform-ants made the point explicitly when describing the kind of wife they were seeking. An office worker from a rural background stated that he hoped to find a wife of a level of education not much less than his own:

> 'I will marry a girl who is of the same education as myself, that is, who has studied to the Eight or Tenth Standard. She will know how to live in society, how to talk and how to behave.'

A shorthand-typist with an MA for which he had studied at evening college declared:

> 'I want an educated wife who will know how to look after and train my children properly. I don't mind whether or not she goes out to work. That is up to her – but she must be at least a matriculate.'

The final choice of bride in such cases would be made not by the young man alone but by his parents who, in the case of farming families, might be more interested in the girl's skills in farm and home management than her educational qualifications. But these statements show that urban men desire education in their brides not simply as an adornment but because they see it as an indication of real attainments which are of practical value to the household.

I should not want to underestimate the part which women's employment plays in creating a demand for female education, especially in a city like Shimla where there are opportunities for educated women to find jobs and where wage work is not generally regarded as intrinsically degrading or inappropriate for women. Many of the women interviewed explicitly stated that they wished their daughters to be educated in order that they be equipped to earn their living. But I do not think that female employment can explain the demand for female education in full; there are many parts of India where women's participation in the labour force is minimal but where girls' schools and colleges burgeon, and even in Shimla the families who wish to see their daughters get jobs are not the only ones to send them to university. This new demand relates more to historical changes in women's domestic roles. The conditions of modern middle-class city life discourage the segreg-ation between men and women in the household which had been a

characteristic of the old urban elites, and encourage a more
unmediated and directly cooperative relationship between husband
and wife. Meredith Borthwick for instance, notes that in mid-
nineteenth century Calcutta:

> 'Having a wife who took part in public society was seen as a career
> asset for those who aspired to succeed under British rule . . .
> Women increasingly took on the function of official hostess to
> actively aid and complement their husbands' careers . . . It
> became part of a woman's role not only to serve her husband but
> to help his career as well.'
>
> (Borthwick 1982:113–14)

These Bengali women appear to have been required to do the very
kind of household service work which the wives of Shimla
bureaucrats have to do today, and it is not surprising that education
became a desirable asset in a bride for a man in certain types of
occupation. As Borthwick points out, this change in what was
expected of a wife did not emancipate women in any substantial
way from the authority of their husbands. Their education was to
be harnessed to the husband's career and comfort and to the welfare
of the household as a whole rather than used for developing the
wife's independent interests, although it was seen as liberating at
the time.

These changes can be interpreted as follows: there comes a point
in the development of modern urban society at which the reproduc-
tive functions of the household have to alter because the social order
which is to be reproduced is now that of industrial capitalism. So far
as women are concerned, what this means in practice is that the
forms of household service work which were appropriate formerly
have to be replaced by new kinds of household service work which
in turn require new skills and competence. Some of these are best
acquired through the formal education system, even though this is
not its ostensible purpose. These changes are likely to be felt very
early on in government bureaucratic circles where competitive
achievement is open and formalized. Men compete with each other
in a rather direct way and benefit from the support and assistance of
their wives in this competition, but they are characteristic of
industrial bureaucracy as well and will be felt in even quite poor
families in so far as they aspire (realistically or otherwise) to upward
mobility.

I do not think it is particularly helpful to see these changes in domestic life in terms of cultural diffusion of 'western' practice, although in both Calcutta and Shimla, middle-class Indian families had the example of the European 'companionate' marriage very tangibly held before them during the British Raj. We can label these patterns of domestic life 'traditional' and 'modern' if we like, but in doing so we do no more than provide descriptive labels. Those who cling to the more segregated domestic roles where education is not such an important qualification in a wife probably do so because they are not yet threatened by the kind of competitiveness I have described, rather than from conscious adherence to 'custom' (for instance established commercial elites, groups still performing traditional caste crafts or occupations).[4] I prefer to see these changes as a response to conditions of living imposed by the nature of capitalist bureaucracy (quite possibly socialist bureaucracy imposes the same conditions of living but I do not have the evidence to decide whether or not this is the case) which penetrate the domestic sphere and demand a response from the woman in her capacity of wife and mother. Looking at the matter in this way it is easier to understand why women at a certain juncture are required to be educated, even though so many of them do not appear to 'do anything' with their education.

Notes

1 The school fees for one child might amount to anything from Rs40 to Rs70 per month at a private school, depending on the type of school and the age of the child. At a high-class day school as much as Rs50 per month may also be required for stationery, books, science charges, extra subjects and special equipment.
2 'Scheduled' castes and tribes are those which are classified in certain articles of the Indian Constitution as being particularly disadvantaged. Most of the scheduled castes are those which were traditionally regarded as 'untouchable', i.e. ritually polluted.
3 Those who have seen the educational inflation rife in many Third World countries as a response to a pathological demand for ever more degrees and certificates as qualifications for the most ordinary jobs – what Dore (1976) has called the 'diploma disease' – have perhaps missed this dimension of the phenomenon. However meaningless the nature of the instruction dispensed in the classroom (and radical critics are surely right to call it schooling rather than education), the school and university provide a social experience as well as an academic one. This holds true for men as well as women, but in India it is often the social experience as

much as the occupational qualification it represents which makes the degree or diploma desirable where women are concerned. I am not arguing that this social experience is intrinsically superior to that which the uneducated boy or girl gets in the street or the family courtyard – the Hindi and English learnt in schools and colleges are not in themselves better than Himachali dialects as means of communication, and the 'good habits' the *balvari* teacher desires in her pupils are largely the habits of docility and dependence – but it is a social experience which is practically useful to those who aspire to upward mobility.

4 This argument is well supported by Susan Seymour's data (1975:757–69). In Bhubaneswar she found a marked difference in domestic practice between the households of the old town (priests, traders, temple servants, traditional caste functionaries, etc.) and those of the new capital (government servants and employees of modern business firms). In the former the husbands and wives had more segregated roles and the women were less likely to continue their education beyond matriculation. In the latter, conjugal roles were more joint and women were educated to college level if their parents could afford it.

8 Women and paid work

India, and more particularly North India, is not an area where the work participation rates of women[1] have been high. The women I shall discuss in this chapter, therefore, do not represent the norm. But if they are a minority they are a highly significant minority, since it is likely that more urban women will undertake paid work outside the home in future. We need to know more about what their earnings mean to the household as a whole, how they are used, what redistribution of other work takes place as a response to the wife's occupation outside the home, and the value which is placed on women's waged work by men and by women themselves.

Much of the discussion of women's employment in India has taken place against a background of concern that Third World women may not be benefiting from the development process to the same extent as men. In many 'developing' countries, men's opportunities for training and earning have increased more rapidly than those of women. Gadgil's rather depressing discussion of the 1961 census statistics relating to the economic activities of women, for instance, reports little expansion in opportunities for women as a result of post-independence industrial and agricultural development, and concludes that,

> 'There appears, in reserve, a potential supply of women's labour particularly in urban areas; the economic situation in the country and the conditions of the female labour market prevent it coming out.'
>
> (Gadgil 1965:27)

To put it more bluntly, many women who could be earning to feed their families cannot find work which suits them.

In the last decade it is certainly true that women's work participation rate has not increased dramatically, having risen from only 12.13 per cent to 14.4 per cent, between 1971 and 1981 (see

Table 12) (although this does not include women who are marginal workers, i.e. in discontinuous or seasonal employment). There are wide interstate variations however, and in some parts of India the female work participation rate has increased more sharply, in others it has actually declined.

Himachal Pradesh is one of the states with a fairly high female work participation rate (18.8 per cent compared with 48.8 per cent among men), even though the adjacent states of Punjab and Haryana have rates which are much lower. So far as urban women are concerned, the work participation rate for urban Himachali women (9.53 per cent) is somewhat higher than the national figure for urban women (7.57 per cent), consistent with the general tendency for Himachali women to play an active economic role. The rate for Shimla is even higher than that for urban Himachal as a whole, being 12.01 per cent. Therefore, although the number of working women in Shimla is small in absolute terms (3,423), it represents a rate of economic activity which is relatively high in the Indian context.

What kind of paid work can women find in Shimla? The main problem for women who seek employment is that there are few jobs for those who have no education. The same problem faces men of course – Shimla is, as we have seen, very much a white collar city – but it is greater for women who generally receive less education than their menfolk. Older women brought up in villages are unlikely to have ever been sent to school and it is common even now for village girls to drop out or be withdrawn by their parents after four or five grades. As Shimla has little industry there is no manufacturing employment for women with little schooling, and almost the only form of manual work where there is great demand

Table 12   *Work participation rates (all India),*
1981

	total persons (%)	males (%)	females (%)
total	33.44	51.23	14.44
rural	34.77	52.21	16.49
urban	29.17	48.18	7.57

for female labour is domestic service. To be a house servant is regarded as a somewhat degrading option though, and it is certainly ill-paid work, especially for women. A few women try to find custom as self-employed seamstresses, but this also is not very remunerative and depends much on the individual women's success in attracting custom through word of mouth recommendation.

The areas of employment where women have benefited most in Shimla have been the traditionally 'female' professions and in clerical/secretarial work. There is a greater demand than ever for female teachers, social workers, nurses, and doctors and this has given a great incentive for middle-class parents of modest means to extend their daughters' education as an investment for the future. Clerical and secretarial work were until relatively recently a predominantly male preserve but the past ten or fifteen years have seen an increase in the training and employment of women in this sphere, and an increase in its acceptability as proper employment for respectable girls. In Shimla, where the main employers of such labour are the government, banks, medical institutions, etc., the rates of pay for clerical and secretarial work are good and more and more graduate girls are finding clerical work in offices or taking courses in stenography.

Table 13 shows the occupational distribution of the employed women in the interview sample, and illustrates very well the points

Table 13 *Occupations of working women in the interview sample*

domestic work	5
tailoring	2
caretaker /*peon*	5
clerical	4
secretarial /stenographer	5
administrative	2
school teacher	4
nurse	4
college lecturer	3
doctor	2
legal	2
own business /shop	2
total	40

I have just made. I do not know whether it is representative of the way in which women in Shimla are employed (there being no detailed employment statistics available, I have no way of finding out). However it is certainly illustrative of the range of occupations in which women in Shimla are employed.

Let us now consider the role of women's paid work in the household economy.

Women's earnings and household income

The data from the present study certainly support the idea that where women are in paid employment their wages are a substantial element in the household resource system. *Table 14* summarizes information on those women in the sample who were in employment at the time of the survey and whose husbands were living with them, indicating the percentage of the total household income represented by the wife's wage. On the whole, these data show that wives' wages are secondary only in the obvious sense that women tend to earn less than their husbands. (None the less, there were five women in the sample who currently command wages equal to or greater than those of their husbands.) But though 'secondary' in this crude sense, these women's earnings were certainly not marginal to the household economy, commonly representing 30 per cent or more of the cash coming into the household. In this sample, the higher the total household income, the greater the proportion of

Table 14 *Employed respondents'*
earnings as a percentage of total
household income (excluding female
headed households)

% of total monthly household income	no. of respondents
< 10	0
10–19	4
20–9	0
30–9	6
40–9	14
50–9	5
> 60	1
total	30

it that is represented by the wife's wages on the whole.[2] However this does not mean that the wages of women in poor households are unimportant. Several of the women in the two lower income bands were in what was effectively less than full-time employment, mostly cleaning, domestic work, tailoring – poorly paid but fitting in well with domestic work. Some of these women were in a position to increase the amount of work they did should circumstances require it. This is exemplified by the case of the one woman whose income represented 100 per cent of the household budget at the time of the interview. She was a domestic servant and had held various part-time jobs until her husband became unemployed due to ill health. Thereupon she had taken a full-time job – poorly paid but the only alternative to starvation or an ignominious return to her husband's village to depend on his parents there. Where the husband's work was irregularly paid or insecure, the wife's work was often regarded as a kind of insurance policy. One woman who was just beginning to attract business as an independent seamstress explained that her earnings were very low at present but she intended to build up trade so as to cushion the family from the effects of irregularities in her husband's income (he was a sign painter). She could, after all, reduce her commitment in good times or if her domestic work required it. The *long-term* significance of the wife's wages cannot be judged solely by the percentage of household income which they *currently* represent.

The importance of this point becomes clearer if we consider the effects of the 'domestic cycle'. In *Tables 14* and *15* I have not given weighting for the factor of household size, nor have I taken into account the ratio of earning to dependent members. Some of the employed women in the sample were members of large nuclear family households or complex households which would in due course divide or disperse, at which point the woman's own wage would come to represent a higher percentage of the income of the household composed of herself, her husband and their dependent children. Shila, for instance, is a sweeper with two adult sons (one married with a small baby) living with her. The monthly earnings of the members of this household are as follows:

Shila (sweeper employed by a private institution)	Rs160
husband (sweeper employed by municipality)	Rs300
married son (works in abbattoir)	Rs200
unmarried son (works in abbattoir)	Rs150

Shila's wages currently represent about 20 per cent of the household's income, but when her elder son eventually establishes a separate home for himself and his wife (an event which Shila expects to happen within the next few years) her wages will represent 26 per cent of the household income, assuming that her younger son earns the same as he does now. This is a very crude account which does not take into consideration the changes in scale of expenditure which are likely to occur when wage earning adults depart from an existing household unit. It serves, however, to reiterate the point that the significance of women's earnings in the household cannot always be judged with reference to the short term only. But even adopting a short-term perspective, we can safely assert that women's earnings are seldom, if ever, marginal to the households in which they live. What their wages represent in terms of what they 'buy' – short-term survival, long-term security, security for children – will differ greatly according to the general level of income and employment situation of other members of the household.

Where widows and divorcees are concerned the importance of women's earnings is even more obvious. *Table 15* shows that in female headed households the respondent's wages seldom represented less than 50 per cent of total household income, the rest being made up from the wages of adult sons or daughters, or from pensions. Indeed in a city with a different employment structure the

Table 15 *Employed respondents' earnings as a percentage of household income (female headed households only)*

% of total monthly household income	no. of respondents
< 50	1
50–9	2
60–9	2
70–9	2
80–9	2
> 90	1
total	10

significance of the income of female heads of household might be more striking, since in Shimla a disproportionate number of widows had been married to men in government service and enjoyed benefits in terms of pension rights not common in the private sector.

So far I have discussed the income-earning role of women as wives and mothers rather than as daughters, since the respondents in the main sample were married women. In Shimla there are increasing job opportunities for unmarried women with education to matriculation or degree level and there is an increasing tendency among white collar households to regard it as legitimate if not actually desirable to send their daughters out to work. Therefore it is relevant to consider also the contribution which working daughters make to household income. Some information is available from the main sample but also from a series of interviews carried out with fifteen unmarried women between the ages of 20 and 30 years who were currently in waged work. These young women were mainly in clerical and professional work of some kind, there being few unmarried women employed in other kinds of work in Shimla. Of the ten women who lived at home with parents or siblings (as opposed to alone or in a hostel) more than half were the main breadwinners in the household and none contributed less than 20 per cent of the total household budget. Of the five who did not live with relatives, two made substantial contributions to the finances of their parents' households. Some respondents claimed that their parents did not like to take money from their daughters, in accordance with the widespread Hindu notion that to accept any gift directly from a daughter is a sin. However such attitudes in no way inhibited parents from permitting daughters to contribute to the expenses of their younger siblings or other dependent relatives. One woman, for instance, was meeting the total cost of bringing up and educating a nephew who was living with her, and several respondents were living in Shimla with one or more younger siblings for whom they took financial responsibility.

The prejudice against enjoying the earnings of daughters cannot, however, be very strong, as a number of the women in the main sample reported the earnings of unmarried daughters as a component of household income. There was a slight suggestion that daughters are rather more reliable contributors to household budgets where they are in employment than married sons, who appeared more likely to make irregular contributions, fail to disclose the precise amounts they earn, keep back substantial amounts as personal 'pocket money', etc. The data from this study would therefore appear to confirm the findings of researchers in other Indian cities. Standing (1985) concludes from a survey in Calcutta that there is a

'shift in responsibility from sons to daughters . . .[and] . . . a significant upward trend in the numbers of such employed non-marrying daughters taking on the main caring responsibility for parents.'

(Standing 1985:36)

Similarly, Blumberg's Bangalore sample indicates that 'the economic duties of the sons of the family are now shared by some of these educated daughters' (Blumberg and Dwarki 1980:99). The effect of inflation is evidently an erosion of middle-class orthodoxy.

Attitudes to women's employment

It must be clear by now that in most households where there are working women, the members of the household would enjoy an inferior standard of living and/or considerable insecurity without the wages of the wife or daughters. In a few cases the household would not even be able to maintain the minimum conditions for independent survival without their contributions. And yet this fact is at odds with a public ideology which subordinates woman's role as actual or potential earner to her domestic roles of housewife and mother. For instance, in the media women are only exceptionally represented as workers rather than as mothers, wives, daughters, or sweethearts. When they are presented as workers, generally their work is problematic in some way (it creates conflicting demands on their time or loyalties) or they have been forced unwillingly into selling their labour by tragic hardship.

A very widespread attitude to women's employment is a kind of conditional approval (it is all right for women to work if they do the right sort of work and for the right reasons). As has been found in many studies of South Asian communities (Blumberg and Dwarki 1980:119) the degree of approval depends very much on the kind of work contemplated, and both men and women were likely to suggest, for instance, that 'respectable' work such as teaching or medicine would seldom be condemned, whereas manual labour or domestic service would be approved only as a last resort in case of extreme hardship. In Shimla, men in particular were likely to make their approval dependent on whether or not a woman could also fulfil her domestic duties, and the husbands of a number of well-educated women stated that they would not like their wives to work precisely because they did not feel this would be possible.

A more detailed reading of the results of the interviews we carried out with men shows that their attitudes to women's employment are often based on a much more perceptive appreciation of women's household activities than crude expressions of general approval or disapproval would suggest. One unmarried man, a college lecturer, said that he was not looking for a working bride since he preferred

> 'a girl who will like to make our home, who can run the house well and is sociable, who can keep up with the progress of my job. That is, if I get promotion she can adjust to my social standing and the living standards of my associates.'

Another man, a technocrat from a farming family, described the woman to whom he was engaged as better employed living with his parents on their farm than getting a job in Shimla.

> 'If she gets a job, she may earn a few hundred rupees a month. But if she is not there to help my parents they will eventually spend that much on hiring labour, and the workers they employ will not work as hard as my wife will. We would be able to trust her with the work completely. So it is all a matter of economics.'

In these examples it is not so much a matter of women's work roles or earnings being undervalued so much as other kinds of economic contributions to the household being given a higher priority (in the first example household service work and in the second, unpaid family labour).

Other men gave changing times and increasing inflation as a reason for modifying an unconditional disapproval of women's employment. One middle-aged administrator, whose wife had once held a job as a teacher, now regretted that she had left this work shortly after their marriage:

> 'Now you have to make [*sic*] your wife go out to work because of changed economic conditions, not for any other reason. People

like us get into the middle income group. We are not highly paid however, and we cannot enjoy life unless both of us are earning. At least, we cannot ensure that our children are well provided for otherwise. When we were born people's needs were less and we were not very conscious that our dress should be of a certain style, that we should have smart neck ties and so forth. In those days we went to school dressed very simply. Now it is quite different.'

A *peon*, 29 years old and from a rural background, regretted that his wife did not have the formal qualifications which would have made it worthwhile for her to leave the farm work she did on his parents' tiny plot of land in order to take up a clerical or professional job in Shimla:

'Had she been of a higher educational level, I should have wanted her to work. She could have come here and got a well paid job and that would have eased our life a bit. Two incomes are better than one. As it is, our land and my wages give us enough to eat, but there is no extra money over and above these basic needs.'

Much work on attitudes to women's employment suggests that in South Asia women's waged work is often evaluated in terms of notions of honour and sexual shame (e.g. Papanek 1982:212). Employment which brings women into contact with men or places them in promiscuous contact with the public violates notions of proper female conduct and is therefore deplored. This is certainly a common notion and explains why occupations such as hotel work or air hostessing, though well paid, are thought of by many as unsuitable for women. But it must also be said that to a large extent the occupations that are thought of as unsuitable for women are also those which have a low status when performed by men. Domestic service, sweeping, and road mending are considered degrading jobs for women in a city like Shimla but they are not considered prestigious for men either. If nursing and midwifery have a low status it is largely on account of notions of pollution (contact with bodily secretions, tending to the bodies of people who are not relatives), considerations which are used to evaluate men's work as well. The difference is, of course, that women's work is always evaluated with reference to a known and approved alternative, that is, domestic work, and as we have seen from the examples quoted above, other forms of household service work. Urban men, on the other hand, are not deemed to have any alternative to employment.

Their work is evaluated only in terms of comparisons within a range of possible waged occupations. The point which I am trying to make is not that judgements about the desirability or otherwise of women's employment are made entirely on the basis of rational calculations about the household's economic interests and that ideological factors are secondary. Rather, I am trying to say something about the structure of the ideology in operation. More fundamental than particular notions about what constitutes 'suitable' work for women, and lying beneath judgements about whether specific occupations are likely to bring about a loss of honour or reputation, is the idea that earning money is *not* an intrinsic part of the female role. It has to be justified in a way that men's employment does not and it is at this point that considerations about possible loss of status versus the economic advantages of women's employment are introduced and weighed up. It is significant that of the women with whom the matter was discussed most thought women's employment a good thing from one point of view or another, but none expressed this approval in terms of waged work being any part of women's normal *duties*. In this respect the structure of gender ideologies in South Asia and in most western industrial societies are basically similar. Where they differ is in respect of the kind of criteria which they allow for evaluating the legitimacy of particular female occupations (compatibility with conceptions about the psychological needs of young children in the west, ideas about *purdah*, family honour, or pollution in South Asia).

Entering the labour market

Let us now turn to the question of how decisions about women's employment come to be made, and why some women enter the labour market readily while others in apparently similar circumstances do not.

On the whole, it appears that women's preparedness to enter the labour market depends as much on the attitudes of parents as those of husbands. It is parents who encourage daughters to think of themselves as potential workers or primarily as dependents. Husbands are then chosen whose attitudes are consistent with choices already made or orientations already established. Not all daughters accept the attitudes of their parents, of course. Some respondents remembered having to overcome parental prejudices as to whether they should train for paid work or not, or over what kind of work they ought to seek once they had trained. Others had had to abandon aspirations which their families strongly opposed. However there were very few cases of women leaving waged work because their *husbands* disapproved.

While most women presently of working age will have been brought up in homes where women have not worked, there appear to be two types of household in which girls are given positive encouragement to think of themselves as actual or potential earners. The first kind belong to service castes where women have traditionally pursued the caste specialism alongside or complementary to their menfolk. Households of sweeper or *dhobi* (washermen) caste where the male members are practising their traditional occupations would fall into this category. Not all married women in such castes do undertake paid work and most would probably like to avoid it, for the work that is available to them is generally unpleasant and of low status. But women's employment in such households is taken for granted as a normal option.

The second category of household in which girls are likely to be brought up to think of themselves as potential wage earners represents a type of middle- or lower-middle class household which is probably growing more common in a city like Shimla. In such households there is an ethos favourable to women getting as much education as the family can afford, usually in the form of training for a fairly specific occupation (clerical work, nursing, teaching). Recalling their parents' attitudes, women made statements such as, 'All my aunts and sisters worked; it never occurred to me not to consider it.'

In some cases this family 'atmosphere' (a word frequently used in this context by English speaking informants) was not necessarily an enduring aspect of family culture, but something that had developed recently in response to new educational opportunities for women. One nurse, for instance, came from a rural family and her father had been a physical training instructor in the army for many years. On his retirement from the army he had worked for a time in a girls' private school as games master and had been impressed by the kinds of career these girls had been encouraged to undertake. He decided that his own daughters, although of humbler family, might also aspire to well-paid jobs, and indeed all three had qualified as either teachers or nurses. The effect of such positive family encouragement is clearly very strong. Only two of the seventeen women in the interview sample who claimed to have been brought up in this way were not currently in employment. Where women were (according to their own accounts) actively discouraged from thinking of paid work as a future possibility for themselves, or where they were given only lukewarm approval for their aspirations, some none the less attained the qualifications they desired or ended up in paid work for one reason or another (twenty-five of the fifty-five in the interview sample who described their parents as having been ill disposed to the idea of women working). It would seem that at the present time a family ethos and socialization process which favours women's employment is much harder to resist than one which discourages it, or that women have more incentive to deviate from the latter in later life.

Where caste differences in attitudes to women's employment are concerned, we are clearly dealing with group subcultures, perpetuated by the practice of caste endogamy and persisting so long as caste members continue to share certain experiences and a sense of common tradition. In the second type of household described it is much harder to understand what is going on; how can we explain why in one lower middle-class household all the daughters are brought up to think of themselves as future wage earners, while in another household of apparently similar income and standing the daughters are directed into forms of education which are unlikely to lead to marketable skills, and are discouraged from thinking of themselves as wage earners? One possibility is to see these differences between households in terms of Wallman's concept of household 'styles' – differences in the way in which domestic groups habitually prioritize possibilities and choices which do not appear to have obvious correlates such as class, income level, ethnic background but which are fairly consistently practised by members of the same household.[4] This does not get us much further in terms of explaining differences between households, but it does have the advantage of enabling us to see households themselves as subcultures, groups capable of developing values and preferences which remain fairly stable over time and which inform the choices which their members make.

It is also true, though, that the time at which this study was conducted was one of rapid change and of reassessment of the way in which the paid work of wives and daughters should be viewed. This is most evident in those strata of Himachali society who have been able to benefit most concretely by the expansion of white collar employment for women, the urban lower middle class and the better off peasant families. Typically, it is the daughter of an urban clerk or prosperous farmer who trains for clerical work or a traditionally 'female' professional job (social work, teaching, nursing) where her mother never dreamt of entering the labour market. And it is in such a family that her earnings are most likely to make the greatest difference to the standard of living her household can enjoy.

This general shift can be most clearly seen if we examine women's comparisons of their parents' attitude to the possibility of their entering employment with their own attitudes to their daughter's working. In *Table 16* we see a marked difference between generations as reported by respondents themselves. Data such as these, of course, have very limited predictive value; some of the women had no daughters of their own and were responding hypothetically, while some women who were in work themselves and desired their daughters to work actually had grown daughters who had never been in paid work. Also the women were not all of the same age or at the same point in the domestic cycle. The data do, however, indicate that further expansions in women's employment and educational opportunities are likely to be well received.

Table 16   *Interview sample: attitudes to daughter's employment*[3]

	respondents' parents (as reported by respondents)	respondents' attitudes to own daughters
daughter expected to seek work	6	17
daughter's employment desirable	9	16
'it is up to the girl herself'	8	21
daughter expected *not* to seek work	49	6
don't know	—	12*
total	72	72

* These were mainly women who had no daughters and found the question too hypothetical to answer.

Women's work histories: patterns of employment

So far I have discussed evaluations of women's employment and the ways in which it is seen by men and women in relation to other female roles and activities. Another way of examining the role of women's waged work in the household economy is to look at the work histories of married women. Do they enter and withdraw from the labour market in response to the changing circumstances of the family? Does the birth of a child, widowhood, divorce, or other crisis bring about a readjustment of the relationship between paid and unpaid work? Are married women committed to paid work or do they regard it as an unsatisfactory if unavoidable solution to economic need? The work histories of the respondents in the interview sample (some aspects of which are summarized in *Tables 17* and *18*) indicate four dominant patterns of behaviour:

1 The woman enters the labour market on or soon after the completion of her formal education (whatever this may consist of) and remains in work, although not necessarily in the same job, with little or no interruption.
2 The woman enters the labour market after marriage, and usually after the birth of children, in response to economic pressures (the needs of a growing family, unemployment or sickness of the husband) and is likely to remain in work at least until her children are independent adults.
3 The woman enters the labour market in response to the death or departure of the main breadwinner and usually remains in work thereafter. In most of the cases I studied the precipitating crisis was the death of the husband or the breakdown of the marriage. A few women, however, had entered work as unmarried girls in response to the death of the father.
4 The woman never enters the labour market at all, or only briefly previous to her marriage before a permanent withdrawal from paid work.

The first pattern of employment (early entry and no subsequent withdrawal) is typical of some service castes and is common among some lower middle-class families where the daughters have been encouraged to see themselves as potential workers or have developed career aspirations during the course of their education (see pp. 130–31). They may change their jobs around the time of

Table 17   *Employed women: occasion of first entering employment*

household income	at or soon after completion of education	divorce/ separation	during married life	widowhood	total
<Rs750	2	—	3	5	10
Rs750– Rs1,500	2	1	4	2	9
Rs1,500– Rs3,000	10	—	1	1	12
>Rs3,000	7	—	2	—	9
total	21	1	10	8	40

marriage if the husband chosen for them lives in a different place, and further changes in employment may take place in response to transfers or changes in the husband's employment. Where a woman has a secure and well-paid job, however, she may stick to it even if her husband is transferred elsewhere, at the cost of a temporary separation.[5]

The second pattern of interaction with the labour market (entry after some years of marriage and the birth of children) is common among poor uneducated women who have not been encouraged to think of themselves as paid workers in the first place but find themselves obliged to seek work owing to the pressure of economic circumstances. The wages of a low-paid husband in a manual or minor clerical job will be hard stretched to cover the food, clothes, and school fees of a growing family and the very high cost of housing and basic foodstuffs in Shimla adds to the difficulties of low income households. The evidence from the interview sample suggests that having once entered the labour market such women are not likely to withdraw from it very soon, even though they themselves see their employment as a stop-gap measure. One woman I knew, aged around 45, started doing part-time cleaning work in the houses of middle-class neighbours about ten years previously. Her husband's wages as a carpenter did not meet the needs of their six children. Her husband had not liked the idea of her working very much, but had not put up too much resistance.

'I started to work because I had so many children and a lot of expenses. I thought, why should it all be on my husband's head?

Table 18 Non-employed women: employment patterns prior to study

household income	left employment at marriage	left work when children born	left work because did not like it (or some other reason)	would work now if suitable job presented itself	have never been in employment and never intend to be	total
<Rs750				1	3	4
Rs750–Rs1,500			1	1	7	9
Rs1,500–Rs3,000	2			1	6	9
>Rs3,000		1	1	2	6	10
total	2	1	2	5	22	32

If we both earn, we can get somewhere. At first he was unwilling, but I told him that there was no shame in such work. So he said, all right, it is up to you – if you can see that the children are well cared for, then it is all right.'

But now that the children are older and one is actually earning, she can even save a little from her wages so she sees no reason why she should leave work just yet, especially as her husband has accepted the new situation.

Women who have lost a husband from either death or divorce usually see themselves as having no choice as to whether or not to seek work. It is the policy in government departments and in some private organizations as well, to offer employment to the widow of a permanent employee who dies before retirement age. (More exceptionally the job is offered to a son or daughter rather than the actual widow.) This policy has benefited many women who would never have entered the labour market otherwise – widows of *peons* and clerks who in some cases were not even living in Shimla at the time of their widowhood. One widow, for instance, stated:

'My husband died three years ago and I was offered a job in his department, so I came to Shimla from our village with our four daughters. I was thankful for the job although it is expensive here in Shimla and I cannot send any money home to our relatives in the village. But I can at least put all the children in decent schools. I want them to be educated so that they can get good jobs.'

This widow could presumably have continued to stay in her husband's village, farming their land as she had done before his death but without the benefit of his remittances and probably dependent on the good will of his relatives. However she opted to leave the more familiar rural world in order to replace her husband as a wage earner. Some widows who adopted this course effectively forfeited their claim to inherit their husband's land by doing so. They could not attend both to a regular job in the city and stand by legal entitlements. These rights are well defined in law, but illiterate rural widows often have difficulties in enforcing them if they are still junior members of a joint family and are unlikely to be able to muster local support to make their claims effective. This happened to Meera, a widow of about 30 years old who had been unable to obtain any land on her husband's death. Her claims had been disregarded as she had no son. She had therefore come to Shimla with her adopted daughter to take up the offer of a job in her husband's office. In yet other cases, widows of farmers had more or less abandoned small plots of land in favour of urban employment. Unlike some of the families described in Chapter 6, they did not find it possible to combine the supervision of rural land with urban employment – an option not easily exploited by a household with only one adult member.

In cases where divorce or desertion had forced the wife to take on the breadwinner role the hardship which the household had to undergo was often even more severe than in the case of widowhood. Most deserted wives had not undergone any formal divorce proceedings and were not in receipt of any kind of support from their former partners. One young woman, for instance, had been married to a soldier but after the birth of their daughter he had visited her at his parents' home less and less and she had come to accept the fact that he had abandoned her. But for the support of her parents, with whom she now lives, she would have been in severe difficulties, and her mother still cares for the child while she works as a seamstress in a large hotel, repairing linen and furnishings. One Christian woman from a tribal area in North East India had parted from her husband many years ago and for a time relied on her mother to look after her children while she underwent training as a nurse. Now she has a job in a mission hospital in Shimla and her children are either grown up or at boarding school in her home state.

I have referred to paid work as an option, yet in cases such as these paid employment was not really perceived as a choice but something *mazburi*, i.e. forced upon one. In fact, of course, several of these women did have alternatives to paid work, in theory at least. The widow could have stayed on in her husband's village, continuing to cultivate the little land he had owned. The deserted wife could have clung to her rights in her in-laws' household rather than return to her parents. But in most cases the women themselves had rejected such alternatives out of hand, either because they involved humiliating dependence upon grudging in-laws or because the positive attractions of urban life, education in particular, were perceived as benefits of which their children stood in greater need, being fatherless.

But if paid work was seen as a forced response to a tragedy or unfortunate circumstances, not all women found it distasteful once they were used to it. One widow, a clerk in a government office, said:

> 'When I first started work here I found everything very strange. I found it difficult to adjust to going out to work. I did not know how to relate to people, how to talk to them. I was very shy and not at all confident. But I got used to it. The people here are very nice and helped me to get used to things.'

Another poor woman, the wife of a bearer, who had started work because her husband's wages did not cover family needs, said that her job as a domestic was not one which she would have undertaken willingly, but in the event the women who employed her turned out to be pleasant and understanding employers, and so she had found the work quite acceptable in the end.

Many of the women who had entered the labour market on account of financial pressure or some household crisis were not doing jobs that satisfied them or even paid very well, and would willingly give up work if the problems that had forced them to take up employment in the first place were resolved. But I mention the positive feelings reported by a number of women from poor households since it is often assumed that employment only brings satisfaction to educated women able to command interesting and responsible jobs. When employment enables a woman to achieve financial independence where otherwise she would have had to beg from unwilling in-laws or see her children destitute, it may give her a sense of worth and confidence even though the content of the work itself is menial or tedious.[6]

Most of the respondents who were not working at the time of the study had never undertaken paid employment in their lives and most of them had never seriously considered entering the labour market, regarding the earning of income as the husband's affair. A few stated that they would have liked to take a job to help with the household budget or because they liked the idea of working outside the home (see *Table 18*) but these stated wishes seemed to me somewhat hypothetical and not accompanied by any real attempt to seek work or gain qualifications at the present time. A fairly typical attitude was expressed by the young wife of a petty shopkeeper:

> 'My job is to do the housework – it is the business of the men of the household to go out to work. I do not have any plans to take up

service. I do not have any objections to other women doing so if they wish, but I do not feel that I should have to myself.'

The 24-year-old wife of a *peon* said:

'I have never thought of going out to work. There is no custom of women doing that among our village people. I did a two-year sewing course in our village but my relatives would regard it as a matter of shame for women to do service. If I were highly educated it might be different, of course.'

A few non-employed women did have regrets about their lack of qualifications but did not see that they could do anything about the matter. The wife of a Punjabi engineer said:

'I never expected to do service – my parents were against it and they did not let me finish my education because a suitable offer of marriage came along. Now I realize that it would have been better to finish the MA course which I started. Then I could have got a job when I wanted one. You cannot manage on one salary these days. But now there is no question of me taking a job. I am too old to find work easily with no experience.'

Only five of the interview respondents who were not currently in employment had any previous work experience. Of these, one had quite willingly left a job as a social worker at the time of her marriage since her husband did not like the idea of his wife going out to work and another gave up a teaching job for similar reasons. Another had worked until the birth of her first child, but when the firm she worked for went out of business she decided not to seek another job. Another two left work after marriage because, according to their statements, they did not care for the work they did. This general lack of work experience makes it harder for them to find well paid employment in the case of financial pressures making it necessary that they should do so, but also highlights a striking difference between patterns of employment in South Asia and in most industrialized countries in the west. In Britain, for instance, there will be few married women who have not had paid work at some stage in their lives, even if there are equally few who have worked full time without interruption. The pattern characteristic of Britain is for entry to the labour market to take place as soon as work is available after the completion of formal education or training. Marriage does not usually constitute an occasion to terminate or interrupt paid employment (although it may have done in the past) but the birth of a child generally does occasion a major readjustment in the household division of labour. Usually the wife withdraws from work, or shifts from full-time to part-time work. A married woman may return to full-time employment at some later stage in her life (e.g. when her youngest child is at school) but the birth of children typically constitutes a critical juncture (e.g. see Oakley 1980:201).

In Shimla neither marriage nor motherhood were experienced as critical junctures by women who were already in paid employment (see *Table 19*). Few women who had jobs at the time of marriage withdrew from the labour market because of marriage itself, although some had had to leave the particular job they were in when marriage involved moving to another town or district. The main reason for the fact that marriage does not precipitate a crisis in a woman's working 'career' is that there are in effect separate marriage markets for women who are in paid work and women who are not. A man who desires a wife who can contribute to household income can seek a bride from among those girls who are already employed or in training for a specific job or profession. A man who does not like the idea of a working wife will be looking out for recommendations for girls who are not employed. The matrimonial advertisements placed in English language newspapers de-

Table 19   *Effect of birth of first child on employment (employed women only)*

household income	had to leave/ change job	continued in same job	were not in employment at the time, entered job market subsequently	total
<Rs750	0	3	7	10
Rs750– Rs1,500	0	4	5	9
Rs1,500– Rs3,000	0	11	1	12
>Rs3,000	0	6	3	9
total	0	24	16	40

monstrate this through the way in which men and women specify the kind of partners they desire and the way in which they advertise their own virtues and qualifications. Some such advertisements are very explicitly worded, others indicate the requirements of the advertiser in a more coded way. The following exemplify the way in which working brides are solicited or advertise themselves:

> 'Arora Khatri bank employed match for Arora, boy, 28, 5ft. 7½ins., bank employee, salary Rs1400.'
> 'Match for Rajput girl, 28, staff nurse, dowry seekers excuse.'

At the moment it would seem that the increase in demand for working brides has taken place in step with the increase in supply of young women who are used to being in employment. There is no need therefore, for a woman who is very committed to her job or who likes to be in paid work to find herself married to a man who will resent her working outside the home. Similarly, there is no need for a girl who has been brought up expecting to be supported entirely by her husband to find herself married to a man who will expect her to contribute to the household income herself. At the moment it seems that it is possible to match expectations about work at the time of marriage, at least if parents take these expectations seriously.

Childcare arrangements

If marriage is seldom a reason for withdrawal from paid work, neither is the birth of the first child. On the contrary, many informants stressed that the birth of their children gave them added incentives to stay in their jobs or to seek work which was better paid; children inevitably increased the demand on the household budget, especially when they reached school age and required fees, uniforms, and books. Not one of the respondents in the interview sample had left a job on the birth of the first or any subsequent child, although it must be remembered that many of them were employed by the government and were entitled to more generous maternity leave than would be offered by most private employers. Several women in clerical government jobs had borne and brought up quite large families with no interruption in employment.

Working mothers employ a variety of arrangements for their

children and *Table 20* summarizes those used by the women in the interview sample.

Many of the poorer women who had only started paid work after marriage had waited until the youngest child was at school before looking for a job since they could not afford servants (indeed they were likely to be employed as servants themselves) and had no relatives living nearby. Such women sometimes relied on neighbours to keep an eye on young children after school hours. Most poor women had used a variety of strategies during their working lives, although 'strategies' is perhaps a somewhat elevated term for what were often *ad hoc* arrangements. Naina, for instance, was a sweeper woman who cleaned the toilets in a group of private flats and offices. She had three young sons and had started her present work when the second son was a baby, simply carrying him with her as she went from house to house. Then a charitable organization had started a creche near her home and she had sent him and the next child there until they went to school. Now that all three boys were at school she relied on neighbours to see that they did not get into mischief after school (she attended a private college in the afternoon where she hoped to pass her matriculation in order, eventually, to get an office job). During school holidays the youngest boy might accompany her to work, being of an age to make himself useful in helping her to empty rubbish bins and to sweep staircases. If one of the children fell ill she was obliged to take time off work and lose income.

Women like Naina, who cannot possibly afford servants, are at a disadvantage in that there is very little part-time work available such as would fit in with the school hours of their children and

Table 20 *Childcare arrangements used currently or in the past by women who were or had been in employment while their children were under school age*

creche	3
servant	10
relative*	12
combination of part-time servant and relative	3
total	28

* Usually the mother or mother-in-law (see Chapter 9).

obviate the necessity for regular child care arrangements. Many women in this category have no choice but to work as cleaners in the homes of lower middle-class women who cannot afford a full-time servant but who are prepared to pay a woman who will come in after breakfast to wash the pots, clean the kitchen, and perhaps do a little laundering also. The only other possibility is self-employment in work such as home tailoring or knitting sweaters to order, work which can be made to fit in with the demands of domestic work and a family. Even here, however, finding custom and delivering finished goods necessitates leaving the home from time to time, and hence arranging child care 'cover'. Shanti, an extremely poor widow of rural origin, made ends meet by knitting sweaters for middle-class women. When she had to go to the bazar to buy wool or deliver the finished garments she frequently had to leave her 1-year-old baby unsupervised if there was no neighbour about to keep an eye on her.

The fact that most women do not leave employment because of motherhood alone does not mean, therefore, that child care is unproblematic, especially where the poorest women are concerned. When asked what they considered to be the main problems of working women the almost universal response was in terms of concern for children's welfare. A stenographer told us:

'Working women are all right if they get help from their families. If your in-laws are helpful then it is fine. Otherwise you are dependent on servants, with all the problems that entails. In any case you worry about the children while you are in the office.'

And in the words of a poor tailoress:

'The main problem working women have is in looking after the house and children. Now my children are at school I can spend more time on my work and earn a little more. If you do not have enough money your home and children will suffer in other ways.'

The women least troubled by doubts of this kind were those who could leave their children in the care of a relative either living in the same household or in the same neighbourhood. However there is clearly a need for more cheap and well-run nurseries for women who have no kin at hand and who cannot afford a servant. The combination of motherhood and paid employment is by no means unproblematic in Shimla in spite of the low drop-out rate due to the birth of children. Poor women are obviously very conscious of the fact that they are obliged to negotiate a compromise between the social needs of their children and the financial needs of the whole family which is difficult to achieve and not always very satisfactory in the end.

Organization of domestic work: double or triple burden?

As we have already seen, the fact that a wife is employed does not usually mean that she bears less responsibility for cooking, cleaning, and childcare than a woman who is not out at work. Women's employment does not lead to any very substantial redistribution of domestic work between the sexes, although it may lead to a redistribution of tasks among the available women. The teenage or adult daughters of employed women may be expected to do more cooking or shopping than might otherwise have been the case, and mothers or mothers-in-law may undertake more or different responsibilities when a daughter or daughter-in-law is working outside the home. According to their wives some husbands, it is true, were helpful in minor ways and might lend a hand when there was a backlog of domestic work or a crisis situation. Many women in lower income households described their husbands as unwilling to join in domestic work in the ordinary way when the wife was present, but reliable in getting things done if for any reason she had to be away from home. Partly, I feel sure, this was the result of the domestic self-sufficiency many husbands had been obliged to cultivate as lone migrants to the city before being joined by their wives. A number of employed wives said that while they did not realistically expect their husbands to do much housework, they did appreciate an understanding attitude. By this they generally meant an undemanding attitude – forbearing to ask for cups of tea at awkward times, not bringing in friends unexpectedly and then asking the wife to cook for them after a tiring day at work, being flexible enough to allow for the demands made on the wife by job and home.

But however understanding the husband might be, for most employed wives domestic work and paid employment combined to form a heavy burden. Those who could afford it might ease it with the help of servants, and those in a position to do so might seek the aid of female kin, but the responsibility of caring for husband and children still lay primarily with the wife. Most employed wives fulfilled these demands at the expense of their own leisure, as replies to questions on social and recreational activities demonstrated. One widow described her feelings about starting a job after the death of her husband as dread lest she should come to resemble an aunt of hers who went out to work and when at home 'always appeared with a broom in one hand and a *paratha* [bread] in the other', i.e. always in the middle of attempting several domestic tasks at once. Or, as another woman put it: 'The main problem for working women is tiredness – you get in from the office and there is all the housework to do. You have no time to relax.'

A few informants explicitly stated that working women in fact had a triple burden – not only must the housework be attended to and the demands of the job fulfilled, but time must be made for those activities which I have termed household service work. A woman lawyer said:

> 'We have more duties than men. We do double work – we have to cook the food and then rush to the office on time. But we also have to impart education to our children, entertain our guests, supervise the children's play – so many things.'

And in the words of a rural migrant working as a clerk:

> 'Working women have two lots of work to do; one at the office and one at home. And some of us have a third as well, when we have to keep visiting our villages to make sure everything is all right there.'

This being so, must not Papanek (1979) be right in conceiving family status production work and paid employment as, on the whole, mutually exclusive alternatives for women? Certainly it is difficult for a woman in regular employment to take time off to visit her village or attend to property. Women in the lower income groups who did full-time work were able to spend less time on developing and maintaining relationships with neighbours and kin than their unemployed counterparts. (Employed women in high income brackets were at less of a disadvantage with respect to entertaining and social life because they could hire servants to help with entertaining and care of the home.) On the other hand, many forms of household service work which were done by non-employed women were done by employed wives also, for instance, keeping in touch with relatives outside Shimla, helping children with school work. This was generally achieved through feats of efficiency and rational organization of time and resources and, as I have indicated, at the expense of the woman's own chance for recreation and relaxation.

All the same, there are forms of household service work which the working wife is in a privileged position to perform. The workplace itself may be a useful place to cultivate valuable contacts or sources of information even if women's workplace networks are less productive than those of men (see Chapter 9), and women no less than men are alert to any opportunity to cultivate or claim fringe benefits which their work may offer in the form of 'perks', access to information, etc. So if paid work limits the time available for household service work of one kind, it may open up opportunities for household service activities of a different nature, much depending obviously on the kind of work which the woman does.

Women's employment and the household: options and constraints

It is perhaps useful to consider here how far the employment of wives represents an option for households.[7] Is it best seen as one strategy among the various possible means for enhancing household resources or as a compulsory response to economic pressures and inflationary tendencies in the urban economy? Obviously the latter is the case for certain types of household – households where there is no adult male breadwinner, for instance, or where the male breadwinner is sick or unemployed. On the other hand there must be an element of choice at some levels, because how else could it be possible to find two households in which the husbands earn comparable incomes, yet where one wife's employment is accepted as the only possible way of making ends meet while the other wife has never contemplated taking employment, and even regards it as detrimental to the interests of the household in some way?

In some cases I have been able to argue that differences in subcultural norms or household 'style' can account for the preference of a particular household. But if we abandon the synchronic 'snapshot' approach which interview surveys are liable to encourage, we can perceive other possibilities. One important variable may be the nature of the husband's job, as will be clear from the following cases. In one lower middle-class household of rural origin the husband, whom I shall call Mr Thakur, was employed as personal assistant to an important Indian Administrative Service (IAS) officer at an income of about Rs1,500. He was regarded as a very promising young man by his superiors and had entered for the examinations leading to selection for the Himachal Administrative Service (HAS).[8] If he passed, his career would be a very bright one, but even if he did not it was likely that he would receive promotion within the department where he worked. His wife, a country girl with a little education, did not work and had not been brought up to consider doing so, but had thrown herself into the role of an urban housewife with energy and enthusiasm. Another couple (let us call them the Agarwals) were, on the other hand, both in employment and both had been in the same or similar employment since before their marriage. Mr Agarwal was a stenographer in a bank and Mrs Agarwal held a similar post in another branch of the same bank. Both were satisfied with their jobs and did not expect to change these or to receive any very dramatic promotions or increments in salary. Mr Agarwal earned Rs1,200 and his wife earned Rs1,100. It is doubtful whether Mrs Thakur would have been able to obtain paid work of a type commensurate with her husband's status even if she had wanted to. But in any case she saw her time as better invested in the education of her two daughters and the cultivation of a useful social circle, an investment whose value would be realized in time to come when her husband, as seemed likely, would land a top administrative post and move in quite elevated circles.

The Agarwals were unlikely to achieve the rather spectacular social mobility attempted by the Thakurs, although they felt that they were materially better off than their parents had been. Neither were on career ladders likely to lead to substantially greater prestige or higher incomes in future, so Mrs Agarwal saw the double income they presently earned as worth maintaining to pay for their children's college fees and (eventually) their marriages. The withdrawal of either partner from paid employment would result in a drastic loss of income which was most unlikely to be compensated for by an eventual increase in the other's earning power. Mrs Agarwal would be a lot less tired if she did not work full time and Mrs Thakur would be better able to pay her daughter's expensive school fees if she did work, but their decisions have to be seen in the light of their expectations for the future, not simply in terms of their immediate circumstances.

This comparison reveals a certain rationality at work, a social accounting system that balances both social and economic losses and gains. But it does not do to assume perfect rationality on the part of all households. I came to know of some low income households whose fortunes undoubtedly would have been improved if the wife had been willing to work, but where such a course was never contemplated. Many women of rural origin saw paid work for women other than a few professional occupations as demeaning and would have regarded the loss of status consequent upon taking a job as not worth the pay, which given their lack of qualifications would not be great in any case. Yet how far are their fears about loss of status justified? Some women in the sample did undertake domestic work and did not feel that they had suffered as a consequence although they clearly stated that they wished they were better paid. Jivan, for instance, had worked for a retired school teacher for some years and was evidently much liked and respected by her neighbours. Indeed, her mistress and her mistress's friends all spoke well of her, describing her as a respectable woman who worked hard, helped people where she could, and spoke ill of no one. Can it be said that Jivan lost status as a result of the lowly work she did? The critical question is perhaps just *whose* judgement the women are afraid of. Most poor women who dismissed paid work as a possibility because of 'what people would say' were clearly referring to their kin and neighbours back in the village, not their urban neighbours who might be working women themselves. As the wife of a *peon* said:

> 'There is no custom of women doing service among our people. Village people would regard it as shameful unless I were doing a very respectable job or were very educated.'

Kamla, who had left her village to come to Shimla over twenty years previously, took a cleaning job to enhance the household budget and knew that her village kin would disapprove. When visitors arrived from the village she would simply take time off work to entertain them, so that they never in fact found out that she was in employment. Her employers did not like this much, but they had a regard for her as an otherwise reliable and conscientious worker and their goodwill enabled her to maintain this deception. Her neighbours and friends of her own social class in Shimla apparently did not think the worse of her for being out at work, and like Jivan she was a popular and well-respected woman. How far fears about loss of status alone will deter poor women from seeking employment will depend very much on the kind of contact such women have with their villages of origin, since it is village kin who still constitute the reference group of more recent migrants. This is not to say that working as someone else's menial is well thought of by city people, but in the case of women like Jivan or Kamla, potential loss of status through doing demeaning work can be offset to some extent by the respect they receive for personal qualities, for good neighbourliness, for the better clothes they can afford to wear. The news that 'So-and-so works as a servant in other people's houses' will reach village ears sooner than the news that 'So-and-so is a generous neighbour'. Women who are in a position to keep their urban 'servant' identity separate from their rural identity as members of a certain caste or household in the village can afford to risk the loss of status which employment may entail, but not all are in a good position to do so. This is especially true of the more recent migrants and younger women, whose junior status might make them more exposed to accusations of insubordination and dubious sexual morals if they undertook activities outside the home not approved by their husbands and their husbands' family.

In conclusion then, it is quite possible to see decisions about women's employment as the result of rational choices between alternative strategies and options, but with two important qualifications. First, the material factor of the income which a woman might earn is only one element in the balance sheet, which may include far more non-material factors such as 'loss of status', 'loss of leisure', 'future earnings or activities of both husband and wife'. Second, we must not assume that either the costs ('loss of leisure', 'less time for domestic work') or the benefits ('more income', 'sense of independence') of paid employment would necessarily mean the same thing to each individual woman and her family members. A household has a history and it has future prospects. Decisions of women as to whether to enter or abstain from the labour market may be made in the light of past experiences (enduring contact with or dependence upon conservative village kin, socialization and education processes) and orientations to the future (the career prospects of employed members of the household, the likelihood of adult children adding to the household income or leaving home, the degree of ambition exhibited by members of the household). As they participate in different 'household histories' individual women may evaluate the same costs or benefits differently. Further than this, I do not think it is possible to generalize.

Notes

1 The female work participation rate is the percentage of the total female population in paid work or otherwise economically active in the terms defined by the Census of India. It does not represent the most sophisticated way of measuring economic activity, but it is the most accessible, being used in the Census reports.

2 This is no doubt partly due to the fact that in many wealthy households husband and wife are in similar types of employment – professional work or government service with pay scales and conditions which do not disadvantage women grossly. In a city with a different employment pattern, e.g. where the main employment opportunities available to women are poorly paid industrial or service work, this generalization might not be valid.

3 It is important to distinguish parental attitudes to *employment* from parental attitudes to *education*. Many women were at pains to stress that while their parents never considered the possibility of their daughters seeking employment, they nevertheless encouraged them in their school work and kept them at school or college for as long as they could afford to.

4 'Even households with similar objective characteristics living in the same urban neighbourhood may have markedly different styles of livelihood. This happens because the values of separate resources that constitute and define the household system are not fixed, and because each of them is combined with or converted into others in different ways through the ordinary process of livelihood . . . in many cases there is more than one kind of successful performance' (Wallman 1984: 41).

5 One college lecturer, for instance, was married to an engineer employed in another Indian state. As his job involved a lot of travelling in areas where the wife would be unlikely to find such a lucrative or interesting job the couple decided to make Shimla their base. The family were together only at weekends, but felt the advantages of this arrangement outweighed the disadvantages, specially the fact that in Shimla the children had access to excellent schools.

6 This confirms what Khanwar Mumtaz found in a study of low-paid female workers in Pakistan: 'despite very low earnings, most of the women felt very positive about their work, claiming that work had given them more confidence in themselves' (Mumtaz 1983: 18).

7 I write here as though decisions about the wife's employment were taken by the household as a collectivity. Most women described themselves as having entered employment in the first place as a result of their own unilateral decisions, certainly not as having been pressured into employment at the instance of other household members. Equally, though, they stressed that they could not consider employment without the consent and support of husbands or other senior members of the household. Young women, in particular, were likely to have chosen a particular kind of work in consultation with the father or husband.

8 Members of the Indian Administrative Service are senior civil servants recruited by the central government and allocated to the various states. Each state also has its local administrative service (in this case the HAS) recruited locally. Members of the IAS may be transferred to other states, while members of the local administrative services remain in the state by whose public service commission they were recruited.

9 Networks, cooperation, and social life: sources of information

In this chapter I deal with the informal marshalling of resources that takes place through the activation of personal networks, and the contribution of women to the construction and servicing of these networks.

There will be many occasions on which members of the urban household rely on others to give help which cannot be got from the state or through the market. In some instances the direction and amount of such help may be determined by specific and conventional norms of obligation. When a woman is married, for instance, custom allows her to expect some help with the wedding expenses from her mother's parents or brothers. But in most situations where help is needed no such prescriptions exist. The members of the household must construct their own aid networks and rescue services from the material available to them – kin, neighbours, contacts in the workplace, fellow migrants.

Some emergencies cannot be predicted or imagined beforehand, but there are problems which most households will experience at some time or another and in which members may well need the assistance of others. Looking for work is one such situation. The labour market in a city is large and complex, yet in most Third World towns it is very largely organized on informal lines. In the search for work it pays to be well informed and well connected. Finding accommodation is another situation in which members of the household benefit from the help they can rally from their friends and kin. Not only is there an acute housing shortage in Shimla, but many of the rooms and flats that become vacant are never advertised publicly. Much information about vacant accommodation passes round by word of mouth and personal recommendation. Looking at the needs of the household in the long term, the help of others will be needed most acutely when it is time to get the adult sons and daughters married. Given that in most parts of North India marriage between consanguines and even unrelated people who are already well known to each other is disapproved, it is clear that information about suitable marriage partners for one's children can only be got by attending to the reports of others. One must turn to one's friends' friends and relations' relations. Finally, apart from these situations which most households will encounter at some time, there are the occasional emergencies such as sudden illness, in which the help of others proves a vital resource.

An urban household in India is likely to be more reliant on tapping personal networks for the kind of purpose just described than is its British counterpart, although it is very likely that sociologists have underestimated the role of informal networks as channels of information in western society. Formal agencies are either poorly developed or absent and, being urban based, are inaccessible to the villager who wishes to migrate to the city, until he or she actually arrives. Employment bureaux exist, for instance, but many jobs are never registered, especially in the informal sector. Newspapers publish advertisements for schools, apartments, and even marriage partners, but the poor or uneducated cannot read them. There is no overall system of social security organized by the state. Government employees are better off than others in this respect, since they enjoy pension schemes and housing entitlements unavailable to most private employees. The household must cope with unemployment, sickness, or disablement as best it can. Some charitable organizations exist but they usually help specific categories, e.g. destitute women or orphans, and even here informal connections often determine who receives help.

This reliance on informal networks and sources of aid is further strengthened by a widespread feeling that such personal connections are more to be trusted than impersonal agencies. This belief, of course, works both ways. If the applicant for a job feels that he or she has a better chance of getting it because his or her name has been recommended by a friend who works in that office, then the individual responsible for the choice of staff is just as likely to feel that a person connected to someone already employed in the organization will be a better risk than an unknown quantity.[1] His obligation to the friend who helped him to get the job ought to ensure that he will work well and will do nothing that will reflect ill upon the reputation of his patron, in case he needs his help again. Such expectations are not always fulfilled, of course; this system of guarantees does not rule out inefficiency or breach of trust but presumably most of the time it works well enough to convince people that it is a reasonable way of doing things. It certainly eases the problem faced by those responsible for the allocation of scarce resources; among the dozens of competitors for a job, a flat, the hand of an eligible bachelor, a sound personal recommendation distinguishes certain candidates from the many equally well qualified. Personal contact simplifies the problem of choice in a buyer's market.

This system of patronage affects everyone in the system. Those who are rich or powerful, it is true, are more often in the position of having to dispense aid or favours than the poor. They are better protected by their very wealth from the effects of crises in the household. On the other hand, when they do require aid it is usually on a substantial scale (help with tax problems, getting foreign currency to travel abroad) and if they have not cultivated relations of trust and mutual obligation with their peers and those who are even more powerful than themselves, then they run risks with the privilege and security they currently enjoy. The resources of the household are best protected if its members cultivate both horizontal links with status peers, with whom they exchange services and information of an approximately equivalent kind, but also vertical links of patronage with those who can be useful to them in both higher and lower levels of society.

There is nothing particularly novel about these observations. Anthropologists discovered the usefulness of the concept of social network as soon as they began to study urban neighbourhoods in depth.[2] What I want to add to this knowledge is the idea of networks as household resources. Anthropologists have generally described networks as though they were series of linkages between individuals, and this is not an inaccurate description. But if we concentrate on the purposes to which networks are put (as opposed to their structures and formal properties) we see that to a greater or lesser degree members of the same household have a stake in each other's networks. This is certainly obvious in the situations discussed above. But there is another sense in which networks are a household's resource and not just the 'property' of individuals. As we shall see, members of the same household contribute to the construction of each other's networks, or, to be more specific, women contribute to the construction and maintenance of their husband's networks. In as much as networks are serviced and extended through the exchange of hospitality, letters, and gifts, the efforts of the household members who cook the meals, write the letters, and buy the gifts must be taken into account. As we shall see in the next chapter, much of this work is done by women.

Constructing and servicing networks is not something that either men or women do quite separately from the rest of their activities. This business is usually embedded in the 'social life' which goes on in the home, in the neighbourhood, among office colleagues or fellow migrants. Therefore we have to ask what are the forms of interaction people engage in which lead to exchanges of help, and how are these interactions sustained over time? Networks may be constructed with a greater or lesser degree of calculation about the usefulness of the contacts they yield. Individuals may make overtures of an appropriate kind to someone they may wish to help them in future in a fairly deliberate way (Carol Stack, for instance, has described how poor black women in a US city would make gifts in order to obligate the recipient, an insurance against the time when they might have to ask for help (Stack 1975: 41)). Or people may simply cultivate relationships with those they find congenial, dipping into their fund of social credit when the need for help arises. Many accounts of networks describe them in such a way as to make the element of self-interest more prominent than it actually appears in everyday life because they omit to describe the context of sociability within which networks grow and flourish.

In this chapter I shall concentrate on the relative effectiveness of men's and women's networks in recruiting aid for the household, especially the way in which they yield information, a crucial resource. When I write of 'men's' and 'women's' networks I am referring simply to the networks of male and female members of the household. Female members' networks need not consist only of women, nor male members' networks consist only of men, although in practice there is a fair degree of segregation (see below, p. 168). However, I am not concerned here with the precise extent or structure of the networks, only with the ways in which they are useful to the household. To simplify my account I have concentrated on some specific situations in which the help or advice of others is needed and which, if not faced by all urban households, are at least fairly common.

Finding accommodation

There is a severe shortage of living accommodation in Shimla, mainly because the city's population has grown much faster than the stock of housing. The situation is particularly difficult for those who migrate to the city from elsewhere, whether as first time migrants from a village, or as a result of a transfer from another city. Some accommodation is advertised in a national English language daily newspaper which has a large circulation in Shimla, but for those seeking the kind of humble living space that a poor clerk or *peon* can afford this is no help at all. There are a few estate agencies but those that exist deal with property for sale rather than property available to rent. When searching for rooms or a house to rent one is more than usually dependent on information provided by personal contacts.

On the whole, accommodation is an area in which husbands' networks contribute more to household resources than those of wives. Many women lived in government accommodation to which their husbands were entitled as government employees. (Some very senior public employees are provided with accommodation automatically by virtue of their function or rank; less senior employees can simply claim for government accommodation as it becomes available.) In several cases a man moved to Shimla to take up a new job and simply moved into the rooms rented by the predecessor in his post, and in others the husband had been told about accommodation by a colleague who knew the landlord or already lived in the same building himself. Accommodation found through male contacts, therefore, usually means accommodation found via the husband's place of work.

Few employed women occupy positions senior enough to give them automatic entitlement to accommodation, but female government employees did not seem to have difficulty in getting government accommodation when they applied for it, or at least none that were not also experienced by men.

Another category of women well placed to find housing through their work was domestic servants. Full-time servants might be offered living-in jobs where their families would be provided with special servants' quarters. Most modern housing in Indian cities which is intended for upper income groups does not include separate servants' quarters and many servants have to trudge miles from the slums and colonies where they live to reach their mistresses' houses, which is why full-time domestic service is not a job which many married women with young children can easily undertake. In Shimla, however, there is still a stock of housing dating from British times, when land was not scarce and government servants lived in sprawling bungalows with spacious gardens and rooms for several servants' families in a separate block.

Finding employment

As in the case of accommodation, I am concerned here with the question of how people come to hear about a job vacancy or opportunity for promotion rather than the question of whose influence, if any, helped them secure it. In many cases a source of information might also prove to be a source of influence, but this is not necessarily the case (a junior clerk may tell his brother about an opening in the office where he works without having any control over the way in which the vacancy is filled). Besides this, it would have been impossible to verify informants' reports about the extent to which they understood personal contacts to have been influential in getting the posts they occupied.

A large proportion of men and women hear about their jobs through public advertisements, employment exchanges, or through information officially circulated in the workplace. However these were almost all government servants and the total picture might be very different in a city where the public sector accounts for a smaller proportion of employment opportunities, since information about government jobs on the whole receives wider circulation than jobs in the private sector.[3]

Women who heard about their jobs through personal contact (about 40 per cent of the respondents in the interview sample had done so) seem to have found male networks more productive than female networks, although this is hardly surprising when relatively few women are employed full-time outside the home at the moment. The women who had heard about their present jobs through female friends, relatives, or neighbours were mainly domestic servants (of whom more below), although a few were

professional women who had been 'tipped' by a female lecturer at
college about a particular opportunity. Many of the women whom I
classified as having found their jobs through male 'contacts'
actually inherited a job, or at least a job opportunity, from a
deceased male relative. Government departments and some private
organizations may offer the widow of a permanent employee a job of
some kind. Occasionally the job may be 'inherited' by an unmarried
daughter instead. (I suppose a dead husband or father counts as a
male 'contact', in the sense that the woman could not have been
offered the particular job but for her connection with him.) We
should expect the new entrant to the labour market to be in a
different position from the 'old hand' in the matter of finding jobs
since she will not have the benefit of information circulated in the
workplace and is likely to have fewer contacts in the places where
she might find employment. However, these factors seemed to be
less important for women than for men. Most employed women
seemed either to have commenced their working careers in Shimla
after a period of residence there or to have moved to Shimla on
marriage to join a husband who had been living there for some time.
In either case, the woman seeking work had access to existing
networks, whether her own or her husband's. Very few had ever
been in the position of trying to find work in Shimla from a base
outside the city. For male migrants, on the other hand, this was a
common situation. A boy from a farming family who wishes to find
a clerical or manual job in town is unlikely to have access to a
newspaper or to live within reach of an employment exchange. He
must rely on some fellow villager (usually a kinsman) who is
employed in the city to pass on information about job opportunities
there.

Hiring servants

It is worth discussing the question of how servants are hired in some
detail since it illustrates very aptly the general way in which
informal information networks operate in the field of employment,
and in particular the way in which vertical and horizontal networks
mesh.

Upper-class women in Shimla believe that servants, or at least
good reliable servants, are very difficult to obtain. The problems
encountered in searching for a suitable *ayah*, a dependable maid-

servant, or a properly trained cook are topics of conversational interest and recounted at length. I had expected that as it was usually the wife who does the actual hiring, i.e. who approves the servant and often takes the responsibility of paying him or her, servants would be recruited almost exclusively through women's networks, but this was not always the case. In about 40 per cent of the cases on which I have information, the servant was found through some connection of the husband, nearly always through his contacts at work. A nurse married to a clerk told me that a *peon* in her husband's office had offered the services of a young relative of his who was seeking work. An engineer's wife had visited her husband in the rural area where he was temporarily posted and had met a young woman related to the family of farmers with whom her husband was lodging. The girl had indicated that she would like to find work in Shimla and the wife hired her on the spot. In another case a senior government servant employed a *peon* in his office to work in his house after office hours. In fact it is not unknown for senior employees to 'borrow' junior employees in their offices to do work of a more or less domestic nature or to run errands for their wives. This is all quite unofficial, but it is regarded as one of the perquisites of such jobs. Occasionally a driver or gardener supplied officially with a senior job or with official accommodation might also be asked to perform personal services for the superior's household, demands which the junior employee can scarcely refuse without fear of offence.

Very few women who are employed have the kind of jobs that would entitle them to use office servants, either officially or unofficially, although a few find that contacts at work make it easier for them to hear about servants seeking work, such as in the case of an employment officer who told me that as she worked in an employment exchange she never had any problems in finding servants. More often they obtain servants by tapping local networks, that is, they ask friends or neighbours to look out for a suitable person. The friends and neighbours may respond by recommending women they have employed themselves in the past, or, if a part-time dishwasher is all that is needed, by recommending a woman whom they presently employ, or they may know of a man or woman related to their own servant who wants a job. In some cases the prospective employer may approach poor women living in her neighbourhood and ask them to spread the word around among their kin or acquaintances. Women with rural connections are often able to get servants from the villages where their parents live or have land. The fact that it is the women of the household who are most likely to make these visits to the village most regularly means that it is they who are most likely to come into contact with the kind of poor rural women who seek servants' jobs in the town. A woman who hires a male servant from the village knows that most likely he intends the job as a stepping stone to some better employment and will probably not stay with her long. But even this arrangement can work to their mutual advantage. As the wife of a retired doctor told me:

> 'I know that Ram Das [her servant] stays with us only because my son is an influential official in his home area and he hopes that we will be able to get him an office job. But I do not mind that. It means that he will work willingly for us while he is here, and when he goes he will almost certainly be able to find us another servant from his village.'

From the employer's point of view, one servant can lead to another; from the servant's point of view, one job can lead to another.

Where a servant stays with the same household for many years, a relationship of mutual responsibility is often established which favours the circulation of information about work opportunities. Servants find out about work for their kin through their employers, and employers find out about servants for their friends. There may well be other perquisites for both parties when the relationship is harmonious and long standing. For instance the mistress may pass on discarded clothes which the servant can give to his or her family. From a grateful servant the mistress can expect to obtain 'overtime' ungrudgingly, or at any rate uncomplainingly, when she has to entertain a group of visiting relatives or gives a party.

This circulation of goods, services, and information between servants and mistresses flourishes best where the mistress is rich and well connected, for only then is she likely to afford this dimension to their relationship. Several servants recounted appalling experiences in middle-income group families where the wife kept a servant to enable her to go out to work. In such cases the mistress was unlikely to 'waste' resources on such things as extra cups of tea or snacks for the *ayah*, and the toddler's discarded clothes would be kept as hand-me-downs for the next baby. Such employers seldom have the kind of useful connections themselves which would induce a servant to put up with poor pay and long hours in the hope of finding jobs for her own kin, so it is not surprising that the turnover among domestics in such households is high. Here, no doubt, is the genesis of the notion that servants are inherently 'unreliable'.

However, where mistresses have enduring and satisfactory relations with both their servants and their neighbours, a very effective system of information exchange is constructed. Information, and sometimes goods and services as well, are exchanged *vertically* across class boundaries between servants and mistresses, and *horizontally* among status equals (as when a servant woman informs a relative about her mistress's neighbour who needs a cook, or when the employer taps her network to find an opening for her *ayah*'s unemployed son). The household is the point at which these channels of information intersect.

Finding help with childcare and domestic work

In Chapter 8 I discussed the arrangements which employed women make for the care of their young children, and we have seen that most women rely on either servants or female relatives (see p. 142). Both men and women seem to regard it as a woman's business to organize a substitute supply for her own domestic labour if she decides to go out to work, or if she has to be away from home for any other reason. The three employed women who used nurseries had all found out about and applied for places on their own initiative, and those who employed *ayahs* to care for babies or toddlers had all found and approved such servants themselves. Where employed women relied on a living-in relation to care for their children, that relation was almost always the mother-in-law. However, looking at the past histories of women presently employed, it became clear that mothers are also an important source of help, especially when the children are very young. Ten of the forty employed women in the interview sample had relied on their mothers for full-time childcare at some time in the past, and several of these still depended on their mothers in matters like collecting the children from school or taking them to the doctors when they were sick. Sometimes the mother is used as a 'back-up' service when the person who usually minds the child is sick or absent. For example, one shorthand-typist took her baby to her mother-in-law's house most days, but if the latter ever went away to visit kin, her mother would have the child for a week or a month as the case might be. A doctor described how her mother had cared for her two small boys every day while she was undertaking postgraduate training in Delhi, without which arrangement she felt it would have been impossible for her to complete her qualifications.

Indeed, where women are living near to their parents there is often a fairly constant flow of domestic help of one kind or another from mother to daughter (less often the reverse). A mother may send her servant to help with some chore in the daughter's house or arrive herself to help prepare food if her daughter is entertaining visitors. In Shimla this is a more common pattern among middle-class families with an urban background; poor women are usually migrants whose parents live in distant rural areas. Elsewhere, though, this pattern of aid seems common enough among the very poor. Contrary to the preference for local exogamy prevalent in most rural areas in North India and still strong in many urban communities, slum dwellers and poor urban labourers seem not to be averse to marrying their daughters to men who live nearby and when mother and daughter are neighbours, they exchange many services and other kinds of aid. Gulati, for instance, compares the often unfulfilled expectations of poor women that their sons will support them in their old age with the ideologically unrecognized reality, namely that, 'surviving men and women are being looked after more often by daughters than sons' (Gulati 1981: 170).

In so far as the flow of aid is mainly from mother to daughter (certainly the case in Shimla if not in Kerala where Gulati collected her case material) then this could be seen as part of the conventional pattern in North India in which the bride's family continue to make gifts to her after her marriage, over and above whatever may have been given by way of dowry at her wedding. The parents of a married woman (and after their death, her brothers) have an obligation to give her or her husband presents when she visits them on major festivals, or on family occasions such as the birth of a child. Alternatively, we could see this flow of aid as an instance of a pattern of female cooperation which is not peculiarly Indian at all, but on the contrary seems common in many urban situations. Willmott and Young (1962) identified a regular exchange of services of a domestic nature among kinswomen who lived in the same area, especially between mothers and daughters (1962: 50). For some time this was regarded as something characteristic of localized working-class and black communities in the west, but work on middle-class families suggests that it is fairly common among them also when mothers and daughters live in the same locality. Stivens (1978) suggests that:

> 'Domestic labour in kin circles outside the elementary family contributes to the reproduction of labour power and is thus necessary to the capitalist system.'
>
> (Stivens 1978:179)

Perhaps what we see in Shimla is a form of female cooperation which is usual in other urban societies but which has been suppressed in North India where the bride is generally removed to another locality on marriage. It reasserts itself where local marriage becomes acceptable or where daughters return to their natal kin after being widowed or deserted. Possibly local urban marriages will become more common in Himachali cities like Shimla, since many migrants come from areas in rural Himachal where village exogamy is not so imperative as it is elsewhere in North India or may not be required at all. Certainly many of the respondents in the interview sample who were of Himachali origin stated that they would like to get their daughters married in Shimla if a suitable match could be found.

The cooperative relationship between mother and daughter is a strong one and brings practical benefits to the household, but it is not the only form of female cooperation in domestic matters. A few women reported such exchanges of services with sisters living in the locality and women whose mothers-in-law lived separately but nearby often found them a source of practical assistance. This, however, depended very much on the kind of relationship which the couple had established with the husband's parents after setting up their own separate home. Some women enjoyed an intimate relationship with their husbands' families, with much informal visiting and giving and receiving of small services. Some either did not get on well with their mothers-in-law or preferred to maintain a more formal relationship.

Finding marriage partners

The majority of marriages in India are arranged by the couple's parents. It is their responsibility when their children reach marriageable age to find suitable partners for them, acting on the information they are able to gather from their relatives and friends. Close kin ought to be prepared to help in this work although the main obligation is the parents'. In most communities the prevalent ideology rules that it is the girl's parents who are supposed to do the searching and come to the boy's parents with an offer, but in reality the system only works because the friends and kin of both girls and boys are prepared to circulate information about young people among their acquaintance whose parents wish to marry them soon.

In my study of rural women I found that it was women who were chiefly responsible for spreading this information and who most commonly acted as intermediaries in the arrangement of marriages, even though the matrimonial deals may be clinched by men (Sharma 1980a: 143ff.). As noted earlier, there is a preference for village exogamy in many parts of North India, although not in all parts of Himachal. Before it became common for men to seek employment outside their villages, a household's main connections with families in other villages would be through its in-marrying womenfolk. Increased opportunities for men to migrate to work have extended men's range of contacts outside their own villages and I found that among army families and households with urban connections there was less exclusive reliance on women's networks where match-making is concerned. However, urban living and urban employment also extends women's range of contacts when they settle in cities. Neighbours, colleagues, the wives of husbands' colleagues – all kinds of new contacts may yield useful information about marriage partners for their own or their relative's children. And in so far as migrant women tend to make more frequent trips back to their areas of origin than men, they often serve as the relayers of such information between town and countryside. A wife goes home to see to family property or to attend a wedding and sees a nice girl who might suit her neighbour's son. Or she hears that her husband's workmate wants to get his daughter married soon and tells her sister, who has a bachelor son in the army.

Collecting data on the way in which marriages are arranged is not a particularly easy task. Formerly village girls were married at an early age – perhaps only 12 or 13 years old – and many older informants may genuinely not remember how their families had come to marry them to the particular husbands chosen for them. I also found that some women found the question 'How was your marriage arranged?' mildly offensive, suggesting that a young girl, supposedly innocent of the discussions being held about her future, might have been unwholesomely curious about the choice of her groom. As one woman put it:

> 'When I got married it was all done by relations. I knew nothing about it. It was not like it is in some families today where the girl picks and chooses according to her own fancy.'

In some cases, especially among women of urban background, the woman could remember that the marriage had been arranged through a family friendship, but could not remember who had mooted the idea first. The wife of a businessman, for instance, knew that her husband had been chosen for her because of the close friendship between his and her own parents, but could not say whether it had been her mother or her father who had originally proposed the match.

In the majority of cases on which I was able to collect data the marriage had been arranged on the basis of information received through networks of female members of the household. But male networks cannot be discounted in the urban context. Where the marriage had been arranged on the basis of information provided by a male contact, this was usually through a near relative on the mother's side. The mother's brother often makes efforts to get his sister's children married well and is regarded as having something of a special obligation in this respect. More often, though, the contact was one connected with the workplace. The wife of a bank employee told me:

> 'My marriage was arranged by my father. He worked in the same office as my father-in-law and they were friendly with each other. Both my parents and my husband's parents liked the idea of a local match and so our wedding was arranged.'

In another instance the educated daughter of a government servant had been found her husband when her father visited another state in connection with his work and met a young IAS officer of his own caste and with excellent prospects. Another woman's husband had been found by her brother who had been studying science at the time. One day the students from his college were taken to visit an engineering college for some purpose connected with their course and while there, her brother had met a student who seemed very suitable for his sister, being good-looking, of the right caste, and a high achiever in his studies. He suggested this boy to his parents who took up the matter and in due course arranged the matter with the boy's parents. Menial jobs as well as professional occupations may yield useful contacts, as exemplified in the case of a domestic servant whose father had been employed as a porter in a college and had come into contact with a suitable groom for his daughter in the place where he worked.

Where information about marriage partners was gathered through female networks, the common connection was almost always through family. The wife of a shop assistant had her match arranged by her elder sister's sister-in-law, who lived near the groom's uncle in another city. A domestic servant of carpenter caste had her marriage arranged by her paternal uncle's daughter-in-law. This young woman went to her own village on a visit and met the prospective groom, a neighbour's son, while he was on leave from his job as a carpenter employed by the army.

Not all information gathered by women is circulated along purely family networks, though. Proximity counts for much, as in the case of a shopkeeper's wife whose husband had been found for her by a neighbour of her mother's, or that of a seamstress employed in a hotel, who married the son of the tenant who cultivated part of her sister's land.

Female networks in the workplace did not seem to be an important source of information about marriage partners, but the workplace might well provide the opportunity for the girl to find a husband for herself. Very few of the marriages in which the girl 'found' her own husband were love marriages, and these are still unusual. More often the workplace provided the setting in which the girl could be seen and known by people outside the family circle and 'viewed' as a prospective marriage partner. A woman doctor described the 'rather peculiar fashion' in which her marriage was arranged.

> 'I was working in this medical college and my boss was very fond of me. My husband was also working here, although I did not know him at that time. But my boss knew him and liked him very much, so he proposed the match to my father. As the boy was the same caste as ourselves and a doctor (which was what my parents wanted for me) my father said 'why not'. So he talked it over with my boss and eventually the match came off.'

In another case, Jyoti had left home before her marriage to take a master's degree course in vocational guidance and had made friends with one of the female lecturers in her college. This lecturer knew a suitable boy, the son of friends of her own family. She mentioned this boy to Jyoti, who presumably liked the idea since she put her friend in touch with her parents and negotiations proceeded in the conventional way. In a third case, Shakuntala, a nurse, had met her husband when he was a patient in the ward where she was working. He had liked the look of her and, being an enterprising young man, had found out where her parents lived and made a proposal. They liked the look of him too, made enquiries about his family, and eventually the marriage was arranged. Parents with daughters might do well to consider that although sending a daughter out to work may bring censure from some quarters, it may also increase her choice of marriage partner in that it extends the range of people who hear about her skills and qualities.

To obtain one's husband through a newspaper advertisement is regarded with disdain by many, who see it as the last resort for men and women who have something very wrong with them, such as a physical disability, over-dark complexion, some kind of bad reputation, and who are forced to use such impersonal means. Certainly there are horror stories in circulation about women who found what seemed to be a splendid match through an advertisement only to find out when it was too late that they had been deceived into marrying a man of low caste or a criminal reputation. This, it is always pointed out, would hardly happen if there were mutual family connections to check on the groom's claims about himself. However those who had found their husbands in this way might equally point out that such disasters were reputedly not unknown among women who had their marriages arranged in the normal way. I only encountered three women who had found their husbands through advertisements, but there seemed nothing about them such as might make them undesirable marriage partners. A doctor stated that her parents had been keen to find her a husband in the medical profession, a preference which she endorsed herself. As they did not have any connections with that themselves, they had advertised in a national newspaper and had found her a husband with whom she seemed very satisfied. Another woman said that her parents had several boys in mind from their own acquaintance but had wanted to widen the scope of choice for their daughters and had therefore put an advertisement in the press. Her husband had responded and they liked him better than the other boys they had been told about, and so went ahead with the match.

Urbanization, it would seem, extends the range of possible means by which parents may hear about suitable marriage partners for their sons and daughters. Lunchtime at the office or shop can as easily provide the occasion for the exchange of such information as the family visit or trip to the village. However it is still *female* networks which are the staple source of this information although these networks may be more varied and extensive than the female networks which operate in villages. The fact that in the city it is still women who bear the chief responsibility for keeping in touch with kin also feeds the vigour of the female grapevine. The making of marriages is a topic of overriding interest and importance in women's circles at all levels of income, and in any kind of social group the talk will turn from time to time to matches desired or completed.

Summary

In this chapter I have discussed some examples of the kind of situation in which members of households tap their networks for information or other kinds of resource. From these data we see that both men and women are responsible for the coordination of information or aid relevant to the household's needs, but there is a degree of specialization. Men are more likely to mediate information on jobs or accommodation whereas women are more likely to find sources of information about marriage partners or of domestic help. There is also a degree of segregation of these networks, in the sense that women's networks tend to be predominantly female and men's networks, largely centred on the workplace, tend to be predominantly male. Men and women are not segregated physically to such a large extent as they are in some other parts of India, but sex appears to constitute a barrier to communication – outside the household at any rate – even though it does not constitute a barrier to interaction. A woman will tell other women about the relative of a servant girl who is looking for work, while a man will tell other men about a vacancy in the apartment block where he lives. It is mainly within the family that male and female information networks intersect.

In most of these networks important information circulates

among people of similar income and status, but at a few key points there is vertical interaction, points at which information or other resources flow between people of different status. The interaction between servant and mistress is a good example of this and it is for this reason that I have discussed it in some detail.

On the whole, employment outside the home extends the range of sources of help and information which are available to the household. This is especially true in a city like Shimla where many people are in government service, which often entitles the employee to valuable perquisites (housing, servants, pension rights, etc.). From some points of view the employment of women may lead to a constriction of the household's invisible assets. They may, as we have seen, have less time to spend on their children's education, but this may be compensated by other indirect benefits accruing from their employment. However, given that there is no seclusion of women in Shimla, even women who do not work are very free to construct their networks to whatever extent their energy, enterprise, and general sociability allow, and to explore channels of practical assistance and useful information which would not normally be available in the village.

Notes

1 I am not suggesting that those who select candidates for jobs ignore such criteria as education, experience, etc., only that personal recommendation is regarded as an additional relevant qualification in many situations.
2 For example, see Mayer (1963), Mitchell (1969), Boissevain (1974). The concept of network seems to have been used more extensively in studies of African and European communities than in studies of Asian cities, although I see no reason why this should be so.
3 Holmström's data on Bangalore, for instance, suggest that factory workers in the private sector are more likely to have found their jobs through what I have called 'informal' means than are workers in the public sector (Holmström 1976: 43).

10 Networks, cooperation, and social life: patterns of sociability

So far I have discussed the kinds of resource which enter or leave the household via personal contacts and have compared the roles of husbands and wives in rallying aid and information. But these transactions take place in the context of relationships which are not usually conceived in a purely instrumental fashion. The anthropologist Mauss (1954) argued that what distinguishes the gift relationship from pure contract is its totality, the fact that it may 'embrace a large number of institutions' and be sanctioned by norms which refer to many different kinds of obligation (kin ties, religious ideas, aesthetic or legal notions) (1954: 76–7). In urban India the gift relationship flourishes, albeit largely in de-ritualized forms. This should become clear in the following discussion in which I examine the structure and style of the social life of the women whose households I studied, the context in which these useful exchanges take place.

Most women, of whatever class, can identify two areas of social life which are of central importance to them – their relations with their kin and their relations with their neighbours. Those who work outside the home will generally also build relationships among the people with whom they work, although different kinds of occupation offer scope for different kinds of relationship. It is only among the middle and upper income groups that women can easily identify separate categories of 'friends' who do not necessarily belong to any of these groups, women whose company they enjoy and seek out even though they are not regularly thrown together by circumstances of kinship, proximity, or work. Indeed, many of the poor women we interviewed, could not make much sense of questions about their social life and leisure time. It seemed self-evident to them that the people you mixed with were your relatives, your neighbours, and the people you met at work if you had a job. You might get on well with them, or badly, but you were unlikely to have *time* for any other kind of relationship. Rupa, employed as part-time dishwasher by several middle-class women described her social life thus:

> 'We meet our relatives here – they are my husband's uncles and their families, plenty of company. They all live and work in Shimla. And then there are the ladies I work for, they are all nice people. I have five daughters and one son so I have plenty of work to do. There is always work to do in the house so I do not go out much. What time do I get for cinema outings or tea parties?'

This was quite different from the upper-class women who could usually describe an elaborate programme of social events, few of which were directly or solely based on either kinship, neighbourhood, or the workplace. They could identify a social circle, usually shared with their husbands to a greater or lesser extent, consisting of friends connected to them by quite diverse ties. Leisure activities, visiting, and formal entertainment were the forms of interaction which sustained this social life. Women on the middle and lower-middle income groups were increasingly being drawn into a comparable pattern of sociability for reasons which I shall discuss below. As we shall see, all this activity, apparently engaged in for its own sake, has consequences for the management of household resources.

Kin

For women of all social categories, kin ties have prior claim on their time and energies, and are of practical and psychological importance. At the very least, they are observed as a matter of duty; at best, they are a source of deep satisfaction and support. Many migrant women have relatives living in Shimla, usually siblings or cousins, and often their husbands have relatives there too. (Fifty-five per cent of the respondents in the interview sample claimed to have relatives other than their own parents or children living in Shimla, and to visit these relatives regularly.) Many women explicitly mentioned the presence of their own or their husbands' kin as a strong inducement to settle in Shimla in the first place and a good reason for making that settlement permanent. In many cases migrants had found their relatives very helpful in the first few months of their residence in Shimla, helping them settle in, find accommodation and schools for their children, and so on. This was true not only of Himachalis but even of some couples whose origins were in distant parts of India but whose close kin had moved to Shimla as well. Home is very largely where one's near relations happen to reside, and the sense of connection with some far-off village or city where neither oneself nor one's husband any longer have siblings or cousins becomes attenuated quite soon.

Single men, and men who have migrated to the city without their wives, will generally send money home to their parents or wives with some degree of regularity. Married couples, however, do not seem to send regular remittances of money to kin who do not live in the same household. Where they do, it is invariably to the husband's parents, although a few working women evidently buy small gifts for their parents out of their own earnings to take with them when they visit. This is in accordance with the dominant ideology which defines it as being the wife's parents' obligation to contribute to her welfare rather than as being her business to support them.

Wealthy women usually felt that such support was not needed either by their own or their husbands' parents. Fathers with professions usually received pensions of some kind when they retired, others owned land or some other kind of property. In some cases the burden of supporting elderly parents was mainly shouldered by the sons with whom they were living; other sons made only occasional contributions. Those who were poor simply stated that the cost of living in the city was such that they could not afford to send regular sums home even if their parents and siblings needed it. Naina, an electrician's wife, told me:

> 'We don't send my in-laws any money, although we used to when my husband's brothers and sisters were little. Now we don't send anything since we have enough problems meeting our own expenses and feeding our own children. Each household must look after itself.'

Informants whose children were grown-up and earning expected and usually received substantial contributions from them while they were unmarried and living at home, but once sons married and settled elsewhere they made only occasional contributions and mothers did not seem to expect them to do more.

But, if regular commitments were rare, it was evident that most households gave occasional help to kin. In many cases the couple would send cash or gifts via relatives when the latter came to Shimla for any reason. Many women reported recent occasions on which they had had to contribute to the wedding expenses of a relative of their husband's. The kinship system provides insurance policies in case of emergency rather than meal tickets, and this insurance is secured through sons and brothers rather than sisters and daughters, whose prime commitment is to their own husbands' families.

Help can be offered in other than financial terms, however, and many migrants were able to offer substantial aid of other kinds. Residence in Shimla itself was a resource which kin from the village might exploit from time to time. One woman had just spent six weeks nursing an aunt of her husband's, who had come to Shimla for a serious operation and had convalesced at her nephew's home. Another woman had accommodated her husband's younger brother for nine years while he was at school, since the village in Uttar Pradesh from which her husband came was not thought to provide such good educational facilities. In another household, the husband's sister had spent a few years with the family while she studied at college. Shimla is, after all, the capital and chief administrative centre of Himachal Pradesh, so any migrant household can expect to have to provide hospitality for relatives in town on business of some kind. Women from wealthy households often found that their relatives in the plains would expect them to provide a holiday refuge from the heat of Delhi or Chandigarh when the children's schools closed in summer.

How far is this a one-sided bargain, and do women resent having to put themselves out for what, in some households at least, seemed like a stream of transient kin, all expecting well prepared meals and claiming a good deal of their hostess's time? And is this work not the more likely to be perceived as a burden since the chief obligation of women is to their husbands' kin and not their own?

There are, of course, ways in which a woman can communicate to such house guests the point at which their presence is no longer welcome to her, without actually violating the norms of reticence and patience which a wife ought to observe in respect to her husband's family.[1] On the whole, though, such demands seem to be tolerated in spite of occasional irritations and resentments. Women find greater emotional closeness with their own natal kin, but they do identify with the interests and business of the husband's family to a large extent. Even if they do not like all his kin, they usually find that they can construct satisfying and congenial relationships with some of them. Also there is a strong awareness that while at times it seems that the urban household gives more than it gets to rural kin in the form of hospitality and services, the latter may yet provide services in return. As noted earlier, many urban households which own property in a village depend on kin to supervise that property from day to day. In some cases the husband's parents or brothers are actually cultivating this land, and there is clearly no point in alienating those who hold your property, or future property, in trust. When members of the urban household return to the village to supervise their land or just to enjoy a holiday, they usually rely on relatives to accommodate them. Looking at the matter in a long-term sense, many parents who live in Shimla expect to marry their children to people of the same caste and from the same original locality as themselves. This being so, they look to their rural links as possible sources of help in arranging such marriages, the more so if they come from a caste or ethnic group which is not very well represented in Shimla itself. Seen in this light, the services and hospitality which urban households provide for rural kin do not seem such a one-sided bargain, although there are undoubtedly cases where much more is given than received.

The effort which goes into maintaining these long-distance kin ties can be considered as a form of work in that it contributes (in the long term) to the welfare or survival of the household. This work is done largely, though not exclusively, by women. We have already seen that it is the regular visits made by women that are the chief means by which migrant households communicate with their places of origin. This is true of women from rural families, and generally of urban women from other North Indian cities. Most women whose parents are still alive try to visit them once a year when the Shimla schools close for the winter break and usually this is the occasion to visit their parents-in-law as well. Those women whose parents or parents-in-law live within easy reach of Shimla may go to see their families as often as every three or four months. Where the wife is illiterate she cannot be expected to keep in touch through letters, but where she has any education at all it will fall to her to keep up much of the correspondence with kin.[2] Few men seem to take the responsibility for maintaining contact with their wives' kin, but many women said that it was they who wrote letters to their parents-in-law and other affinal kin. It was often they who took responsibility for choosing suitable gifts for kin on weddings, festivals and other ritual occasions, although as we have seen in Chapter 6, they would usually consult their husbands as to the amount of money that ought to be devoted to such purposes. The servicing of kin links through hospitality, correspondence, visiting, and gifts could be regarded as a form of household service work which claims the time and energies of women of all classes.

Neighbours

Neighbourhood is another dimension of social experience common to women of all classes, although it has more practical importance to women of the middle- and lower-income groups, who are also likely to live in closest proximity to their neighbours. There is a well-developed notion of what it means to be a good neighbour and the kind of things neighbours should be prepared to do for each other. All women interact regularly and often intimately with some or all of the women who live in their vicinity. Housewives who inhabit the same tenement or block of flats will congregate on a shared balcony or any patch of ground where the sun strikes through the deodar trees. When their early morning chores are done they will sit together knitting or mending, perhaps slicing the vegetables they will use at lunchtime, chatting in companionable groups. There is little formal visiting among neighbours unless they also happen to be kin, but the women will drop into each other's houses to borrow small items, for instance, inquire after a sick child, or pass on a portion of the sweets they have received from a wedding in the family. The children, who may attend the same school, will be in and out of each other's homes and a house where there is a television set will automatically draw neighbours when a good film is being shown.

In these respects, neighbourhood life in Shimla seems to resemble that in any other large town in India. Where it differs would seem to be in the absence of any well-developed formal or ritual dimension to neighbourhood life, although this might simply be due to the fact that Shimla has grown very rapidly in recent years

and most people have not lived long enough in the same neighbourhood for anything more than informal relationships to develop. I did not find, for instance, the kind of formalized gift
exchange described by Vatuk (1972) in a suburb of Meerut, nor did
neighbours generally use fictive kin terms very readily or very
extensively (1972:177ff.). There are few neighbourhood temples
which might serve as centres where women can meet, indeed there
are few temples of any size in Shimla generally and these are mostly
situated near the centre of the town, further than most women
would have time to walk for personal devotions, although a visit to
Kali Bari or the Hanuman temple is often favoured as a Sunday
outing for the whole family. Major life-cycle rituals in migrant
families are frequently held outside Shimla, in the family's village
or town of origin. Festivals such as Divali (the Hindu festival of
lights) or Karva Chauth (on which women fast in order to secure
long life for their husbands) are observed, but as household affairs
rather than as neighbourhood celebrations.[3] Some of my Punjabi
informants regarded this as evidence of what they saw as typical
Himachali reserve ('they are all just concerned with their own
family and no one else'), but I think that this absence of ritual
involvement among neighbours is more likely to be because of the
immaturity of many Shimla neighbourhoods, considered as social
groups. The ritual dimension of neighbourhood may well establish
itself in the future.

Relations with neighbours tend to be more important to women
than to men. Men who live in the same street or complex of houses
need not have much to do with each other unless they also work in
the same place or live in the kind of crowded quarters where
interaction is impossible to avoid. Women, on the other hand, form
their perceptions of the area they live in very much in terms of the
kind of neighbours they have, and their relations with neighbours
are based on a regular exchange of pleasantries and small services.
A neighbour can be asked to keep an eye on the children when they
return from school if the mother expects to be late home from
shopping or work, to lend a little sugar if a guest calls unexpectedly
for tea, or to loan bedding or kitchen utensils if a party of relatives
descends on the household for a visit. Potentially useful information of the kind discussed in the last chapter – about the children's
schools, about kin seeking marriage partners, about servants – is
passed about and evaluated when neighbours gather to chat in their
yards or on their balconies.

It would be a mistake to portray such relationships as always amicable. There may be friction as well as amity among neighbours and the potential for friction is always higher among those who live in greatest proximity to others, usually the poorest. Disputes over the use of shared yards or standpipes, conflict between the children, strains where one woman feels that another has borrowed more than she has been prepared to lend – all these can lead to bad relations. A few interview respondents claimed that they tried hard to keep themselves to themselves for fear of such strains intruding on their peaceful domestic lives. But most women preferred to take the risk of finding that they could not get along with one or other of their neighbours, since they valued the practical benefits of a pleasant neighbourly relationship. Friendships among women who are neighbours do not often seem to survive a transfer to another town or removal to another part of Shimla. But although brittle, these relations are of great practical and emotional significance while they last.

Relationships in the workplace

Women who worked outside the home often expressed the import-ance of their relations with the other women at work. None claimed to work *in order to* meet people, but the kind of people they met at work was one of the considerations that made a job satisfactory or unsatisfactory. Some evidently found quite tedious jobs acceptable because they enjoyed the company of the women they worked with. A servant employed in the linen room of a big hotel said:

'This job is really hard work, nine o'clock in the morning to five at night with not much of a break. But I like it because of the company. The woman in charge of the linen room is very kind and her two daughters who also work there are nice people.'

Those who worked alongside men sometimes found this rather stressful since they had to be very careful that nothing in their behaviour towards fellow workers gave rise to gossip or misunder-standing. A well-educated and perceptive secretary put it like this:

'There is one problem I face in my work, although I like my job very much. I am the only lady in our office. The men here ask me to do this, that or the other in the course of my work. You have to be equally obliging to all or they will gossip. It is not so bad if

there are other women in the office. I can't tell my husband a
thing like this or he will say "Don't bother about work then, leave
the job". Fortunately my boss is very understanding, otherwise
my position would be difficult. It requires a lot of tact and
diplomacy.'

Women were consequently less free to cultivate sociable relationships with superiors at work in the hope of making a favourable
impression or obtaining help of one kind or another, unless those
superiors were female. This was not usually the case except in
certain occupations such as nursing or teaching. Other exceptions
were domestic servants and sweepers who certainly expected a
pleasant relationship with the mistress of the house to result in
numerous small perquisites, such as discarded clothes for their
children, a share of sweets or other luxuries at festivals or children's
birthdays.

The noticeable thing about women's relations with colleagues is
that they seldom extend beyond the workplace. A few teachers and
office workers said that they sometimes went shopping or called on
women whom they had met and become friends with in their
present or some previous job, but otherwise women seldom met
their workmates outside the workplace unless they also happened to
be neighbours. Women who work in the same office, hotel, or school
may well live at opposite ends of the city and will have little time to
visit one another after work or at the weekends if they have
husbands and children to attend to. Unmarried middle-class
women, on the contrary, were much more likely to meet women
friends from the workplace for a trip to the cinema at weekends or
just to call on one another at home. But here again, working women
who had domestic responsibilities such as a large number of
younger siblings to help care for, were unlikely to have the leisure
for this kind of social life.

These observations indicate a marked contrast with the pattern
of sociability among male colleagues or workmates. A remarkable
sight in Shimla is the large crowd of men, mostly office employees,
who congregate at the top of the Mall every evening after about five
o'clock. They stand around or saunter up and down chatting with
one another, apparently doing nothing much yet seemingly unwilling to disperse to their suburban homes. This amused some of my
women friends, who would remark that the men must have 'nothing
better to do than hang about on the street' or that 'perhaps they

don't want to go home to their wives'. However, I think that such sociability is not very different from that of women who live near each other and spent the slack periods of the day in each other's company. It is only the more conspicuous for being conducted in a central public place. Like the intercourse of neighbours, this apparently idle 'hanging around' is the means by which numerous small items of political or office gossip are passed around, and the flow of useful information is maintained. If, as we have seen, the husband's networks at work are frequently a source of aid, then presumably these networks have to be cultivated somehow.

Male colleagues who are friendly at work still stroll down the Mall in the evening, perhaps stopping at a tea shop for snacks before going home. Such friends may well visit each other's homes at the weekend, especially if they happen to be migrants from the same district or have some other common interest or association. And while women who meet their workmates outside the workplace are unlikely to involve their husbands in such relationships, quite the reverse is true of men. Friendship between two men at work is likely to result in exchanges of family visits, and if their wives take to each other then the pattern of sociability is reinforced. This seems a continuation of the principle that a wife is incorporated into her husband's set of relationships, but he is not necessarily incorporated into hers.

Entertaining

The social lives of most women are encompassed by their everyday interactions – at work, in the home and neighbourhood – and their interactions with their husbands' friends and kin. They usually have few friends outside the categories I have described and little leisure in which to attend social gatherings or pursue personal interests or hobbies. Higher up the social ladder, however, the wives of high ranking bureaucrats and rich businessmen have a long-standing tradition of female sociability and women's organizations.

Rich women who have leisure usually have a circle of female friends with whom they play bridge or golf, enjoy kitty parties (see p. 84) or cookery classes, or attend social clubs. Shimla is, as one would expect of a hill station, well provided with associations oriented towards leisure activities. Some, such as the Drama Club, date back to British times and owe their origin to the hectic social life the imperial elite enjoyed in Shimla in the days of the Raj, but most Indian cities of a comparable size would be likely to boast a similar variety of associations and activities.

Women of the middle income groups may have the leisure for activities of this kind but they seldom have the resources. For instance, Suman, a 'technocrat's' wife, does not belong to the kind of family who can afford to join the Naldehra Golf Club or play tennis or squash. Indeed, a young woman from a rather conventional Punjabi family like herself might regard such pursuits as not very suitable for women anyway. But she has a number of women friends, many of them wives of her husband's colleagues, and they organize their own modest kitty parties, picnics, and family outings, enjoying the more inexpensive pleasures of urban life in each other's company.

A form of female sociability open to wealthy educated women is membership of the various women's organizations which exist in Shimla as in any large Indian town. These perform a number of functions, charitable and social (see Caplan 1981 for a fuller account of such associations). The Shimla branch of the All-India Women's Conference, a very large national organization, for instance, funds a training school at which poor women can learn tailoring under a qualified instructress. Some of the members meet at the training centre each week to help organize orders for the women who work there, and the group also funds a creche for working mothers. In addition to this there is an annual dinner and various other outings and social events during the year.

Not all the women who participate in these organizations are exceedingly wealthy. Some are women of modest means who are otherwise well connected or known in public life – retired professional women for example. However, membership in such associations would be difficult for women with low incomes and many dependents; there is always a membership fee and the various social events arranged by the clubs must be paid for and require the appropriate dress.

Many such associations do what is termed 'social work', which in the Indian context means charitable activities of one kind or another. 'Social work' is considered a highly suitable way for a wealthy woman to spend her time and many find it provides a satisfying outlet for their energies outside the home as well as a pleasant way to meet women of similar background.[4] On the other hand, a few find the expectation that they will do 'social work' turns into a kind of pressure. The rather retiring wife of a very senior civil servant, whose children claimed less of her time now that they were all at school, was being constantly exhorted by various active ladies of her acquaintance to get involved in 'social work'. It was almost as though she was failing to carry out her duty as a woman of rank by failing to take an interest in their charitable endeavours.

Many of the professional women who belonged to these organizations seemed to feel that 'social work' was a healthy antidote to the tendency of rich housewives to fritter away their days in bridge parties, frivolous shopping expeditions, and other pursuits which they saw as a hedonistic waste of time. I did wonder whether there was not a tendency to regard leisured and wealthy females as something of a threat when their energies were evidently not fully absorbed by their domestic duties. Be that as it may, many women of this class clearly find such activities an agreeable way of meeting other women, exchanging ideas and information, and enjoying themselves in a socially acceptable way.

Much of the social life of upper-class women, however, is not of a totally female kind, indulged in separately from husbands. Women married to senior government servants, professionals, and wealthy businessmen are likely to find themselves involved in an elaborate round of sociability in which they participate as couples. A good deal of this social life may be related to the husband's concerns at work. A senior official's wife may have to preside at a drinks party held in honour of some foreign guests of the Himachal Government, or the wife will be invited to go to a party which she knows will be attended mainly by her husband's colleagues and their wives. Whether or not she is interested in the people who go to such gatherings or in the topics of conversation which prevail, she is expected to go willingly and be a credit to her husband. This could be seen as an instance of the process of 'incorporation' into the organizations for which their husbands work, which Callan and Ardener have described. The 'incorporated wife' is 'socially identified as "wife of" a particular kind of worker' and may have to do certain kinds of work which relate to her husband's occupational interests (Callan and Ardener 1984: 1). This is particularly true of senior civil servants' wives, who are expected to entertain and generally organize their lives around their husband's official duties.

In some cases the tendency to absorb the wife in her husband's work persona is far less formally articulated and consists of no more than a general expectation that the wives of colleagues will be prepared to service their husbands' relationships with their work-mates in their leisure time. The wife of a hospital specialist, herself a doctor also, found this tendency problematic:

'I like to be a bit reserved, I don't mix much. I would prefer to stay at home with the children or read some books. As a doctor's wife you are expected to mix with other doctors and their wives, but if you do there is a lot of politics and gossip about work, which I do not like at all.'

But most women felt that not to go to such social events would be to fail in their wifely duties. In any case, how could the husband reciprocate such hospitality without their cooperation, and how might his career be affected if he did not? Whether or not they enjoyed this entertaining, it obviously involved a certain amount of effort. Parties at this level of society are often the vehicle for elaborate and quite sophisticated forms of status display in which it is not just one's wealth which is on show, but also one's taste and imagination. The right kind of buffet supper should include both meat and vegetable dishes to suit all tastes, but one would not serve just spiced potatoes, and the meat dishes ought to be something out of the ordinary. The addition of one or two western dishes would also be the sign of a skilled hostess. This might be some kind of cake or pastry, or perhaps a cheese dish such as pizza. Attention must be given to the way all this is presented: elegant crockery should be provided, not just the steel or brass dishes from which Indian families eat their everyday meals, and there should be napkins or paper serviettes. Servants must be deployed in a proper manner, with constant discreet replenishing of dishes, but they can hardly wear the old coats and cotton pajamas acceptable for serving the family on ordinary occasions. Entertaining at this level of society becomes a fine art for which some training is required, and it is not surprising that domestic science continues to be a popular subject for college girls from wealthy families. They do not study it in order to learn how to make chapattis for their children (they may never have to do this, for they can afford servants). They need to know about cookery to a more sophisticated level than the ordinary middle-class girl. It is perhaps for the same reason that women's magazines are so popular among wealthy educated women. Magazines such as *Femina* and even the Hindi journals read by women who have not been to English medium schools and colleges, contain recipes which always seemed to me to require such elaborate and obscure ingredients or equipment that I wondered how the ordinary housewife could ever contrive to make them (I certainly seldom succeeded). But perhaps that is the point; they are the kind of dish one serves to impress others.

In the context of this kind of entertainment, more attention has to be paid to the way the house is furnished. The decoration of the home has not hitherto been very important as an area of status display. Wealthy merchants and landlords in the past lavished money on their wives' saris and jewellery, which were displayed at weddings and festivals, rather than on new curtains or kitchenware. Nowadays friends and colleagues are likely to enter one's home and cast a critical eye upon it, so it becomes a matter of more importance to have as tasteful and imaginatively furnished home as one's income makes possible.

At the very highest level of society, being a hostess is a semi-public activity. Women's magazines contain features on women whose main claim to fame is as givers of parties and receptions, in which they describe how they go about selecting guests for a party or organizing a menu. We can, if we choose, regard all this activity as pointless consumption ritual, but I prefer to see it as a kind of *work*. It requires a considerable input of time and energy and for women above a certain level of society it is not really optional. It is a form of household service work since the household's social position, and often the husband's professional position, is less easily maintained if it is omitted. Just as the coffee shop gatherings of humbler employees are the occasion for the circulation of useful gossip and scraps of information, so the buffet suppers of the great may be the occasion for the exchange of information relating to the politics of the husband's workplace, or other matters affecting the household's position. Social life is not by any means divorced from the practical concerns of the household and the higher up the social ladder, the more this social life is likely to be related to the husband's occupational life, yet the more it is likely to be undertaken jointly by husband and wife.

The increasingly 'joint' nature of social life in upper- and middle-class families in Indian cities has been noted by several authors. Seymour (1975), for instance, remarks upon the differences between conjugal roles in the Old Town area of Bhubaneshwar and in the New Capital, mostly inhabited by government servants, businessmen, and other functionaries of the modern industrial economy, almost all migrants. In the Old Town most families were long established residents, the joint family was a common household form and men and women led segregated lives even if the women were not actually secluded. In the New Capital most couples did not have close kin living nearby and lived in neo-local nuclear family households. Women were less often secluded and were likely to engage in many activities in the company of their husbands. Seymour sees this as due to the fact that in the absence of a strongly localized kin network men and women in these households

'have been forced to rely on and interact with one another to a greater extent, regardless of sex, which has resulted in some striking changes in sex role behaviour.'

(Seymour 1975:768)

A similar tendency was observed in Meerut by Vatuk, who comes to a similar conclusion, in that

'couples who have resided neolocally since their marriage . . . have thus depended only on each other for primary emotional sustenance in the early years of marriage, rather than on extended household members of the same sex.'

(Vatuk 1972:196)

although she also admits the possibility of emulation of western family patterns. These explanations are certainly relevant but the data I have just presented may suggest other possible reasons. In Shimla husbands and wives do not (negatively) rely on one another's company because the traditional alternatives are unavailable, but because there is a (positive) need for a joint effort in their social life if they are to make the best of the opportunities for consolidating and improving their social position which the urban milieu offers. Entertaining, both formal and informal, rather than ritual events become the occasion for status display and for the extension and reinforcement of social networks. Husbands need not just their wives' cooperation but also their *presence* – to grace the table, pour the drinks, direct the servants, and make polite conversation with colleagues and their wives.

The importance of this pattern of interaction should not be exaggerated. Even among the elite there are women's networks and men's networks which function fairly independently much of the time. However, the pattern I have described as characteristic of high status households is beginning to filter down to ordinary middle-class families and here, more than ever, it involves an extra dimension to the domestic work that women do. Middle-class women cannot afford the sumptuous parties and elaborate buffets of the rich; they do not own a battery of kitchen gadgets and are unlikely to employ servants trained to cook fancy dishes. Their home furnishings are simple and they do not own a stock of saris adequate to a hectic round of entertaining. But if they are to help their husbands develop the social resources which the household needs if it is to flourish and advance, some extra input on their part on the domestic front is demanded.

Summary

One has the impression that everyone in Shimla, or at any rate everyone with any hope or ambition for upward mobility, is busily engaged in constructing and extending the social networks to which members of their household have access.[5] It is up to husband and wife to build up a stock of useful contacts through which information or concrete assistance may be sought in future. But such contacts cannot be made if one is passive: they have to be sought out and cultivated. Ideally households need access to networks which extend both horizontally (among status equals) and vertically (to include status superiors). Neighbours and kin of a similar social standing may provide many kinds of help but there are also occasions when the assistance of a more powerful patron needs to be enlisted.

Women contribute to the construction of these networks in that they establish relationships with their neighbours, local kin, or colleagues in their own right, but they also cooperate in servicing their husband's networks. Not only do they play a major role in maintaining connections with the husband's kin (and there is nothing very new in that) but they reinforce the relationships which their husbands are able to establish among colleagues and other associates through entertaining and visiting undertaken as a couple. Networks can be represented as a chain of connections between individuals, but they can also be a household resource and servicing them is therefore to be considered as a form of work which women perform.

Notes

1 For instance, through what Appadurai calls 'gastro-politics', the process by which women communicate views of a person's status in the household either by manipulating the food itself, in terms of quantity or quality, or by manipulating the context in which it is served, either in terms of precedence or of degrees of commensal exclusivity (see Appadurai 1981: 501).
2 Where a marriage broke down, the wife usually lost contact with her husband's kin without regret and often with relief, but widows married for any length of time usually maintained some contact with their husband's family, especially if they had children. The exceptions were cases where the widow herself was too poor to spend the money on travel or postage and her in-laws were likewise too poor for her to expect much assistance from them. In another case contact broke down completely when the husband's siblings cheated the widow out of the portion of her husband's land to which she was entitled by law.
3 Although major festivals like Divali or Durga Naumi may be the occasion for religious or social gatherings organized by groups of migrants from the same area or by other kinds of urban association.
4 According to Caplan it may indeed bring other benefits such as the public prestige associated with philanthropy or even access to a political career (Caplan 1981: 18–19).
5 Satish Saberwal has written a good account of how this operates among upwardly mobile men in a Punjabi city:
    'Although everyone is free to join in the game, what networks one can assemble are a function of one's own resources. One starts with the skills of social navigation, but whether or not alter agrees to help ego is a function of ego's overall standing – his kinsmen, his bearing, his language, etc. – and of his specific capacities for reciprocity.'
                                                        (Saberwal 1976: 162)

11 Conclusion

Household service work and class: the positive case

I hope that the ethnography presented in this book will have convinced the reader that much work is done in the household which is not subsumed by the conventional categories which social scientists use, and that much of this work is done by women. Household service work includes many activities, some definitely seen as work by those who do them and others which they do not distinguish from the web of ordinary social interactions.

I have concentrated on women's contribution to household service work because in the community I studied most work of this kind is done by women, although it will be clear from my account that some is done by men or with the assistance of men. There is no intrinsic reason why household service work should be a female task, indeed one can think of circumstances in which it is more likely to become a male task. In a community where women were strictly secluded in the home, for instance, the kinds of household service work which they could undertake would be circumscribed and more liaison work, network building and resource management would have to be done by men. This is not the case in Shimla, but it may well be true of certain urban communities in other parts of India.

Household service work has an added importance to the domestic group in a situation such as obtains in Shimla – the competitive atmosphere of a town that has recently expanded and allowed a good deal of social mobility, while still not providing jobs sufficient for the aspiring migrants from the villages who hope to fill them. The household service work which women do, I have argued, contributes to the household's attempts to establish, maintain, and perhaps improve its position in this fluid situation. There is an inherent insecurity in the position of those who depend for their livelihood on wage labour, even so privileged a form of wage labour as government service. Those households which do not own property have little which they can be certain of passing on to their children in any tangible form. The child of a well-paid technocrat may be in no better a position than the child of the lowly *peon* next door when they both come to enter the labour market, but a certain amount of work can be put in to help ensure that he or she maintains the lead his or her parents have acquired. They can choose the best school they can afford, organize tuition, or tutor their child through examinations themselves, cultivate contacts that may help find him or her work, arrange an advantageous marriage with a well-connected wife or husband – the kind of efforts which have been charted in this book.

Another way of trying to maintain the class position of one's children is to diversify household resources, usually by acquiring property. One might buy urban land on which to build a house for oneself, a part of which may be rented out to provide a sure source of income. Or one might acquire rural land to be used for commercial farming, providing an income from fruit or grain production. In either case, the children of the household can hope to maintain the life-style their parents have achieved even if they are less successful on the job market. As we have seen, much of the work involved in organizing and managing these resources is performed by women.

Much mobility in Shimla is neither upwards nor downwards, but sideways. That is, migrants move from a position in an agrarian class structure to a position in an urban class structure, or rather they keep a footing in both. Some urban dwellers maintain an interest in rural property, many rural dwellers depend on remittances from the city. At the top of the scale, the wealthy have a substantial stake in both systems, a fact which must have political consequences, although a discussion of these would be beyond the scope of this book. In many Indian cities there is also an underclass of those who never had any stake in the rural system and can scarcely be said to have acquired one as yet in the urban system. These are the landless labourers who migrate to take up uncertain and ill-paid work in the most menial urban employment. This class is not yet much in evidence in Shimla because the employment structure of the city is such that it does not attract this kind of migrant in large numbers (it is a 'white collar' city). Also in most parts of rural Himachal migration from the villages has taken place from the 'top downwards', that is the better off and better qualified farmers sought urban employment first; the exodus of the landless labourers and sharecroppers is only just beginning.

Urban migrants, as we have seen, do not necessarily shed their sense of position in the rural community through residence in the city. This is not just a matter of 'culture lag' or the reluctance of conservative peasants (or ex-peasants) to shed old identities and adopt new ones. The rural identities they retain are often changing and developing since the nature of the stakes they retain in the village may also change (unproductive land is abandoned, new holdings are acquired with cash earned in the city, land used for subsistence farming or share leased to share croppers is turned over to commercial farming, the household extends patronage to fellow villagers who seek work in the city). As I have shown in Chapter 6, the relationship between the household's rural and urban bases is sustained by work, especially (though not solely) the work of women who travel from city to village to collect harvest dues from tenants and sharecroppers, transmit decisions about tenancies, view a piece of land which they might decide to buy, organize labour for the apple or wheat harvest. The articulation of rural and urban class positions takes place through the household and depends on activities fitted in between the demands of employment, housework, and the care of children – activities which are seldom recognized in accounts of either urban or rural economies.

As a theoretical notion, I believe that the concept of household service work has wide applicability. It could be used in any situation in which the household is a significant and relatively persistent unit of organization, although obviously the actual content of this category of work will vary considerably; household service work might not everywhere take the specific forms I have described here. Also the societal (as opposed to domestic) consequences of this form of work need not always be the same. I have argued in this study that in Shimla household service work not only services the household, but can be identified as one of the means by which class formation is facilitated (along with institutions such as the education system, the mechanisms of the labour market). This is true at this particular juncture of social development in India but

I do not conclude from this that the household service work must always have these effects.

Household service work and class: the negative case

So far, I have argued that in the community I studied the household service work of women contributes, albeit indirectly, to the 'firming up' of a fluid urban class hierarchy. But to make a theoretical assertion like this does not cost the theorist much. Functionalists were castigated for explaining institutions in terms of their 'functions' when no one could possibly demonstrate what would happen to the system were these functions not fulfilled. Some Marxists tend to structure their arguments in a comparable way. When we say that a particular practice contributes to the reproduction of class divisions, gender inequality, etc., such a statement may facilitate our understanding of the social processes in which we participate. But to claim any explanatory value for such a statement we should need at the very least to be able to show that if these practices did not exist the consequences might be different. One can almost always identify some aspect of any activity or institution which contributes to the working of the 'whole' whether that whole is conceived in a functionalist or a Marxist sense, but without the discussion of the negative case, such identification has only descriptive value.

What might constitute a negative case such as might enable us to identify the consequences of household service work not being performed?

One possible example is that of the widower or divorced man, i.e. the man who does not have a wife to perform this work for his household. Does such a household suffer from this deficiency, or are means found to remedy it? Since the focus of the study was on the work of women in the household I do not have a great deal of material on households which lack female members. However it would seem unusual for a widower or divorced man under the age of 45 not to seek a second wife if he can afford to do so. In the short term other female relatives may perform some of the services his wife used to perform (attend to the daily needs of children, cook, and clean). Mothers and sisters-in-law can act as substitutes in this way, and those who can afford to may hire servants. A widower is generally protected from the immediate consequences of his lack of a wife by these means.

The same is not true for solitary women. A widow or divorcee will not find it easy to find male substitutes for the services her husband performed in the household and in many[1] communities it is not easy for her to think of remarriage. The ideology of Hindu marriage stresses the wife's dependence not just on a husband, but on a *particular* husband for whom there can be no substitute in the case of his death or desertion. A husband is dependent on his wife, to be sure, but it is a generalized dependence; one wife may substitute for another who dies or is unsatisfactory. Like a woman, a man is regarded as incomplete as an adult unless he is married, but he may remarry if widowed and in many parts of India may marry a second wife if the first is childless (with the sanction of custom if not of modern statutory law). These factors tend to disguise the actual dependence upon wives which must obtain if widowers and divorcees are as anxious to remarry as the classified matrimonial advertisements in national newspapers indicate. We may presume, though we cannot prove, that this dependence is for sexual and 'status producing' services which female kin and servants cannot easily provide.

Another possible 'negative case' might be that of households or individuals who have suffered downward mobility or who were at the bottom of the urban hierarchy to begin with. Has inattention to the kinds of work I have been describing produced or contributed to their misfortunes? Most of the households which appeared to have suffered or be in danger of suffering downward mobility in the class hierarchy and of which I had personal knowledge, were in fact female headed households in which the male breadwinner had been lost through death or desertion. In such cases a frequent response on the part of the wife was to put an enormous effort into securing the best education possible for the children through the kind of activities described in Chapter 7 while earning a livelihood as best she could, seldom at the level of income enjoyed while the husband was alive or present. Loss of income and lack of material resources is the chief cause of downward mobility in such cases, but may be compensated to some extent by concentrated investment in certain types of household service work.

What about those who are already down and therefore fear no

fall, the resourceless urban poor? At this point my own data are not very helpful since, for reasons I have already indicated, Shimla does not as yet have a substantial urban underclass of resourceless day labourers. Those construction workers, coolies, and sporadically employed manual workers who are found in the city often stay for limited periods of time and seldom bring their wives and children. However the work of other sociologists will answer the question posed very adequately. There have been a number of studies of urban *bastis*, the shanty colonies where the poorest migrant labourers build their flimsy huts.

The Majumdars, for instance, give detailed case histories of a number of families in a New Delhi squatters' colony, mostly living lives of extreme poverty and insecurity (Majumdar and Majumdar 1978). I will reproduce only a couple of examples, indicating the principal incidents which have served to peg these families firmly into the lowest slot of the urban hierarchy.

Radha, for example, lived on what she could earn through building huts for other squatters. She and her family had suffered the following succession of problems since their stay in Delhi:

– prolonged illness of Radha's husband, the main breadwinner;
– main breadwinner sacked from temporary job;
– destruction of Radha's hut and all the family's possessions in a fire;
– miscarriage and subsequent illness suffered by Radha;
– desertion of Radha by her husband.

In the case of Gularam and Dakshana, construction workers, we find a similar string of catastrophes since their migration to Delhi:

– loss of all family possessions and ornaments when their hut was burgled;
– serious illness of Gularam, leading to eventual unemployment;
– death of three of Dakshana's four children;
– sporadic unemployment of Dakshana, who was partially paralyzed after the birth of her last child.

It is clear from the Majumdars' account that families in circumstances such as these do make attempts to extend their range of useful contacts, consolidate whatever little temporary advantage they may gain in periods of good health and full employment. But such attempts are ineffective in the face of crises such as those just listed, which arise from the kind of conditions in which these households are obliged to live. At this level of society kin relations tend to be brittle, especially those that are otherwise the most usual sources of aid – the ties between brothers, and the ties between parents and sons. Those who seem to be on the path to a slightly better life do well to consolidate their luck by marrying their children well and cutting off ties with poor relations who are likely to make claims on their precarious resources (Majumdar and Majumdar 1978: 72).

Circumstances usually lead to frequent removals from place to place and the dislocation of any useful local networks the migrants are able to establish. Furthermore, at this level of poverty households are subject to periodicity constraints which make the establishment of any kind of stability in their lives difficult. Mary Douglas has demonstrated the anthropological usefulness of the concept of periodicity in studying class differences in styles of consumption behaviour (Douglas and Isherwood 1978: 114ff.), but it is also useful in studying other aspects of household behaviour. The processing of resources in a poor slum dweller's household has a very short cycle. Earnings are received daily and will be spent there and then on the immediate necessities of the family. A day's unemployment means a day's hunger. There is no opportunity to build up reserves to be drawn upon in times of crisis, and the force of the periodicity constraints may even inhibit the family from taking up opportunities which in the long run might help them improve their circumstances; in such a situation there can be no 'long' run. For instance, the Majumdars cite the case of a beggar woman who was offered a job as a servant, but refused it since she could not see how she would be able to feed her children while she was waiting for her first pay at the end of the month (Majumdar and Majumdar 1978: 61). In such a situation there is also little chance that a woman will ever be in a position to build up any very solid relationships with neighbours or kin on the basis of reciprocity. Even if she is ever in the position of having anything that might be shared with others, there is no guarantee that the recipient will return the favour, and the kind of neighbourly relationship based on the regular exchange of practical aid that obtains among even quite poor families who live in more stable circumstances will be hardly worth striving for. It is clear that in some of the cases the Majumdars describe, individual men and women did make attempts to cultivate cooperative relationships and sometimes the contacts they made yielded useful information and help. But such relationships were difficult to sustain throughout the vicissitudes characteristic of their lives – periods of bare survival interspersed with the crises of destitution.

At this level of poverty and insecurity the benefits of household living itself are not very pronounced for those who are in employment and must share their meagre resources with numerous dependents. For this reason the abandonment of wives by husbands and parents by grown sons is not uncommon; the household group itself has an unstable and uncertain existence, and so the concept of household service work may not be very useful here since it presumes a degree of continuity and stability which cannot be guaranteed. Failure to perform household service work is not responsible for the plight of such families, nor can its diligent performance possibly remove the poor health, low pay, and unemployment which are the immediate causes of their poverty. Household service work becomes a useful concept at a level where households have some kind of advantage, not necessarily material, which can be conserved for transmission to the next generation. The requirement for this is probably security rather than any absolute level of income. As we have seen from the data I have presented, even lowly *peons*, domestic servants, and shop assistants may, if their employment has any stability and their residence any permanence, attempt to consolidate what little security they possess through the kind of activities I have described. Household service work is not an activity open only to women in elite households, although the actual forms of household service work appropriate to the wife of an IAS officer or affluent businessman may be quite different from those which the wife of a *peon* or porter might usefully engage in, and there is a level of degradation at which it can scarcely be attempted at all.

One last type of 'negative case' is that of the 'singleton' migrant men who come to the city without their wives. Do they lose out because their wives are not present to perform either household service work or other ordinary domestic duties? I suppose one could argue that in a sense the question is irrelevant, since a man whose wife and children live elsewhere is presumably not seeking status in the urban class hierarchy and therefore cannot 'lose out' in a competition in which he chooses not to participate. However a man who is employed in a city still has the option of establishing a household position there so it is instructive to examine the way in which choices are made in this matter.

Certainly it is unusual for a migrant man who is earning more than about Rs1,000 not to have his wife living with him in Shimla, regardless of the kind of position the household enjoys in the village. Above this level a man cannot easily guarantee his children a position similar to his own unless he ensures their education to a fairly high level, which may be better done (though at greater cost) in the city. And for the reasons discussed in Chapters 9 and 10, his social life will be much easier if he has his wife present to help entertain and contribute to the consolidation of urban relationships. Otherwise the decision about whether or not the wife is to join her husband in Shimla seems to depend on a variety of considerations. One might be the value of any property the family owns in the husband's village and whether there are other relatives willing and able to supervise it. If there is a holding which is worth careful supervision for the kind of income it brings, then the wife may be better deployed working it or managing it in the village. Some migrants' wives are clearly fully occupied with the kind of family status production work appropriate to the rural situation. One migrant explained that his wife was competent not only to do much of the manual work on the family farm, but was also educated enough to do things like deal with legal problems (in case of disputes over land, etc.), communicate with agricultural extension workers over improvements to the land, and cope with correspondence, so that her presence was indispensable at home. The wife of a clerk spent some of her time in the village and came to Shimla for a while each year:

> 'She manages the land very well herself. She is a independent sort of person and only has to bother me with things she cannot do herself. But most matters like the sale of cattle and produce, shopping and writing letters, she can cope with on her own. I just send her some money each month.'

Another government clerk also gave his wife's competence in agricultural matters as his main reason for her not staying permanently in Shimla, as well as the high cost of family accommodation. In many other cases the wife was obliged to remain in the village because the husband's parents were either too elderly to run the land themselves or had no other sons, and the couple were afraid of losing control to tenants if one of them were not present to manage it personally. These were the migrants who were unlikely to abandon their ancestral holdings as they were of a size to be well worth cultivating themselves. But the cost of this kind of decision obviously lies in the fact that the children will then be brought up in the village. They will not have the advantage of the more prestigious education offered by city schools, nor the chance to make useful contacts in the town such as may lead to employment or other urban benefits.

Male migrants who do not bring their wives to Shimla do not become 'de-classed' as a result (indeed they often strengthen their village bases), but they are not in a position to consolidate their *urban* gains. Above a certain level a man needs a local base from which to exchange services, construct networks and launch his children into urban careers, and he has little choice but to bring his wife to the city. And there are some cases where the wife is obliged to live in Shimla because the family has no land remaining in the village. Where there is an option, the decision as to whether the wife should reside in the village or in Shimla will be the outcome of numerous factors – the value of the land or other source of income in the village, the wife's skills and the possibilities for their deployment in either place, the accessibility of adequate schooling for the children in the village, family structure and size. Since most sociologists have studied migration either from the point of view of its effects on those who remain behind in the village, or from the point of view of the fate of migrants once they arrive in the town, few have been in a position to scrutinize the process by which such decisions are made (Parry's excellent discussion of decisions about household partition in Kangra, a district of Himachal Pradesh, might provide a useful paradigm. See Parry 1979:150–94.) However my own material suggests that it is not so much a matter of the lone male migrant losing status or opportunities because his wife is not with him in the city; rather his solitary state is the outcome of decisions already made about where and how the resource management competence of the wife is best deployed.

In conclusion, we cannot quantify the *negative* effects of household service work not being performed at the level of the individual household. We can say no more than that households are likely to enjoy *positive* benefits from its being performed, in terms of consolidating or expanding their resources of all kinds. Where a household suffers an obvious and drastic loss of status there are usually other factors involved besides the question of whether or not this kind of work was carried out with sufficient skill or energy.

Envoy

In the first chapter of this book I argued for a 'reconstruction of the household as a unit of study, this time informed by a feminist scepticism about any supposed symmetry of rewards or indivisibility of interest among its members' (see p. 4). Members of households in India, even at the highest levels of society, depend upon each other for guarantees which can usually be provided in no other quarter. There is not, as in most industrial societies, a statutory welfare system nor (for most people) any other institution designed to provide insurance against the various kinds of crisis they may experience. There is no doubt that men are better equipped than women in this respect, having more autonomy and usually, greater earning capacity. Even so, both men and women normally rely on the efforts which they and the other members of their household have made in the past to construct their own insurance schemes, whether through saving, accumulating property, investing in education, or other 'invisible' assets, or simply through the creation of effective aid networks. The intent of this monograph has been to indicate the enormously important and largely unrecognized input made by women in this area, work that shares the cloak of invisibility that covers so much of the work done by women. The point about household service work, however, is that whoever does it, it is not done solely on one's own behalf but on behalf of the household unit. Indeed it is not the kind of work that can easily be undertaken by a solitary individual: it predicates the existence of a group which enjoys some degree of continuity and among whom any status security obtained is shared in some way. This should be clear from the examples of household service work which I have given.

If the household is a necessary reality in a community such as the one I have studied there is no reason at all, of course, why feminists should accept the way in which it is structured, its form of internal authority, or distribution of rewards or resources. Indeed, this kind of challenge is being made by feminists in India as elsewhere. But it must be recognized that in India, as in most other Third

World countries, there are few if any alternatives to a family based household at present. This has been a source of misunderstanding between feminists in the west and many Third World feminists, since the latter have found the emphasis placed by western women on sexual individualism and autonomy from men unrealistic so far as their own societies are concerned. A Nigerian writer, for instance, writes of her confrontation with the individualistic assumptions underlying western feminism:

'One was always aware of the self *Chi* [presence or aura] in Africa, but one was taught that this self could never operate in isolation. It operated in communities and among friends. In England, circumstances forced me to operate alone, talk to my *Chi* by myself.'

(Emecheta 1984:249)

Such writers do not feel it is useful at the moment to advocate women's total independence of the family group, although they are ready to question their place within it and work for an open and explicit acknowledgement of the work they do in and on behalf of this group. If this monograph has a political purpose it is intended as a contribution to a proper understanding of that work.

Note

1 This qualification is necessary because Himachal is an area where there are a number of castes and local communities in which the remarriage of widowed and divorced women has traditionally been accepted.

References

Allen, V. (1977) The Differentiation of the Working Class. In A. Hunt (ed.) *Class and Class Structure*. London: Laurence & Wishart.

Appadurai, A. (1981) Gastro-politics in Hindu South Asia. *American Ethnologist* 8(3):494–511.

Barr, P. and Desmond, R. (1978) *Simla: A Hill Station in British India*. London: Scolar Press.

Bernstein, B. (1973) *Class, Codes and Control*. St Alban's: Paladin.

Blood, P. and Wolfe, D. (1960) *Husbands and Wives*. New York: The Free Press.

Blumberg, R. and Dwarki, L. (1980) *India's Educated Women*. Delhi: Hindustan Publishing Corporation

Boissevain, J. (1974) *Friends of Friends*. Oxford: Basil Blackwell.

Borthwick, M. (1982) The Bhadramahila and Changing Conjugal Relations in Bengal 1850–1900. In M. Allen and S. N. Mukherjee (eds) *Women in India and Nepal*. Australian National University Monographs on South Asia no. 8. Canberra: Australian National University.

Bose, A. (1971) The Urbanization Process in South and South-East Asia. In L. Jakobson and Ved Prakash (eds) *Urbanization and National Development*. Beverley Hills: Sage.

Bruner, E. (1982) Models of Urban Kinship. In H. Safa (ed.) *Towards a Political Economy of Urbanization in Third World Countries*. Bombay: Oxford University Press.

Buck, E. (1904) *Simla Past and Present*. Calcutta: Thacker, Spink

Callan, H. and Ardener, S. (1984) *The Incorporated Wife*. London: Croom Helm.

Caplan, P. (1978) Women's Organizations in Madras City, India. In P. Caplan and J. Bujra (eds) *Women United, Women Divided*. London: Tavistock.

—(1981) Women's Voluntary Social Service in India: Is it Work? Paper presented at the Seventh European Conference of Modern South Asian Studies, London.

Caplan, P. and Bujra, J. (1978) *Women United, Women Divided.* London: Tavistock.

Davidoff, L. (1973) *The Best Circles.* London: Croom Helm.

Desai, I.P. (1964) *Some Aspects of Family in Mahuva. A Sociological Study of Jointness in a Small Town.* London: Asia Publishing House.

Dore, R. (1976) *The Diploma Disease.* London: Allen & Unwin.

Douglas, M. and Isherwood, B. (1978) *The World of Goods: Towards an Anthropology of Consumption.* Harmondsworth: Penguin.

Edholm, F., Harris, O., and Young, K. (1977) Conceptualising Women. *Critique of Anthropology* 3(9 and 10): 101–30.

Edwards, M. (1981) *Financial Arrangements Within Families.* Canberra: National Women's Advisory Council.

Emecheta, B. (1984) Culture Conflict. *New Society* 69 (1133): 249.

Erikson, R. (1984) Social Class of Men, Women and Families. *Sociology* 18(4): 500–14.

Finch, J. (1983) *Married to the Job: Wives' Incorporation in Men's Work.* London: Allen & Unwin.

Gadgil, D.R. (1965) *Women in the Working Force in India.* London: Asia Publishing House (for University of Delhi).

Goffman, E. (1959) *The Presentation of Self in Everyday Life.* New York: Doubleday.

Goldthorpe, J. (1983) Women and Class Analysis: In Defence of the Conventional View. *Sociology* 17(4): 465–88.

—(1984) Women and Class Analysis: A Reply to the Replies. *Sociology* 18(4): 491–514.

Gulati, L. (1981) *Profiles in Female Poverty.* Delhi: Hindustan Publishing Corporation.

Heath, A. and Britten, N. (1983) Men, Women and Social Class. In E. Gamarnikow, J. Purvis, and D. Taylorson (eds) *Gender, Class and Work.* London: Heinemann.

—(1984) Women's Jobs Do Make a Difference: a Reply to Goldthorpe. *Sociology* 18(4): 475–90.

Hobson, D. (1978) Housewives: Isolation as Oppression. In Women's Studies Group Centre for Contemporary Studies (eds) *Women Take Issue.* London: Hutchinson.

Holmström, M. (1976) *South Indian Factory Workers; Their Life and Their World.* Cambridge: Cambridge University Press.

Hoselitz, B. (1960) The Urban-Rural Contrast as a Factor in Socio-Cultural Change. *Economic Weekly Annual*. 12:145–62.

Hunt, P. (1980) *Gender and Class Consciousness*. London: Macmillan.

Kanwar, P. (1983) The Changing Profile of the Summer Capital of British India: Simla 1864–1947. *Modern Asian Studies* 18(1).

Kapadia, K.M. and Pillai, S.D. (1972) *Industrialization and Rural Society: A Study of Atul-Bulsar Region*. Bombay: Popular Prakashan.

Kapur, P. (1970) *Marriage and the Working Woman in India*. Delhi: Vikas Publications.

Kincaid, D. (1973) *British Social Life in India 1608–1937* (2nd edn). London: Routledge & Kegan Paul.

King, A. (1980) Colonialism and the Development of the Modern Asian City: Some Theoretical Considerations. In K. Ballhatchet and J. Harrison (eds) *The City in South Asia*. London: Curzon Press.

Majumdar, P. and Majumdar, I. (1978) *Rural Migrants in an Urban Setting*. Delhi: Hindustan Publishing Corporation.

Manohar, K. Murali, Shobha, V., and Rao, B. Janardhan (1983) Selected Case Studies: Construction Workers. In K. Murali Manohar (ed.) *Socio-Economic Status of Indian Women*. Delhi: Seema Publications.

Marceau, J. (1976) Marriage, Role Division and Social Cohesion: The Case of some French Upper Class Families. In D. Barker and S. Allen (eds) *Dependence and Exploitation in Work and Marriage*. London: Longman.

Mauss, M. (1954) *The Gift*. London: Routledge & Kegan Paul.

Mayer, P. (1963) *Townsmen or Tribesmen. Conservatism and the Process of Urbanization in a South African City*. Cape Town: Oxford University Press.

Meillasoux, C. (1981) *Maidens, Meal and Money*. Cambridge: Cambridge University Press.

Miller, B. (1981) *The Endangered Sex: Neglect of Female Children in Rural North India*. Ithaca and London: Cornell University Press.

Mitchell, J. Clyde, (1969) The Concept and Use of Social Networks. In J. Clyde Mitchell (ed.) *Social Networks in Urban Situations. Analyses of Personal Relationships in Central African Towns*. Manchester: Manchester University Press, for the Institute for Social Research, University of Zambia.

202   *Women's work, class, and the urban household*

Mumtaz, K. (1983) The Housewife Myth. *Manushi* 3(5):17–18.

Netting, R., Wilk, R., and Arnould, E.J. (eds) (1984) *The Household. Comparative and Historical Studies of the Domestic Group*. Berkeley and Los Angeles: University of California Press.

Oakley, A. (1976) *Housewife*. Harmondsworth: Penguin.

—(1980) *Women Confined: Towards a Sociology of Childbirth*. Oxford: Martin Robertson.

Oakley, A. and Oakley, R. (1979) Sexism in Official Statistics. In J. Irvine, I. Miles, and J. Evans (eds) *Demystifying Official Statistics*. London: Pluto Press.

Pahl, J. (1983) The Allocation of Money and the Structuring of Inequality within Marriage. *Sociological Review* 31(2):237–62.

Papanek, H. (1979) Family Status Production Work: the 'Work' and 'Non-Work' of Women. *Signs* 4(4):775–81.

—(1982) Purdah in Pakistan: Seclusion and Modern Occupations for Women. In H. Papanek and G. Minault (eds) *Separate Worlds: Studies of Purdah in South Asia*. Delhi: Chanakya Publications.

Parry, J. (1979) *Caste and Kinship in Kangra*. London: Routledge & Kegan Paul.

Patnaik, U. (1978) On the Mode of Production in Indian Agriculture. In Ashok Rudra (ed.) *Studies in the Development of Capitalism in India*. Lahore: Vanguard Books.

Rao, M.S.A. (1972) *Tradition, Rationality and Change*. Bombay: Popular Prakashan.

Ross, A. (1961) *The Hindu Family in its Urban Setting*. Toronto: University of Toronto Press.

Roxborough, I. (1979) *Theories of Underdevelopment*. London: Macmillan.

Saberwal, S. (1976) *Mobile Men: Limits to Social Change in Urban Punjab*. New Delhi: Vikas Publishing House.

Safilios-Rothschild, C. (1976) A Macro- and Micro-Examination of Family Power and Love: An Exchange Model. *Journal of Marriage and the Family* 38(2):335–62.

Sen, A. (1982) *The State, Industrialization and Class Formation in India: a Neo-Marxist Perspective on Colonial Development and Underdevelopment*. London: Routledge & Kegan Paul.

Seymour, S. (1975) Some Determinants of Sex Roles in a Changing Indian Town. *American Ethologist* 2(4):757–69.

Sharma, U. (1969) *Hinduism in a Kangra Village*. University of London: PhD Thesis.

—(1977) Migration from an Indian Village. *Sociologia Ruralis* XVLL (4): 282–304.

—(1980a) *Women, Work and Property in North-West India*. London: Tavistock.

—(1980b) Purdah and Public Space. In A. de Souza (ed.) *Women in Contemporary India*. New Delhi: Manohar.

Singh, A. Menefee (1977) Women and the Family: Coping with Poverty in the *Bastis* of Delhi. *Social Action* (27) July–September: 241–65.

—(1984) Rural-to-Urban Migration of Women in India: Patterns and Implications. In J. T. Fawcett, Siew-Ean Khoo, and P. C. Smith (eds) *Women in the Cities of Asia*. Boulder, Colorado: Westview Press.

Stack, C. (1975) *All Our Kin: Strategies for Survival in a Black Community*. New York: Harper & Row.

Standing, H. (1985) Women's Employment and the Household: Some Findings from Calcutta. *Economic and Political Weekly* XX (17) April 27: 23–38.

Stivens, M. (1978) Women and their Kin: Kin, Class and Solidarity in a Middle Class Suburb of Sydney, Australia. In P. Caplan and J. Bujra (eds) *Women United, Women Divided*. London: Tavistock.

Vatuk, S. (1972) *Kinship and Urbanization. White Collar Migrants in North India*. Berkeley: University of California Press.

Wallman, S. (1984) *Eight London Households* London: Tavistock.

Whitehead, A. (1981) 'I'm Hungry, Mum': The Politics of Domestic Budgeting. In K. Young, C. Wolkowitz, and R. McCullogh (eds) *Of Marriage and the Market*. London: CSE Books.

Willmott, P. and Young, M. (1962) *Family and Kinship in East London* (revised edn). Harmondsworth: Penguin.

Name index

Allen, V. 24, 45
Appadurai, A. 186n1
Ardener, S. 181
Arnould, E.J. 2

Barr, P. 12
Bernstein, B. 3–4
Blood, P. 86
Blumberg, R. 126
Boissevain, J. 169n2
Borthwick, M. 116
Bose, A. 20, 31n2, 62n3
Britten, N. 31n3
Bruner, E. 62n2
Buck, E. 30n1
Bujra, J. 11n1

Callan, H. 181
Caplan, P. 11n1, 82, 180, 186n4
Curzon, Lady 12

Davidoff, L. 7
Desai, I.P. 51
Desmond, R. 12
Dore, R. 117n3
Douglas, M. 193
Dwarki, L. 126

Edholm, F. 6
Edwards, M. 86, 87, 88–9
Emecheta, B. 198
Erikson, R. 31n3

Finch, J. 6, 8

Gadgil, D.R. 119
Gill, B. 34, 37, 38
Goffman, E. 66
Goldthorpe, J. 31n3
Gulati, L. 162

Harris, O. 6
Heath, A. 31n3
Hobson, D. 84n2
Holmström, M. 169n3
Hoselitz, B. 22–3
Hunt, P. 84, 86

Isherwood, B. 193

Kanwar, P. 31n1
Kapadia, K.M. 51
Kapur, P. 11
Kincaid, D. 12
King, A. 13

Majumdar, P. and I. 10, 42–3,
    192–93
Manohar, K. 73
Marceau, J. 6
Mauss, M. 170
Mayer, P. 169n2
Meillasoux, C. 21, 23
Miller, B. 29, 101n1
Mitchell, J.C. 169
Mumtaz, K. 150n6

Netting, R. 2

Oakley, A. 64, 84n2, 140
    and R. 2–3

Pahl, J. 2
Papanek, H. 8, 9, 128; 'family status production work' 8–9, 145
Parry, J. 196
Patnaik, U. 23
Pillai, S.D. 51

Rao, B.J. 73
Rao, M.S.A. 48
Ross, A. 51
Roxborough, I. 26
Russell, W. 12

Saberwal, S. 186n5
Safilios-Rothschild, C. 86–7
Sen, A. 26
Seymour, S. 118n4, 184
Sharma, O.P. 34, 38

Sharma, U. 5, 20, 21, 30, 84n4, 102n4, 164
Shobha, V. 73
Singh, A.M. 42, 51
Singh, Ranjit 14
Stack, C. 7, 155
Standing, H. 11, 126
Stivens, M. 6–7, 163

Vatuk, S. 11, 48, 51, 176, 184

Wallman, S. 131 150n4
Whitehead, A. 2, 3
Wilk, R. 2
Willmott, P. 69, 162
Wolfe, D. 86

Young, K. 6, 162
Young, M. 69

Subject index

accommodation *see* government
service; property; Shimla,
housing
All-India Women's Conference
see India
apple belt *see* Himachal Pradesh
Atul colony 51
ayah see domestic service

Bangalore 126, 169n3
bastis see migration
Bengalis, 15, 41
Bhubaneswar 118n4, 184
bourgeoisie 7, 24–6; state
bourgeoisie 26
Brahmans 22
British in India *see* India; Shimla,
British history
bureaucracy 15, 24, 25, 61, 77,
102n3, 116; bureaucratic elite
16, 27, 104; capitalist
bureaucracy 25, 117; socialist
bureaucracy 117; and state
socialism 25–6; *see also*
government service; Shimla

Calcutta 116, 117, 126
capitalism 20–6, 116, 163; and
agriculture 24, 61; capitalist
industry 23–4; *see also* modes of
production
caste 19, 130–31, 133, 149,
166–67, 198n1; barriers 33–4;
contacts 22, 103; endogamy
131; exogamy 162–64; loyalties
15, 117, 174; 'scheduled' 112;

see also names of individual
castes (Sikhs, Hindus, etc.)
Chaili 22, 33–4
Chandigarh 173
children 8, 82, 103–17, 133, 138;
child care 1, 5, 21, 189, for
working women 56, 136–37,
141–45, 161, within
joint/complex household 54,
56, 137, 143, 161; cost of 29,
141; and rural links 41, 60; *see
also* education; gender
chowkidar see occupations
class formation *see* social class,
formation
cleaning *see* housework
cooking *see* housework

Dehra Dun 28
Delhi 48, 51, 92, 162, 173, 192
'developing' countries *see* Third
World
divorcees 48–9, 54, 104, 191,
198n1; and employment 124,
133, 136–37; *see also*
households, female-headed
domestic cycle *see* household cycle
domestic service 66–8, 71–2,
75–8, 104, 143, 148–49, 194; as
an expression of status 66,
76–7, 182; as an ill-paid and
degrading occupation 78, 121,
123, 127–28, 148–49; *ayahs* 72,
158, 160, 161; cooks 67–8, 72,
159, 161; methods of hiring
157–61, 168; servant–mistress

relationship 75–8, 138, 148,
160, 169, 178; training 7, 75,
77; working conditions 46–7,
52, 72, 75, 148, 156–57, 160,
161; *see also* gender;
occupations

'economic' migration *see*
migration
education 103–17; as a reason for
living in Shimla 55, 74, 104,
108, 137, 150, 195; cost 107–09,
110, 113, 117n1, 141, 147, 195;
female education 103, 112,
114–17, 117n3, 118n4, 120,
130, 132, and family
encouragement 129–32, 149,
150n3; help from kin 10, 125;
homework 65, 73, 109–12;
improved 61, 109, 110, 112,
113; influence on employment
prospects 22, 27, 60, 74, 103,
112, 115, 117n3, 120, 121,
127–28, 136, 188, 195; and
marriage prospects 105, 106,
114–17, 188; mother's role 36,
103, 106, 108, 109–12, 114,
117, 146, 169; pre-
school/kindergarten 107, 108,
113, *balvaris* 113, 117n3;
private 107, 108, 130; rural 22,
106, 107, 120, 173, 196; and
social class 4, 114, 117n3, 189;
system 107–09; *see also*
children; gender
employment: as a source of
independence for women 11,
70, 138, 149; competition for
15, 22, 104, 114, 116, 117, 154,
169n1, 187; exchanges/bureaux
153, 157, 158, 159; of husbands
outside Shimla 54–5, 89–90, 94,
134, 150n5; improvement of
prospects through education 22,
60, 74, 103, 105, 112, 114, 115,
116, 120, 136, through property

27, 60; *jajmani* 24; *nokri* 25;
opportunities for women 44–5,
115, 119, 120, 121, 132, 136,
142–43; *see also* education;
government service;
occupations; women, working
women
endogamy *see* caste
entertaining *see* social life
exogamy *see* caste

family *see* households
famine 20
feminism 2–4, 11, 37, 45, 63; and
the household 2–4, 197; and the
Third World 198; *see also*
housework, the female role
festivals 1, 15, 175, 183; Divali
176, 186n3; Karva Chauth 176,
186n3

gender 3, 11, 28–9, 51, 102n4,
119–20, 190, 191; and
contribution to household
resources 125–26, 172; domestic
training for girls 73, 182; and
education 106, contemporary
encouragement of girls to work
129–32; and household service
work 187, 190–91; preferences
29–30; and servants 84n3, 128;
survival rates 29, 101n1
Ghanyari 22
gift exchange 1, 6, 155, 170, 173;
traditions 5, 162, 175, 176
government service 15, 16, 40, 59,
61, 118n4, 121, 147, 157, 188;
benefits of 27, 52, 59, 125, 141,
150, 153, 159, 169; jobs for
widows 136, 158; hierarchy 27,
100–01, 156; and
'incorporation' of wife 147,
181–82; provision of
accommodation 53, 62n4, 65–6,
153, 156, 157, 159; 'scheduled'
castes 112, 117n2; *see also*
bureaucracy

'green revolution' *see* Himachal Pradesh, agriculture

Harbassi 33, 34
Haryana 13, 19, 28, 120; Haryanvis 15
Himachal Pradesh 13, 14, 18, 19, 21, 25, 30, 34, 120; Himachal Administrative Service (HAS) 147, 151n8; agriculture 19, 21, 22, 29, apple belt 19, 27, 59, 67, capitalist 23, 24, 61, 'green revolution' 19, 97; industrial backwardness 14, 18, 19–20, out-migration 29; Himachalis: characteristics 176; population 28, 29, 120; private enterprise in 24, 61; *see also* India; Shimla
Himalayas 13, 14
Hindus 13, 102n4, 176; beliefs 125, 191
home ownership *see* property; Shimla, housing
homework *see* education
Hoshiarpur 28
household budgeting 37, 62n4, 80–1, 85–95, 98–101; to cover cost of education 112; division of labour 55, 88–95, 98–101, effect of unemployment / retirement 90; influence of income /class 87, 88; payment of bills 88, 90, 93, 95; use of credit 85, 88, 90; women's role in managing 1, 2, 86, 88–95, 98–101, 175, mother-in-law's role 74, 90–1; *see also* housework, shopping; income; women, working women
household cycle 3, 35–6, 50, 91, 123, 132; variations in 35, 52, 62n5, 94, 98, 123–24, 172, 181, 193–94, effect on women's employment 133–37, 139–44, 150; *see also* divorcees; retirement; widows

household decision-making 55, 85, 86, 87, 98–101; division of labour 88–95, 98–101; 'orchestration' power 86–7, 95, 98–101
household finance *see* household budgeting
household resources 2, 6, 7, 98–101, 152, 154, 155, 170, 185–86, 188, 193, 197; allocation of 2, 3, 29, 98–101, 101n1, 197, resulting power 86, 87, 98, 100, 102n3; contribution of unmarried children 125–26, 150, 172; education as household resource 103, 114–16, 117n3; management of 85–7, 98–101, 171, 187, 196, effect of income /class 87, 'implementation' power 86–7; women's employment as household resource 146–50; *see also* gender; household budgeting; networks; women, working women
household service work 1, 3, 34, 114, 116, 127, 128, 175, 183, 186, 187–98; changing role of 116, 185; definition 5–11; and job satisfaction 5; Papanek's 'family status production' 8–9, 145, 195; and social class 7, 8–9, 11, 34, 35, 185, 187–98; *see also* household budgeting; household decision-making; housework; networks; social class; social life, entertaining; social mobility
household work *see* household service work; housework
households: as a collective entity 1–4, 151n7, 189, 197; as subcultures 131, 146, 150n4; composition of 2, 45, 47–56, effect of income on 48, 50, and hiring of servants 76; and

domestic consumption 82–3, 193, periodicity 193–94; female-headed households 49–51, 74, 88, 124–25, 191; joint/complex household 47, 49–52, 62n5, 70–2, 74, 76, 90, 100, 143, 184, as cultural ideal 54, family business 55, 72, and working women 56, 72, 74, 76; male migrant households 50, 61, 84n3; nuclear family household 47, 48–51, 71, 76, 77, 172, 184; power structure within households 2, 86, 87–8, 102n3, 197; rural households 5, 48, 55, 61, 67; sub-nuclear family household 47, 48–51, 71, 76; unmarried siblings household 50, 125; urban household 1, 10, 40–62, 73, 101, 152, 153, 156, 174; urban/rural continuum 23, 27, 28, 40–8, 57–62, 164, 168, 174, 188–89; *see also* divorcees; migration; networks; women; widows

housewifery *see* housework

housework 1, 2, 6, 8, 9, 63–84, 128, 189; as source of esteem 64; cleaning 1, 6, 64, 67–8; conditions of work 64–8, space 64–6; cooking 1, 6, 65–8, 78, 79, 81; and the female role 63–4, 78–9, 115–17, 118n4, 126, 129, 138–39; and feminism 2, 63; housewifery: influence of women's magazines 81–2, 183, models and expectations 80–4, 84n5; laundry 65–8, 77, 79; leisure activities 63–4, 170, 179, knitting 70, 79, 175, sewing 63–4, 67, 79, 81, 175; men helping with 63, 72–3, 84n3, 144; privatization in western societies 68–9; shopping 16, 80, 88, 90–5, 99, 181; and social class 64, 66–8, 80–2; and social relationships 11, 68–72, 175–77, 179; teamwork 70–2, 79, 162–63; use of gadgets 66–8, 82, 185, instead of servants 66, 68, 76; use of servants 67–8, 70, 72, 75–8, 79; for the working woman 70, 72–3, 144–45, 149; *see also* household service work; women

income: from property 27, 57, 58, 59, 60, 95, 172, as valuable extra 96, 188, 195; *see also* household budgeting; income groups; women, working women

income groups 35–7; and access to labour-saving gadgets 66–8; and household type 48–50; and housing 53, 64–6; and migration 20, 43; and models of housewifery 64, 80–2, 84n4; and property 58–60, 95–8; and resource management 85–95; and servants 71, 75, 78; and women's work histories 134–35, 140; *see also* sampling methods

India; All-India Women's Conference 180; the British in India 12–14, 18–19, 61, 117, 180; 1961 Census 119; 1971 Census 17; 1981 Census 17, 35; health services 4; Indian Administrative Service (IAS) 147, 151n8, 165, 194; population sex ratios 28–9; public welfare provision 4, 152, 153, 197; state socialism 25–6; *see also* education; employment; names of individual towns and regions (Shimla, etc.); occupations; women, in India and the west

joint/complex households *see* households

Kalka 12, 20
Kangra 15, 196
Kerala 28, 41, 162
kinship 11, 61, 62n2, 85, 143,
  144, 152–69, 170–86, 191;
  financial obligations 162,
  172–73; links with villages of
  origin 23, 57, 96, 148, 149, 160,
  164, 166, 172–76, and visits to
  Shimla 173–74; networks 1, 2,
  4–5, 6, 152–69, 170–75, 184–86,
  186n2, 193, between mother
  and daughter 161–63, for
  accommodation and
  employment 44, 50, 152–53,
  157, 158, 160, 161, 168, 169n1,
  n3, 171–72, maintenance by
  women 6–7, 145, 146, 160, 168,
  174–75, 185–86, 193; and social
  life 170–75; *see also* education;
  gift exchange; households;
  networks; property
'kitty' parties *see* social life

languages, use of 118n3; English
  114; Hindi 114, 183; Pahari 114

marriage 3, 36, 118n4, 139,
  140–41, 162, 163–69, 183–85,
  191; arranged marriages 10,
  115, 129, 141, 163–69, 188,
  193, role of women in 5,
  164–69; dowry and continuing
  presents 162, 172; and
  education 105, 106, 114–17;
  expenses 21, 29, 147, 152, 173;
  'love' marriages 166; newspaper
  advertisements 141, 167–68,
  191; separation/desertion 54,
  186, 194; *see also* divorcees
Marxism 24, 190; reproduction of
  labour power 6, 9, 21, 163
Meerut 51, 176, 184
migration 16, 20–3, 40–8, 149, 153,
  156, 171, 172, 177, 193–96;
  bastis 192; effect on population

ratios 28–30; of husbands
  leaving women in village 21–2,
  23, 37, 44–8, 55, 58, 172,
  194–96, living conditions in
  Shimla 46–7, 144, 196; of men
  to find work ('economic') 42,
  96, 158, 164, 172, 187; of most
  employable member of
  household 21, 48, 61; of single
  women ('economic') 44–5; of
  widows 136–37; of women
  because of husbands ('social'
  and 'domestic') 10, 22, 40, 42,
  44, 45, 92, 134, 196; of women
  on marrying 41, 42, 44, 92, 134,
  140, 158, 163; push/pull factors
  20–1, 31n2; rural/rural
  migration 42, 164; and socio-
  economic status 40–1, 188–89,
  196; urban/rural continuum 10,
  18, 20–3, 40–8, 164, 168, 174,
  188–89; *see also* employment;
  households; networks
modes of production: agrarian 23,
  27; capitalist 23, 24; *see also*
  capitalism

neighbourhood 155, 159, 164,
  193; social relationships 170,
  175–77, 185; urban 4, 11,
  68–70, 145, 148, 154, and child
  care 142, 176; *see also*
  housework, social relationships;
  networks
Nepalis 41, 63
networks 152–69, 170–86, 187,
  197; as a resource system 4, 6,
  7, 34, 37, 103, 152–69, 170–86,
  188, 193–94, 196, for
  accommodation and
  employment 44, 50, 152–53,
  156, 158, 161, 168, 169n1, n3,
  188, 196, in times of crisis 4,
  153, 173, 192–94, 197; as a
  source of information 152–53,
  155–69, 176, 179, 183, 185,

194; as a system of patronage
153–54, 169n1, horizontal and
vertical links 154, 158, 161,
185; formation and
maintenance by women 4–7, 83,
114, 145, 147, 152, 155, 159,
160, 164, 174–75, 185–86, 193,
197; male networks 155–59,
164, 165, 168, 178–79, 186n5,
187; social/professional 83, 146,
147, 152, 154, 158, 164–66,
179, 183–85; *see also* gift
exchange; kinship;
neighbourhood
New Delhi 192
nokri see employment
'nuclear' families *see* households

occupations 17–18, 64–5, 105;
army service 21, 164, 166;
caretakers (*choukidar*) 46; *dhobis*
84n1, 130; doctors 6, 121, 162,
166, 167, 182; needlewomen 36,
121, 123, 143; nurses 121, 130,
131, 132, 137, 159, 167, 178;
peon (office messenger) 46, 52,
73, 104, 112, 121, 128, 136,
148, 156, 159, 188, 194;
policemen/women 30, 91; shop
assistants 30, 41, 194;
shorthand typists 46, 79, 115,
162; social standing of various
126–27; social workers 121,
132, 139; stenographers 91,
104, 121, 143, 147; sweepers 37,
46, 64, 70, 72, 77, 112, 123,
128, 130, 142; teachers 17, 79,
91, 110–17, 121, 127, 131, 132,
178; 'technocrats' 15, 52, 127,
180, 188; university lecturers
36, 41, 55, 90, 121, 150n5, 167;
see also bureaucracy; domestic
service; employment;
government service; social class;
wage labourers

Paharis 14, 15, 114
Pakistan 150n6
participant observation 32, 35,
101n2; criticisms of 32–3; *see
also* sampling method
Parwanu 20
periodicity *see* households,
domestic consumption
Phagwara 28, 29
politics of scarcity 15
population: sex ratio 28
professions *see* occupations
property 9, 23, 57–62, 95–101;
accumulation 60–2, 96, 101,
188–89, 197; as a factor in
social mobility 59, 188; as
investment/security 21, 23, 52,
58, 59–60, 61, 96, 98, 172, 188,
197, rented out to tenants 27,
59, 60, 188; family property 10,
21, 46, 48, 54, 57, 59, 101,
supervision of 46, 55, 57, 96–8,
100, 137, 174, 195; in villages
of origin 58–60, 96, 174, 188,
189, non-productivity of 58, 59,
96, 189, reversion of 58, 59, 96,
196; inherited 57, 58, 60, 95–8,
102n4, 136–37, 186n2, 196;
women as managers 46, 97–8,
100, 101, 145, 189, 195; *see also*
Himachal Pradesh, agriculture;
income; migration; Shimla,
housing; women, agriculture
Punjab 14, 28, 29, 34, 41, 55, 120;
area of economic growth 19, 21,
29, 61, 97; partition 13, 40;
Punjabis 13, 15, 20, 52, 60, 92,
139, 176, 180

Rajputs 22
religion 6, 8, 34, 103, 170; as part
of social life 176, 186n3; *see also*
festivals
reproduction (labour power) *see*
Marxism
retirement: consequences within

household 3, 36, 62n5, 90; rural (back to village) 21, 22, 23, 59
rural/urban continuum *see* households; migration; property

sampling method 34–9; conduct of interviews 35–8, 101n2; *see also* income groups; participant observation; relevant *Tables*; Shimla, as base for fieldwork
share croppers 25, 96, 97, 189
Shimla 12–31; as administrative and bureaucratic centre 10, 13, 14, 16, 104, 173; as base for fieldwork 10, 33–9; British history 12–13, 14, 18–19, 30, 108, 117, 157, 179–80; class structure 24–8, 83, 185, 188–89, 192; climate 12, 69; differences from other Indian cities 13, 69, 84n1, 104, 175, 187, 188–89; high cost of living 37, 52, 54, 74, 134, 136, 172, 195; housing 16, 36, 47, 52, 53–4, 60, 64–6, 69, 156, 195; the Mall as social centre 16, 17, 79, 93, 94, 178–79; physical description 12, 16, 69, 93; population numbers and composition 15, 17, 24, 30n1, 40, proportion of women 28, 120; rapid expansion 9, 16, 17, 156, 175–76, 187; white-collar city 17, 120, 189; *see also* bureaucracy; education; employment; migration
shopping *see* housework
Sikhs 13; Ranjit Singh 14
Sirmur 15
social class 24–8, 187–98; formation 1, 3–4, 28, 31n3, 114, 187–98, and household service work 1, 5, 8–9, 11, 81–3, 181–83, 187–98, and property 59–62, 188; *see also* education; household service work;

migration; social life, entertaining
social life 1, 7, 145, 155, 170–85; at work 177–79, 182, 185; and charitable work 180–81, 186n4; entertaining 1, 17, 65, 66, 78, 81, 145, 162, 171, 179, 181–83, and assessment of household 83–4, as status display 7, 78, 82, 83, 181–83, 184–85, of relatives 173–75, 179; 'kitty' parties 81, 84n5, 85, 108, 179, 180; lack of for working women 145, 146, 149, 178; *see also* gift exchange; government service, 'incorporation' of wife; housework, social relations; kinship; networks; women, working women
'social' migration *see* migration
social mobility 1, 7, 59–62, 116, 147, 186n5, 187, 193; and household service work 7, 8, 184–85, 187, 191; and migration 40, 188–89, 196; and the role of women 7, 181–85; *see also* property; social class; social life, entertaining
status *see* social class
sub-nuclear families *see* households
Sundernagar 28
sweepers *see* occupations

thapi see housework, laundry
Third World 14, 26, 83, 119, 197–98; urbanization 32, 42, 62n2, 152; *see also* urbanization
tourism 20

unemployment 4, 61, 153, 192; as a cause for migration 20; benefit 4; effect on household 90, 94, 123, 133, 146, 192, 193, 194; *see also* migration
urban/rural continuum *see*

households; migration; property
urbanization 10, 22, 23, 47, 168;
Third World 32, 42, 62n2, 152;
women's role in 10; *see also*
households; migration;
networks
Uttar Pradesh 28, 173

villages of origin *see* households,
urban/rural continuum;
migration; property

wage labourers 22, 24, 27, 188; *see
also* bureaucracy; domestic
service; employment;
government service;
occupations
washing *see* housework, laundry
the west *see* women, India and the
west
widows 4, 44, 48, 104–05, 111,
112, 163, 186n2, 191, 198n1; as
managers of rural property 55;
and employment 124, 133,
136–37, 145, 158, *mazburi* 137;
see also government service,
benefits, jobs for widows;
households, female-headed,
joint/complex
women: and agriculture 21, 29,
30, 46, 58, 127, 195; birth
control 29; dependence on
husbands 2, 42, 86, 87, 100;
identification with household
interests 4, 50, 63–4, 78–9, 126,
138, 198; in India and the west
(similarities and distinctions) 1,
6, 11, 62n5, 63, 66, 68–9,

106–07, 115–17, 118n4, 129,
139–40, 162–63, 198;
isolation/seclusion 11, 30, 92,
93, 128, 168, 169, 184, 187,
purdah 129; maternity leave 27,
141; population ratio 28;
unmarried women/daughters
38, 72, 74, 106, 125, 129–32,
133, 144, 150n3, 178, training
in domestic skills 73; visibility
30, 69, 93; working women 8,
11, 37, 38, 50, 67, 75, 95,
119–51, 157, 159, 169;
attitudes: husband's 72–3, 127,
129, 130, 133, 134, 136, 144,
149, personal 111, 136, 138,
143, 145, 150n6, 177, society's
11, 115, 119, 126–29, 132, 133,
148; as financial necessity
123–26, 133, 134, 138, 139,
144, 146; and joint/complex
households 56, 123, 137, 143;
pressures on 70, 72–3, 76, 95,
111, 126, 144–46, 178, 189; use
of servants 75–6, 142, 144, 145,
160, 161; use of wages and
salary 11, 42, 99–100, 119,
122–26, 132, 147, 148, 149; *see
also* children, child care;
divorcees; education;
employment; feminism;
household budgeting;
household decision-making;
household resources; household
service work; households;
marriage; migration; networks;
property; social class; social life;
social mobility; widows